DIGITAL NARRATIVE SPACES

There is a broad consensus that digital narrative is "spatial," but what this critical term means and how it is used varies greatly depending on the discipline from which it is approached. *Digital Narrative Spaces* brings together essays by prominent scholars in electronic literature and other forms of digital authorship to explore the relationship between story and space across these disciplines. This volume includes an introduction with Marie-Laure Ryan's typology of space, followed by thought-provoking individual chapters which explore innovative explorations of electronic literature, locative media, literary tourism, and the mapping of real-world literary spaces. The collection closes with an essay analyzing continuities and discontinuities in theory of space across the chapters. This volume will provide an important framework for establishing a dialogue across disciplines and future scholarship in these fields.

Daniel Punday received his PhD in English at The Pennsylvania State University. He is currently Head of the Department of English at Mississippi State University. He has published on contemporary literature, digital narrative, and narrative theory. He has recently completed his term as the president of the International Society for the Study of Narrative. His previous publications include *Computing as Writing* (2015) and *Writing at the Limit: Searching for the Vocation of the Novel in the Contemporary Media Ecology* (2012).

DIGITAL NARRATIVE SPACES

An Interdisciplinary Examination

Edited by Daniel Punday

NEW YORK AND LONDON

Cover image: © Getty Images

First published 2022
by Routledge
605 Third Avenue, New York, NY 10158

and by Routledge
4 Park Square, Milton Park, Abingdon, Oxon, OX14 4RN

Routledge is an imprint of the Taylor & Francis Group, an informa business

© 2022 selection and editorial matter, Daniel Punday; individual chapters, the contributors

The right of Daniel Punday to be identified as the author of the editorial material, and of the authors for their individual chapters, has been asserted in accordance with sections 77 and 78 of the Copyright, Designs and Patents Act 1988.

All rights reserved. No part of this book may be reprinted or reproduced or utilised in any form or by any electronic, mechanical, or other means, now known or hereafter invented, including photocopying and recording, or in any information storage or retrieval system, without permission in writing from the publishers.

Trademark notice: Product or corporate names may be trademarks or registered trademarks, and are used only for identification and explanation without intent to infringe.

Library of Congress Cataloging-in-Publication Data
A catalog record for this title has been requested

ISBN: 978-0-367-51444-0 (hbk)
ISBN: 978-0-367-51443-3 (pbk)
ISBN: 978-1-003-05388-0 (ebk)

DOI: 10.4324/9781003053880

Typeset in Bembo
by codeMantra

CONTENTS

Notes on Contributors   vii

   Introduction: Four Types of Textual Space and their Manifestations in Digital Narrative   1
Marie-Laure Ryan

1   Transmedial Unnatural Spatiality and Postdigital Dystopicalization in *The Pickle Index*   20
Astrid Ensslin

2   *Tailing Rebus*: Plotting a Consipiracy in Digital Space   36
Brian L. Greenspan

3   Virtual Wandering: Embodied Spatial Narrativity in Walking Simulators   49
Gregory Whistance-Smith

4   Mapping Imaginary Spaces: From Database to Folk Cartography   70
Paul Wake

5   From Screen to Silicon: Reverse Engineering the Computational Infrastructure of Nick Montfort's *Round*   88
Lai-Tze Fan

6 The Digital Terrain of the Literary Anecdote   109
   David Ciccoricco

7 Footprints in Spatial Narratives: Wearable Technology,
   Active Reading, and a New Digital Literary Mapping of
   Dorothy Wordsworth's Scafell Pike Excursion   125
   Joanna E. Taylor and Christopher Donaldson

8 Archival Interface and Nationalist Memorializations of 9/11   143
   Dhanashree Thorat

   Conclusion: Digital Space and the Keyword   160
   Daniel Punday

Index   *173*

NOTES ON CONTRIBUTORS

David Ciccoricco, Department of English and Linguistics, University of Otago. He is the author of two books on contemporary literature, cognitive theory, and digital media: *Reading Network Fiction* (Alabama, 2007) and *Refiguring Minds in Narrative Media* (Nebraska, 2015).

Christopher Donaldson is Lecturer in Cultural History at Lancaster University. He works on 18th- and 19th-century cultural history, especially changing perceptions of the value of landscape and the environment. He has co-edited *Literary Mapping in the Digital Age* (Routledge, 2016), and has published extensively in journals such as *International Journal of Humanities and Arts Computing*, *Digital Humanities Quarterly*, *Journal of Victorian Culture*, and *Review of English Studies*.

Astrid Ensslin is Professor of Digital Culture at the University of Bergen. She is the author or editor of eight books, including *Literary Gaming* (2014), *Analyzing Digital Fiction* (2013), and *The Language of Gaming* (2011).

Lai-Tze Fan is an Assistant Professor of Sociology and Legal Studies at the University of Waterloo, Canada, and a Faculty Researcher of the Games Institute. She researches digital storytelling, media theory and infrastructure, research-creation or critical making, and systemic inequalities in the technological design and labor. Fan is an editor and the Director of Communications of *Electronic Book Review* and an editor of *The Digital Review*. She is co-editor of the collection *Post-Digital: Dialogues and Debates from Electronic Book Review* (Bloomsbury 2020), and is the Editor of special journal issues on "Canadian Digital Poetics" and "Critical Making, Critical Design."

Brian L. Greenspan, Department of English Language and Literature, Carleton College. He has published essays on digital humanities in the influential *Debates in the Digital Humanities* collection and in journals such as *Digital Studies/ Le champ numérique* and *MediaTropes*.

Marie-Laure Ryan is an Independent Scholar. She is the author or editor of more than a dozen books, including *Narrative as Virtual Reality: Immersion and Interactivity in Literature and Electronic Media* (2003), *Avatars of Story* (2006), and the influential collection *Narrative Across Media; The Languages of Storytelling* (2005).

Joanna E. Taylor is Research Associate in the Data Science Institute at Lancaster University. She works on literature and culture of the long nineteenth century, particularly Romantic poetry and environmental history. She has published in journals such as *International Journal of Geographic Information Science*, *International Journal of Humanities and Arts Computing*, and *Essays in Romanticism*.

Dhanashree Thorat is Assistant Professor of English at Mississippi State University. Her research is situated at the intersection of Asian American Studies, Postcolonial Studies, and Digital Humanities. Broadly, she examines how colonial and racial ideologies shape the technological imagination, specifically in technical infrastructures, platforms, and policies. She has published in journals such as the *South Asian Review* and *Asian Quarterly*.

Paul Wake is Reader at Manchester Metropolitan University. He is the author and editor of four books, including *The Routledge Companion to Cultural and Critical Theory* (2013) and *Conrad's Marlow: Narrative and Death in "Youth", Heart of Darkness, Lord Jim, and Chance* (2007).

Gregory Whistance-Smith holds graduate degrees in Architecture and Digital Humanities from Dalhousie University and the University of Alberta. His research explores the interplay of design, technology, and culture in the built environment, and he practices architecture in Edmonton, Canada.

INTRODUCTION

Four Types of Textual Space and their Manifestations in Digital Narrative

Marie-Laure Ryan

The first thing that comes to mind, when we think about the relations of space to narrative, is the space in which characters live, act, and move—the space of the storyworld. Let's call it mimetic space (mimetic being taken here as synonymous with representational without implying that this representation must be faithful to reality). But the space of the storyworld is not the only kind of space that artistic and more particularly narrative texts can make significant. In Ryan, Foote and Azaryahu (2016), four types of textual space are defined:

1. The spatial form of the text
2. The space materially occupied by the text
3. The spatial context of the text
4. Mimetic space, or space of the storyworld

In this chapter, I will explore these four kinds of space, first in terms of their manifestations in print-based literature and second in terms of the digital narrative applications they have inspired, and of how these applications put into play the distinctive affordances of computer technology. For type 4, however, I will skip discussion of non-digital manifestations because they are too well known.

Spatial Form

The concept of spatial form was introduced in 1945 by the critic Joseph Frank to describe a type of literary meaning that emphasizes internal relations between parts of the text at the expense of temporal progression and of the traditional narrative effects of suspense, curiosity, and surprise (Sternberg 1992). While Frank envisioned spatial form as a mode of organization typical of

DOI: 10.4324/9781003053880-1

twentieth-century novels by which readers must fit fragments together into a global pattern, as in James Joyce's *Ulysses*, it can also be conceived as the extension to prose narrative of a reading strategy typical of poetry which consists of constructing a network of relations—semantic, phonic, visual, thematic—between elements separated in the temporal flow of discourse. Frank's concept of spatial form relied on a metaphorical conception of space, built on the idea that it takes a complete apprehension of the text, like seeing a territory from a high point, to detect systems of analogies and oppositions. Spatial form can therefore be appreciated only retrospectively or, because of the limitations of memory, on a second or third reading.

But literature can shape space much more literally than through internal relations. Here I will extend the term of spatial form beyond Frank's conception by using it to describe the typographical realization of language and the arrangement of words on the page. With standard narrative texts, it does not matter whether the font is Garamond or Helvetia, the paper thin or thick, or the margins large or small, because the meaning of the text transcends its material support and visual realization. (Or if these features do matter, their effect is not verifiable, because it varies from reader to reader.) Poetry however has traditionally given more attention to visual presentation than prose. For instance, the seventeenth-century poem "Easter Wings" by George Herbert imitates the spread-out wings of an angel. In the nineteenth century Mallarmé's "Un Coup de Dés" and in the early twentieth century Apollinaire's *Calligrammes* reproduced visually the subject matter of the poem. Even when not representational, the spatial form of a poem attracts the eye before the mind reads the text. The word-image combinations of comics and graphic novels put great emphasis on the arrangement of frames on the page and, within each frame, on the visual relations between text and picture. Even novels become more and more dependent on spatial combinations of visual and verbal elements, as demonstrated by such experimental texts as *House of Leaves* by Mark Danielewski or *S* by J.J. Abrams and Doug Dorst.

The spatial organization of information takes two highly medium-specific forms in digital narrative. The first is known as the graphic user interface (GUI). The most distinctive feature of digital media is interactivity: the process by which users provide input to the computer, and the computer responds by displaying information, in a repeated feedback loop. In a GUI, users communicate with the computer by means of what Bolter and Grusin (1999, 31) call a hypermediated display: a screen divided into multiple areas, or windows, in which various types of information are displayed, such as textual, visual, or aural. Some of these windows contain information that form the target of the user's interest, while others are tools that enable users to access, create, or manipulate the target information. In a word processor, the target information is the text created by the user, while the tools are the functions on the toolbar, such as cut, paste, search, format page, and so on. In a computer game, the target information is the gameworld, or playfield, in which players perform actions, and the tools are the menus that allow players to equip themselves for action or the icons (such as maps) that help them move around in the gameworld. Daniel Punday (2017, 93) calls these two types of information "primary" and "orienting" space, though they are spaces in different senses: the primary space is an experienced environment which users inhabit in make-believe, but the orienting space is simply an area of the screen—a window— through which tools can be accessed. Moreover, the tools are not always located outside the primary space, so that the two kinds of space are not necessarily distinct: in a hypertext, the links that allow navigation are underlined words belonging to the text that forms the user's focus of attention, and in a computer game, the tools may be objects found within the gameworld.

An even more medium-specific type of spatial form resides in the architecture of the underlying code that controls the navigation of the user through a digital text. Insofar as it determines the succession of textual or visual data on the screen, this architecture is temporal, but insofar as it can be represented on a diagram, it presents a spatial or topological configuration. In a standard print narrative, progression through the data is usually linear, since readers are supposed to scan the text line by line and page by page, but in a digital text, the system of choices that determines reading or viewing progression can take a variety of forms (Ryan 2015, ch. 7): the tree, typical of "choose your own adventures" texts, which allows the author to control the reader's itinerary, since there is only one way to reach the end of every branch; the wheel, a topological variant of the tree popular in commercial websites, because it allows returning to the home page in one click from every node in the system; the flowchart, common in games, because it makes it possible to reach the same node through multiple paths, allowing a variety of solutions to the problems presented to the player; and the network, or maze, common in hypertext narratives, which—in contrast to the tree—presents loops where users may be caught.

Here I would like to compare two hypertext narratives in terms of how their underlying spatial architecture affects the experience of the reader. The first (Figure I.1) is *Twelve Blue* by Michael Joyce, a text from the 1990s, which unfortunately is not adapted to contemporary screens; Figure I.1 is therefore a reconstruction of the interface and not an authentic screen shot. The text consists of about 150 fragments (or lexias); to move from one fragment to the next, the user clicks on one of 12 differently colored threads, shown on the left. Each choice leads to a different lexia (shown on the right); then, 12 more choices are presented, many of which lead back to previously visited fragments. This looping back or recycling of nodes avoids an exponential proliferation of elements. Figure I.1 shows the interface presented to the reader, but not the underlying architecture: if the global structure of the text were represented on a diagram, this diagram would consist of 150 nodes, each connected to 12 others (not to mention some additional links contained in the text, marked by underlined words). This architecture gives lots of choices to the reader, but the

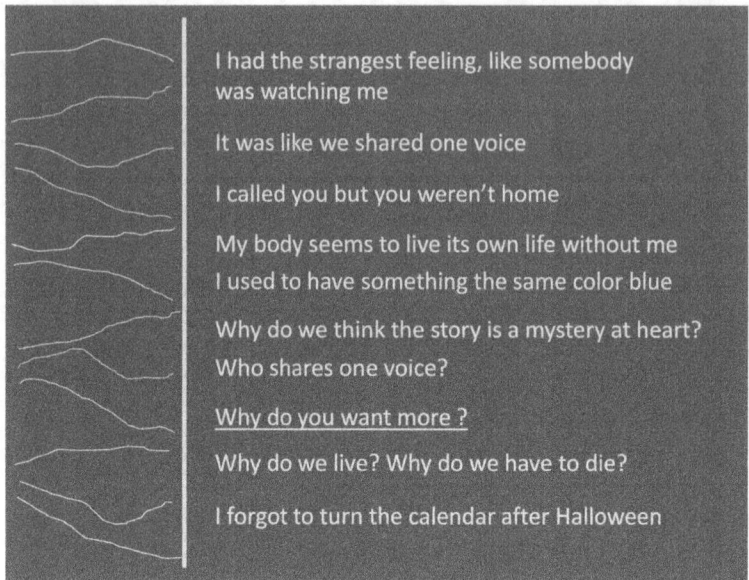

FIGURE I.1 The interface of Michael Joyce's *Twelve Blue*. (Recreated by Marie-Laure Ryan).

choices are blind, because there is no reason to click on one thread rather than on another. The author determines the reader's passage from one fragment to another by placing links between them, but he cannot determine the reader's global itinerary. The lack of control over the path of the reader prevents this type of spatial architecture from allowing the temporal effects of suspense, curiosity, and surprise. Nor is it compatible with a dramatic structure (often known as "Aristotelian") of exposition, conflict, and resolution, because the loops, as well as the sheer complexity of the system, prevent the reader from reaching an endpoint. As a network-based narrative, *Twelve Blue* frustrates interest in temporal development and redirects attention toward thematic relations between the various lexias. Instead of an overarching plot, the text presents a number of small stories concerning multiple characters whose lives intersect with each other. These stories illustrate recurring themes, such as water, drowning, love, family relations, and multiple shades of blue. None of the strands provides closure; rather, meaning arises from the juxtaposition of fragments into a synthetic totality. The spatial architecture of *Twelve Blue* thus supports the kind of semantic organization and reading strategy that Frank describes as spatial form.

While the readers of *Twelve Blue* progress blindly and do not know how much of the text they have seen (instead of closure, the text offers a sense of exhaustion when readers run in circles and cannot access new fragments), my second example of underlying architecture, a French hypertext by Daniel Bouillot titled *Annalena*, is much more user-friendly, in the sense that it seeks a compromise between freedom of choice and a global narrative structure leading to a satisfactory ending. *Annalena* tells the story of Pierre, a photographer who travels from Paris to Antibes to take pictures of the brilliant light of the French Riviera. On his way, he takes a mysterious hitchhiker named Anna. During his stay in Antibes, Pierre runs several times into Anna, and she initiates him into the landscape as well as into the work of the painter Nicolas de Staël, who lived in Antibes and committed suicide by throwing himself from a roof. Anna convinces Pierre that the true way to capture the light of the Mediterranean is through painting, not photography. Pierre falls in love with Anna as much as with the places she helps him discover, and he tries to capture her by taking her photo unbeknownst to her. In so doing, he violates a taboo and she disappears forever from his life. The diagram on Figure I.2 represents the spatial architecture of the text. It begins with an introduction (D) narrating Pierre's trip from Paris to Antibes and his meeting with Anna. Then, readers reach node IC, a slightly overexposed photo of Antibes (to signify the inferiority of photography) on which they click randomly. Depending on where they click on the screen, they activate an episode which unfolds linearly: each screen contains only one link, and after completing the sequence, readers return to node IC. After each episode, a whole area of the Antibes photo turns into a painting with much richer colors. The process repeats itself 19 times for the 19 episodes, each of which contains an autonomous episode, so that they can be read in any order. At any point in the reading, users know exactly how much they have read and how much remains to be read. When all the episodes have been visited, the photograph is fully transformed into a painting, in accord with the thematics of the text, and an epilogue (node F) puts an end to the narrative arc, giving users the satisfaction of having concluded their journey.

The lesson to be drawn from the comparison of these two types of underlying architecture is that in order to maintain narrative tension, it is necessary to limit the choices of the reader. When the choices are so numerous that the author does not control the long-range succession of elements, interest must shift from following a temporal development to the detection of spatial relations.

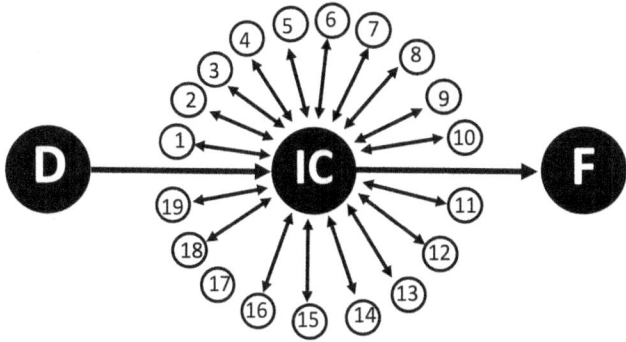

FIGURE I.2 The architecture of Daniel Bouillot's *Annalena*.

While the reader of *Annalena* wants to know how it ends, the reader of *Twelve Blue* finds satisfaction in the lyrical structure of the text.

The Space Materially Occupied by the Text

This space is the space of the physical support of the text. It can present zero, one, two, or three spatial dimensions: zero for oral texts (unless one counts the body of the storyteller); one for moving lines of text, such as ticker tape style news on TV or public buildings; two, the default case, for pages; three, but with one very short dimension, for engraved inscriptions or Braille texts; and a full three for books, if one considers their thickness, which tells the reader how much has been read and remains to be read. Literature has recently begun to play with the dimensionality of texts in creative ways. For instance, the novel *S* by J.J. Abrams and Doug Dorst is full of detachable flat objects inserted between the pages that can be considered two-and-a-half-dimensional because the third dimension is very limited: postcards, written notes, newspapers, and a wheel for decoding hidden messages. In *Bats of the Republic* by Zachary Thomas Dodson, a long band of text contained in an envelope must be twisted by the reader into a three-dimensional Moebius strip to reveal a secret connection between two seemingly distinct stories. And in *Tree of Codes* by Jonathan Safran Foer, a book is sculpted into a three-dimensional object made of plateaus and valleys (Figure I.3). Foer took an existing text, a translation of *Street of Crocodiles* by the Polish author and Holocaust victim Bruno Schulz, and created a new text by cutting out part of each page and retaining only selected words. The cut out parts often overlap with the holes of the next few pages, so that readers can see not only the words on the page they are reading ("page-words," in Katherine Hayles's terminology [2013]), but also words or sometimes individual letters located in deeper layers of the text ("hole-words"). These signs appear at the bottom of crevasses cut through the thickness of the book. Since it would take a superhuman grasp of complexity for the author to foresee and control them, they represent a random element, an informational noise that breaks the syntax of the page words. Judging by the responses on Amazon, some readers hide the hole words by sliding a white sheet of paper behind the page they are reading, while others try to make sense of the noise. Needless to say only the first kind of readers manages to retrieve some kind of narrative meaning, but at the expense of the depth of the text.

In digital texts, the idea of a material support is problematic, because the text exists as code and data inscribed as zeros and ones on a microchip hidden in the memory of the computer; it is only when the code is executed that the text becomes accessible to the user, either as display on a screen or as virtual image. While a flat screen can only convey a sense of depth through perspective, virtual reality (VR) technology can simulate three-dimensionality through holographic display and stereoscopic effects. One type of support that allows a genuine three-dimensional virtual experience is the Cave Automatic Virtual Environment (CAVE) system of Brown University, a cube of 2.5-meter sides

Introduction 7

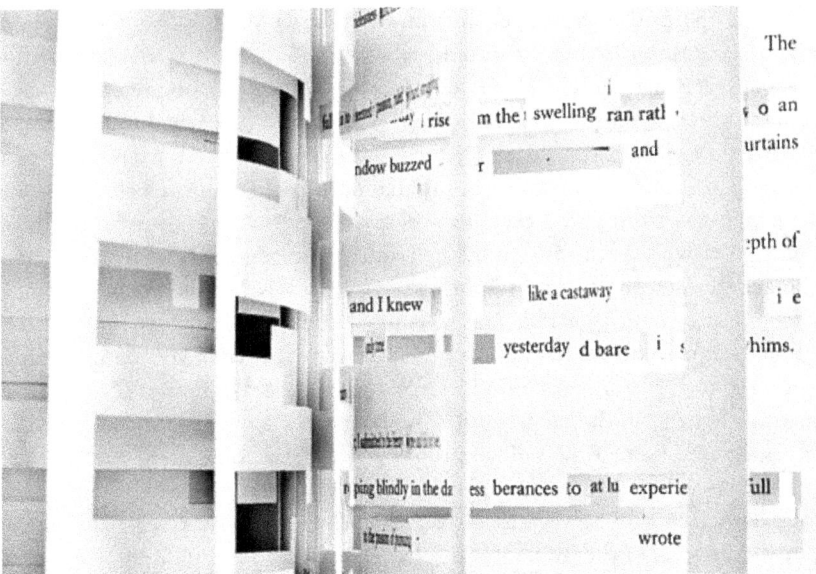

FIGURE I.3 Three-dimensional print writing: *Tree of Codes*, by Jonathan Safran Foer.

mainly used for scientific visualization, but also available for literary experiments. An example of such experiment is a text titled *Screen* by Noah Wardrip-Fruin and his colleagues (Figure I.4). The general theme of the text is memory loss, and memory is represented by the CAVE, in the middle of which the user is located. Fragments of texts, representing personal experiences, appear on the walls. As long as the words are readable, the experiences they relate are accessible to memory; but after a while, words begin to fall off from the walls. Users throw them back on the walls, using their hands like ping-pong rackets, and initially succeed in putting them back in place. But the words fall down faster and faster, as in the game *Tetris*, and when the user no longer manages to catch them, they fall on the ground and break. The length of the experience depends on the user's ability to catch the falling words, but sooner or later nothing is left on the walls and amnesia is complete. This inevitable ending makes *Screen* indifferent to the meaning of words: different texts, personalized to represent the experiences of different users, could be used as data, because we are all threatened by the nightmare of memory loss. It is, moreover, unlikely that the user, entirely absorbed by the task of catching the words and putting them back in place, will have time to read them; in this installation, words are turned into opaque objects. The narrativity of *Screen*, if it exists at all, is not a meaning signified by its particular words, but rather, a meaning symbolically enacted through the corporeal interaction of the user with the materiality of words. As Rita Raley writes of three-dimensional (3D) textuality, "this is less a reading experience than an anti-reading experience."

8 Marie-Laure Ryan

While the user of *Screen* remains aware of the CAVE as the container in which text is projected, most instantiations of VR technology render the notion of "space materially occupied by the text" inoperative, and replace it with a contrast between the virtual space of the world represented by the text and the real space in which the text is projected and experienced. An example of this contrast is Alejandro Iñarritu's VR installation *Carne y Arena*, which represents the experience of migrants trying to cross the US/Mexico border in the Arizona desert, while being chased by the border patrol. As a user, you are ushered into a large room where, after being fitted with a VR helmet, you experience a 6½-minute simulation that puts you in a dark desert landscape; gradually, migrants come into view; then a helicopter hovers over them in a deafening noise; the people scamper around, terrorized, while fragments of dialogue are heard in both Spanish and English. The helicopter moves away, and a period of calm ensues. Then the police return, yell orders, point guns, and unleash attack dogs. Chaos breaks out. You are blinded by an intense light, but when you try to turn away to regain your sight, you are frozen in place. You realize that you are one of the migrants and that you have been caught by the border patrol. At this point, the simulation comes to an end. Until then, you can move around the scene and observe the events from various angles and at a variable distance; but if you come too close to the walls, an attendant gently pulls you back and redirects you toward the center of the room. Her friendliness, which stands in sharp contrast to the hostility of the border patrol, temporarily breaks the illusion but prevents you from bumping into real objects. Even though VR

FIGURE I.4 Three-dimensional digital writing: *Screen*, by Noah Wardrip-Fruin *et al*

technology cancels awareness of the material world (in contrast to augmented reality [AR]), it cannot cancel its existence, since it remains dependent on real space for the display of the virtual world.

The Spatial Context of the Text

By spatial context, I mean the physical space where the material support of the text is located and from where the story can be accessed. By facilitating the multiplication of copies, the invention of print has made narrative texts relatively mobile compared to manuscripts: you can take a book almost anywhere and books can take you anywhere in imagination. The relation between the spatial referent of the text (i.e. the place that the text tells about) and the spatial context is normally variable; but in a type of narrative widely known as "locative," or "location-aware," or "site-specific," this relation is fixed, and the story must be accessed in the presence of its spatial referent. Consider this inscription commemorating an event in WWII: "The memory of France, and the city of Seyssel, invite the passer-by to remember the fights of June 22, 1940," followed by a brief narrative of the events that took place there. In such an inscription, the "where" of the story coincides with the "where" of the reader's location, a coincidence which turns this particular "where" into a special place of almost sacred significance. The text would lose most of its emotional impact, and therefore of its meaning, if the plaque were moved to a museum elsewhere.

Location-specific narrative permeated our urban landscapes long before digital technology gave it a boost and a name. We may not think of grave inscriptions as stories, but they present a clear beginning and ending and the middle is left to the imagination. A more elaborate form of site-specific narrative is found in the design of historical and heritage sites. Kenneth Foote (Ryan et al. 2016, Chapter 7) distinguishes several ways in which narratives of historical events can be "draped" across real spaces. In "point narratives," stories are told from a single location in space where the events took place; in "sequential narratives," events took place in a relatively broad area, and visitors follow a designed narrative trail that takes them through the story from beginning to end; in "area narratives," the story covers a large expanse, and visitors move freely around it or see only parts. The design of narrative information must consequently take these variations into consideration. The main support of non-digital locative narrative is written signs or engraved plaques, but it can also take the form of oral storytelling or of dramatic enactment. In so-called "cemetery crawls," costumed performers positioned on graves bring the past to life by narrating or enacting the lives of the most notorious dead. In the 1950s, a type of night-time spectacle known as *Son et lumière* was developed to tell the stories of history-rich buildings such as the Loire castles or the palace of Versailles. These spectacles brought to life kings, queens, royal mistresses, and other significant figures through dialogue, music, and light effects. In contrast to historical and heritage sites, whose purpose is to convey reliable factual knowledge, the *Son et lumière* spectacles dramatized history through a blend of fact and fiction, similar to what is found in historical novels. Fully fictional stories rarely occur in the non-digital forms of locative narratives, arguably because it takes the official approval of cultural authorities to install material signs in public locations, and authorities prefer to commemorate historical events because they represent a common past, but literary fiction can be made site-specific through the phenomenon of literary tourism. Beginning in the late nineteenth century (Bulson 2009), readers have flocked to Dickens's London, Joyce's Dublin, or Proust's Combray, driven by the conflicting desires to see the places described in literary works as they are in themselves and to experience these places through the eyes of the author, who is credited with the ability to capture their essence.

The advent of digital technology and the development of GPS systems made it possible for site-specific narratives to get rid of the permanent physical markers that had to be approved by the authorities and that favored officially sanctioned versions of history. Now everybody could, in principle, upload narrative content in the cloud and attach it to certain locations. As site-specific narratives multiplied, they also diversified not only in terms of the type of data involved (which now includes images projected through AR technology as well as textual narrative), but also in terms of genre. According to Scott Ruston's useful typology (2010), the three major types of locative narrative are spatial annotation projects, games, and mobile narrative experiences.

A classic example of spatial annotation is *[Murmur]*, a project initially developed for Toronto, but expanded to other cities such as Montreal, Vancouver, and San Jose, California. Inspired by treasure hunts, by Baudelaire's notion of *flânerie* (wandering through a city off the main traffic paths with a mind open to random discoveries) and by Debord's notion of *dérive* (dropping ones usual reasons for moving and "letting [oneself] be drawn by the attractions of the terrain and the encounters [one] finds there" (Wikipedia, Dérive entry), *[Murmur]* encourages people to explore the city in search of stories. Users receive a map showing where stories are offered and they reach these locations by selecting their own itineraries. Once there, a visible sign shaped like an ear shows a phone number that they can call to get narrative content. No GPS is therefore needed, and technically, the project only depends on digital technology to the extent that it uses mobile phones. The purpose of *[Murmur]* is to capture the *genius loci* of a city, not by taking users to its main tourist attractions or by commemorating the deeds of the personalities considered important, as does official history, but by collecting stories told by ordinary people about ordinary places. As the authors of the project write:

> The city is full of stories, and some of them happen in parking lots and bungalows, diners and front lawns. The smallest, greyest, or most

nondescript buildings can be transformed by the stories that live in it. Once heard, these stories can change the way people think about a place and the city at large.

[Locative Hypertext]

Urbanism is particularly well adapted to locative narrative because cities are continually evolving landscapes. We have all experienced the transformation of farmland into a freeway or shopping center, the gentrification of an old, decrepit neighborhood or the social revival of a decayed city center through green spaces and pedestrian malls. Many of the stories of *[Murmur]* recount how neighborhoods have changed and how ethnic specificity has been replaced by soulless expensive dwellings that the original inhabitants cannot afford. By digging into this urban archaeology, *[Murmur]* creates what human geographers call a sense of place: for it is the memories that tie people to certain buildings, neighborhood, communities, and the stories that capture these memories that turn the grey, seemingly undifferentiated spaces of the city into a web of lived places.

Location-based games, our second type of locative "narratives" (scare quotes explained below) follow a basic formula. The playground is the real world; the game is persistent, in the sense that it can be played at any time; the purpose of the game is to find and then to kill or capture creatures whose image is superposed upon the real world through AR technology. The position of the creatures, as well as that of the player, is shown on a map that tracks the movement of the player through GPS techniques. The more creatures you catch or kill, the more points you acquire and the more you rise in the game hierarchy. These games, which include *BotFighters* (2001–2005), *Ingress* (2013), and the tremendously popular *Pokémon Go* (2016), are credited with promoting physical activity and with allowing players to discover their city, for the creatures and strategic areas are often placed by the game designers near interesting landmarks. On the negative side, they have been accused of causing accidents, users being sometimes too focused on their cell phone screen to notice incoming traffic. The games differ from each other through additional rules that complicate gameplay and through the visual appearance of the creatures, but their narrative content is too rudimentary to be a source of interest. In *Botfighters*, which is probably the first location-based games, the players are robots in some futuristic world and their mission is simply to locate and destroy other players. In *Ingress*, according to Wikipedia:

> An unknown, transdimensional force called Exotic Matter (XM) was discovered as a byproduct of the Higgs Boson research (Large Hadron Collider) by a team of scientists at CERN in Switzerland. This substance has been associated with the Shapers, a mysterious phenomenon or alien race.

The basic us vs. them structure of competitive games is dramatized as a fight between two factions: the Enlightened, who believe that harnessing (XM) energy is beneficial to mankind, and the Resistance, who see XM as a potential threat to humanity and want to destroy it. Players select one of these two factions and see each other accordingly as either allies or enemies, but since the game is persistent, the story cannot end. *Pokémon Go* does not even try to narrativize the player's activity. The creatures encountered (there are 146 of them) differ from each other through their names, appearances, preferred habitat (for instance, near the water), and how many pieces of candy they bring for being captured, but they have no personality or biography, even though it would have been easy to tell their stories on a companion website. The game designers must have thought that an overload of narrative information would be distracting players from the game goals, and given the success of the game, one cannot argue with their decision.

Ruston's third category, "mobile narrative experiences" (which can hybridize with the other two, as in Chapter 3 of this book), differs from locative games in that it makes narrative into a focus of attention rather than using it as an incentive to play, and from spatial annotation in that the project is spanned by a global narrative arc rather than consisting of little stories. Moreover, the narrative is fictional rather than factual, even though it refers to real locations. Harnessing the narrative potential of mobile technology is the ambition of the research project "Ambient literature," a "two-year collaboration between UWE Bristol, Bath Spa University and the University of Birmingham, established to investigate the locational and technological future of the book." (Book must be broadly understood as the technological support of literature rather than narrowly as bound collection of pages, for the texts developed by the project use cell phones rather than print.) Traditional literature is context free; the book and the story it tells are the same wherever you take them. Ambient literature wants to give significance to the context by mobilizing the resources of digital technology to make texts dependent on their spatial environment. This context awareness can be understood in two ways: as pulling data from the surroundings and bringing it into the text so that it will tell a different story to different readers situated in different contexts or as taking readers to the locations referred to in the text in order to stage an encounter between the spatial referent and its description. An example of the former is Kate Pullinger's *Breathe*:

> *Breathe* is a literary experience delivered through your smartphone that responds to your presence by internalizing the world around you. Using APIs – application programming interfaces – the story leverages data about you, including place, weather, time, in order to create an experience that is personal and uncanny.

An example of the second strategy is James Attlee's *A Cartographer's Confession*. The author describes the plot as follows:

> My story concerns a young boy and his mother who arrive in [London] as refugees at the end of the second world war, who find a home among a community of market traders and who are then separated; it follows that boy's attempt to manage both the city and his loss by becoming a cartographer and ultimately by confronting the part of his history that has caused him pain, resulting in a violent denouement. Against this narrative is set a non-fictional account of events in the winter of 1931. These two narratives, one fiction the other non-fiction, play against each other.
> *(Writing the City)*

But the real subject matter (or main character) of the story is the London of the late 1940s and early 1950s, a London scarred by the war with low buildings, streets devoid of traffic, and numerous outdoor food markets. The cell phone app takes readers (or rather, hearers) to the plot locations and enhances their experience with multimodal documents that allows them to compare the prosperous present-day London with the London of the 1940s, such as vintage photos, illustrations, videos, newspaper articles dealing with the site, and soundscapes specifically created for the project. One problem with this kind of project is respecting the basic linearity of narrative time and of causal relations while granting users some freedom in their choice of itinerary. This is done in *Cartographer's Confession* by structuring the narrative as a series of semi-independent flashbacks that can be heard or read in a relatively free order. Another solution to this problem would be to use mobile technology to augment a standard print narrative. The user would first read the story in a book and would then visit the principal plot locations with the help of an app which would provide additional site-specific information. But whether the locative app is the main support of the story or an augmentation, site-specific fiction limits its audience to a certain region, and ambient literature is therefore unlikely to overtake the book.

By superposing the setting of a fictional story upon an actual spatial context, mobile technology blurs the boundary between category 3 and the next category.

Mimetic Space or the Space of the Storyworld

Scholars who have addressed the issue of the representation of space in narrative such as Ronen (1986) and Zoran (1984) have generally focused on the case of language-based literary fiction. But narrative can be supported by a variety of media, and media differ widely in how they convey an experience of space. Take language, the principal narrative medium; if it wants to represent a specific spatial setting, such as a house, room, or city, it must describe it item by item and readers must reassemble these elements in their minds in order to form a global representation of the setting in question. Moreover, even though language is temporal, it does not make it easy to represent movement though space as a gradual progression: if a character in a novel is said to walk out of the house and into the garden or to travel from Paris to London, the character experiences space point by point, but the text describes the event as instantaneous and the reader's imagination only visualizes the beginning and the end of the trip. With still pictures, spatial settings can be shown all at once instead of being described feature by feature, but the representation of movement must be divided into distinct moments separated by gaps, as done in graphic novels. Moving pictures, by contrast, are able to represent a continuous movement though space, not just by filming moving objects, but also by placing the camera on a mobile support. With digital media, users can not only experience space as evolving surroundings, they can inhabit it by identifying with an avatar and by controlling its movements. They can also modify their point of view, for instance, by getting closer to objects or by turning around, so as to experience space under different angles. But navigation in digital environment is not entirely free, because the smooth image of space presented on the screen hides a structured organization determined by the code (Nitsche 2008). In a computer game, it may be impossible to stray away from a path and to walk cross-country, even though the screen image shows no obvious obstacles to doing so, because the code creates an invisible barrier; conversely, it may be possible to walk through walls, thanks to a bug in the code which can lead to a shortcut known as a "cheat."

Enacting geographer Yi-Fu Tuan's distinction between space and place, most computer games are based on a contrast between inert space and active places. In standard adventure games as well as in massively multiplayer online role-playing games (MMORGs) such as *War of Warcraft*, players are wandering knights who travel through vast expanses of land where nothing happens, except for changes of scenery, in the hope of finding hot spots where they meet non-playing characters who give them "quests," that is, missions that will give them a chance to demonstrate their skills. In this game model, travel through space is subordinated to finding opportunities for action, since it is only by fulfilling difficult tasks that players can gain experience and advance in the game. But in another type of game, the relation between the journey and the game goals is inverted, and the experience of space takes precedence over the performance of tasks.

An example of this priority is *The Path*, an indie game by Michaël Samyn and Aureia Harvey, inspired by the fairy tale of "Little Red Riding Hood." The user selects one of six girls of different ages and is told to take her to the grandmother's house by following the path. But if the player stays on the path, she will get too easily to the grandmother's house, she won't see anything of the woods, and the game will conclude with a "failure" message. Ironically, the game wants the player's character to disobey the directions, to leave the path, and to get lost in the woods. Early in the game, the woods charm the player with their fog-shrouded landscapes, their fantastic vegetation, and their strange, slightly disturbing atmosphere. But after wandering for a while with nothing happening (it is a very slow game), the player feels frustrated of getting nowhere, and the woods become a prison. The more the player progresses, the more the landscape repeats itself and the more she moves in circles. But once in a while a faint light appears on the horizon, promising a different landscape. It is the anticipation of the pleasure of finally getting somewhere that motivates the player to perseverate in her journey through the sameness of the woods. But when she finally reaches a distinct place, her avatar meets the wolf and a violent death, which is shown in a cut scene. The fulfillment of the player's desire to reach a final destination, rather than wandering forever in the woods, has ambiguous consequences, since on one hand it spells doom for the avatar, but on the other it means success for the player.

Games like *The Path* that require no other skills than moving around the gameworld are known as walking simulators. These games connect a story to a landscape and the player unlocks the narrative by exploring the gameworld. The relative interest of the landscape and of the story and the strength of the connections between the two is variable. In *The Stanley Parable*, the player moves through an empty office building motivated by curiosity about what happened to Stanley, an employee whose job consists of pressing buttons on a computer keyboard as instructed by data on the screen. One day the screen remains blank, and totally disoriented by this lack of guidance, Stanley leaves his office and wanders aimlessly through the building. Finding how it ends (there are six different outcomes) is the player's main reason for moving through a dull maze of corridors, rooms, and doors that offers no aesthetic gratification. In *What Remains of Edith Finch*, by contrast, interest is fairly evenly divided between the landscape and the story. The gameworld is varied and beautiful, and by entering a mansion, finding secret rooms and examining objects, notes and diaries left by the characters, the player discovers a macabre story about a family haunted by a curse that kills all of its members: a story literally told by the things that fill the storyworld. In *Dear Esther*, by contrast, the story is relatively divorced from the environment to be explored and from the rare objects found in the game world, but the game offers a stunning landscape simulation. Moving through its world is almost like hiking on a windswept island off the coast of Scotland: blades of grass, sound of crashing waves, texture of driftwood and pebbles on the beaches, stalactites and stalagmites in a cave are so realistically rendered that players only miss the smell of the ocean and cold blasts of wind on their face—though the wind can be heard as well as seen in the swaying of the grass. Once in a while, when players traverse hidden hot spots, they hear fragments of a rather cryptic story about a dead woman named Esther and a car crash on an island with no roads told by a delirious narrator who may or may not be a ghost and whose past is unknown. The story not only blurs dream and reality, its elements are randomized, so that it will differ with every replay of the game. The cost of this randomization is a loss of connection between landscape features and narrative information, since the communicated information is not dependent on specific locations. All this makes *Dear Esther* into an everchanging, antinarrative text that offers no certainty. But the player is too absorbed in the task of finding a way through the landscape to really pay attention to the story. Even though the landscape looks smooth, the player's movements are starkly restricted by the code, and completing a chapter is more a matter of solving a maze than of absorbing narrative information. *Dear Esther* is all atmosphere, but totally devoid of narrative tension.

Virtual reality, the most life-like form of space representation, enhances the user's experience of simulated environments by making them three-dimensional and panoramic, and by letting people interact with the display by using their own body rather than by manipulating external controls. Through its ability to continually calculate and update the position of the user's body and by modifying the display accordingly, VR technology turns space exploration into a first-person truly embodied experience. The most promising applications of VR technology are indeed spatial experiences, such as climbing mountains without danger of falling, exploring underwater worlds, flying airplanes, flying like a bird, or visiting archeological sites and viewing them from various angles.

Yet, while VR can provide an amazing sense of being there in a variety of environments, this does not make it into a particularly efficient or powerful narrative medium. The narrative possibilities and limitations of VR are illustrated by a VRwandlung, a project developed by the Goethe-Institut Prague based on Kafka's "Metamorphosis" (no longer available). The project exploits VR's ability to manipulate the brain's image of the body and to lead to alternative experiences of embodiment by putting the user in the situation of Gregor Samsa, who one day wakes up and discovers that he has been transformed into a giant insect. An important theme in Kafka's story is Gregor's progressive acquaintance with his new body, how he uses it to move around his room, and how space is reconfigured to fulfill the needs of an insect body. For instance, Gregor can now hide under the bed to spare his mother the awful sight of his body and he can crawl on the walls to entertain himself. This theme is uniquely suited to the affordances of VR. Ideally, users should be able to experience what it feels like to control a body with six legs and giant antennae that impede their movements. They should be able to explore the room. And if they move in front of the mirror, they should also discover their new body from a third-person perspective. But even if VRwandlung succeeds in putting users in an insect body, it does not grant them agency beyond the ability to move around the room, and it does not recreate the human conflicts that make Kafka's story so poignant.

I am not saying that narrativity and VR are totally incompatible. VRwandlung could create virtual characters who would interact with the user and bring the project closer to Kafka's story; but this would be at the cost of the user's freedom of action, for participants would have to be steered along a certain plot line. One can also imagine artistic VR projects that would create surreal landscapes, where users would interact with magical objects rendered in three dimensions, would enter into bodies widely different from their own, and would cause unpredictable transformations by simply pointing at things. This would be like a dream, a hallucination, but dreams are fluid, ever-morphing experiences that rarely maintain narrative coherence. No medium can outdo VR in creating dynamic interactive environments and in conveying a sense of their presence, but there is more to narrative than spatial immersion; this is why VR developers prefer to call their creations "experiences" rather than stories. An influential school in narratology equates narrativity with "experientiality" (Fludernik 1996) and a feeling of "what it is like" (Herman 2009) at the expense of plot, but there is a world of difference between climbing Mt Everest—the topic of *Everest VR*, an ultra-realistic VR game that conveys a powerful sense of being there, but gives little freedom to the player—and having to choose between summiting Everest and rescuing other climbers caught in a storm. The first is a spatial experience, the second a narratively designed spatial experience. So far, VR has specialized in the former.

Conclusion

Digital technology brings something new to each of the types of space defined above, though with some types, it is more productive than with others. It redefines type 1, spatial form, as interface design and as the underlying architecture that determines the user's progression through the text. Space 2 is the least productive, both in old and new media, but VR technology such as the CAVE can give some material, three-dimensional substance to words and turn them into objects that the user manipulates. By tying narrative texts to certain location, GPS-based mobile technology and AR effects gives visibility to space 3, the spatial context of the text, which is normally taken for granted or considered irrelevant to the reading or hearing experience. But the strongest impact of digital technology on narrative concerns the most significant of the four kinds of spaces, the space of the storyworld. While other media merely represent space, the computer provides a lived, first-person experience of space by turning it into a habitable environment with which the user can interact and which can be navigated either through the substitute body of an avatar manipulated by external controls or, in the case of some VR applications, through the user's own body. None of these innovations would be possible if digital texts depended exclusively on language, as does the traditional conception of literature. It is to the extent that it orchestrates diverse modes of signification and absorbs all media that digital technology can produce new forms of art and new spatial experiences.

Works Cited

Abrams, J.J., et Doug Dorst. *S*. New York: Little Brown (Mulholland Books), 2013.
Ambient Literature. https://research.ambientlit.com/
Attlee, James. *A Cartographer's Confession*. https://research.ambientlit.com/cartographersconfession
———. Writing the City: Interview with Emma Whittaker. https://research.ambientlit.com/index.php/2017/07/22/writing-the-city-james-attlee-explains-his-approach-to-his-first-ambient-literature-commission/
Bolter, Jay David, and Richard Grusin. *Remediation: Understanding New Media*. Cambridge, MA: MIT Press, 1999.
BotFighters. Computer Game. It's Alive Mobile Games, 2001.
Bouillot, Daniel. *Annalena*. http://www.lisiere.com/annalena/
Bulson, Eric. *Novels, Maps, Modernity: The Spatial Imagination, 1850–2000*. London: Routledge, 2009.
Danielewski, Mark. *House of Leaves*. New York: Pantheon, 2000.
Dear Esther. Computer Game. Produced by Dan Pinchbeck. The Chinese Room and Curve Digital, 2012.
Dérive (Guy Debord). Wikpedia Entry. https://en.wikipedia.org/wiki/D%C3%A9rive
Dodson, Zachary Thomas. *Bats of the Republic*. New York: Doubleday, 2015.
Electronic Literature Organization. http://collection.eliterature.org/
Everest VR. Computer Game. Solfar Studios RVX, 2016.
Fludernik, Monika. *Towards a 'Natural' Narratology*. London: Routledge, 1996.
Foer, Jonathan Safran. *Tree of Codes*. Visual Editions, 2010.
Frank, Joseph. *The Idea of Spatial Form*. New Brunswick: Rutgers University Press, 1991 [1945].
Hayles, N. Katherine. "Combining Close and Distant Reading: Jonathan Safran Foer's *Tree of Codes* and the Aesthetic of Bookishness." *PMLA* 128.1 (2013): 226–231.
Herman, David. *Basic Elements of Narrative*. Mahwah, NJ: Wiley-Blackwell, 2009.
Iñárritu Gónzalez, Alejandro. *Carne y Arena (Virtually Present, Physically Invisible)*. VR installation, 2017. Trailer at https://www.youtube.com/watch?v=zF-focK30WE
Ingress. Computer Game. Niantic, 2013-present.
Joyce, Michael. *Twelve Blue*. http://collection.eliterature.org/1/works/joyce__twelve_blue.html
Locative Hypertext. http://www.eastgate.com/locative/
[Murmur]. http://murmur.toronto.ca/about.php [No longer available; see instead http://cfccreates.com/productions/76-murmur]. See also Locative Hypertext.
Nitsche, Michael. *Video GameSspaces: Image, Play and Structure in 3D Worlds*. Cambridge, MA: MIT Press. 2008.
Pokémon Go. Computer Game. Niantic, 2016-present.
Pullinger, Kate. *Breathe*. https://research.ambientlit.com/

Punday, Daniel. "Space Across Narrative Media: Toward an Archaeology of Narratology." *Narrative* 25.1 (2017): 92–112.
Raley, Rita. "Editor's Introduction: Writing.3D." *The Iowa Review Web*, 2006. https://elmcip.net/node/1445 [No longer accessible]
Ronen, Ruth. "Space in Fiction." *Poetics Today* 7.3 (1986): 421–438.
Ryan, Marie-Laure. *Narrative as Virtual Reality 2: Revisiting Immersion and Interactivity in Literature and Electronic Media*. Baltimore, MD: Johns Hopkins University Press, 2015.
Ryan, Marie-Laure, Kenneth Foote and Maoz Azaryahu. *Narrating Space/Spatializing Narrative: Where Narrative Theory and Geography Meet*. Columbus: Ohio State University Press, 2016.
Sternberg, Meir. "Telling in Time (II): Chronology, Teleology, Narrativity." *Poetics Today* 13.3 (1992): 463–541.
The Path. Computer Game. Tales of Tales, 2009. (Auriea Harvey et Michaël Samyn). http://tale-of-tales.com/ThePath/
The Stanley Parable. Computer Game. Written by Davey Wreden and William Pugh. Galactic Café, 2011.
Tuan, Yi-Fu. *Space and Place: The Perspective of Experience*. Minneapolis: University of Minnesota Press, 1977.
VRwandlung. The Metamorphosis VR (Goethe Institut, Prague), online: https://www.youtube.com/watch?v=ML8H69E6zB0
Wardrip-Fruin, Noah, et al. *Screen*. http://collection.eliterature.org/2/works/wardrip-fruin_screen.html
What Remains of Edith Finch. Computer Game. Directed by Ian Dallas, produced by Alvin Nelson and Michael Fallik. Annapurna Interactive, 2017.
Zhai, Philip. *Get Real: A Philosophical Adventure in Virtual Reality*. New York: Rowman & Littlefield, 1999.
Zoran, Gabriel. "Towards a Theory of Space in Narrative." *Poetics Today* 5.2 (1984): 309–336.

1
TRANSMEDIAL UNNATURAL SPATIALITY AND POSTDIGITAL DYSTOPICALIZATION IN *THE PICKLE INDEX*

Astrid Ensslin

Introduction

This chapter approaches digital spatiality from the vantage point of unnatural, transmedial, and cognitive narratology. Focusing on Eli Horowitz, Russell Quinn, and Ian Huebert's cross-platform sci-fi fantasy novel, *The Pickle Index: A Novel in 10 Days* (2017; henceforth "TPI"), I examine how, in contemporary transmedial fiction, unnatural in the sense of impossible, defamiliarizing narrative structures can permeate all four types of textual spaces delineated by Ryan et al. (2016): the spatial form(s) of the text, the space(s) materially occupied by the text, the spatial context(s) of the text, and the mimetic space(s) of the text. The parenthetical plural endings are placed deliberately to demonstrate the necessity to approach each type of textual space pluralistically in transmedia narratives that involve multiple entry points, multiple material manifestations, and multiple temporalities in their episodic design. This spatio-temporal multidimensionality calls for a dynamic combination of cognitive and material reading strategies, which are, in turn, contingent upon the reader's extradiegetic spatial constraints.

Narratives across media can "denaturalize our knowledge of space" (Alber 2016: 186) and our perception of the possibilities of spatialized storytelling in diverse ways. Spatial distortion can, for example, take the form of interior spaces exceeding their exterior boundaries. Kings Cross' railway platform 9¾ in J.K. Rowling's *Harry Potter*, for example, is part of an ontologically distinct space (the wizards' world) impossibly contained within the spatial parameters of a pillar between platforms 9 and 10 in the muggle world. Impossible spatiality can manifest as humanly incomprehensible, infinite labyrinths, as in Jorge Luis Borges' short story "The Aleph." It may involve logically incompatible changes to objects and

DOI: 10.4324/9781003053880-2

settings within the same storyworld that defy the principles of non-contradiction, as exemplified by the infinitely looping staircases and ever-morphing corridors in Davey Wreden's indie game, *The Stanley Parable*, or it can manifest as chemically and physically impossible geographies like the burning lake in Milton's *Paradise Lost* and the floating island of Laputa in Swift's *Gulliver's Travels*.

In postclassical narratology, narratives that exhibit impossible and thus potentially defamiliarizing structures are referred to as unnatural narratives, because they employ "strategies or aspects of discourse that do not have a natural grounding in familiar cognitive parameters or in familiar real-life situations" (Fludernik 1996: 11). Many unnatural narrative structures, such as supernatural, utopian, and dystopian elements in fantasy, science fiction, and children's stories are fully conventionalized within the repositories of their respective genres. Likewise, epistemically impossible narrative perspectives like omniscient narration, for example, have over time become conventionalized as integral components of novelistic discourse (Nielsen 2011). Other unnatural structures, whilst not fully conventionalized, are nevertheless readily naturalized as readers deploy specific cognitive reading strategies that may, for instance, attribute unnatural spatiality to a specific psychological state (e.g. a surreal dream) or a transcendental realm (e.g. the assumption of supernatural forces). Of particular interest to this study are spatial arrangements that defy conventionalization *and* naturalization, as often seen in poststructuralist and/or experimental fiction. Such unnatural spatialities operate anti-mimetically (Richardson 2015): they break reader expectations, and they urge readers to bend and flex their experientially developed categorization strategies, and embrace "cognitive uncertainty" (Zunshine 2008: 164).

Digital media afford a medium-specific array of embodied experiences that draw from a wide repository of semiotic modes – from the more conventional linguistic and audio-visual forms of representation known from print and cinematic narrative to the gestural (Bouchardon 2014), environmental (Jenkins 2004), ergodic (Aarseth 1997), and procedural (Hawreliak 2019) forms of narrative interaction characteristic of interactive screen media such as video games and digital-born (or digital) fictions (DFs). DFs are fictional, interactive texts made and perused in a variety of computational technologies ranging from standalone hypertext to three-dimensional (3D) narrative games, touchscreen story apps, and virtual reality/augmented reality (VR/AR) fictions. In DFs, conventional forms of textual and narrative space can become medium-reflexively amplified, foregrounded, and/or anti-mimetically subverted. DFs can therefore break not only the conventions of linear storytelling but those of digital-interactive narratives themselves (Ensslin and Bell 2021). These medium-specific conventions include, for instance, forms of interactive-multilinear storytelling, intradiegetic-navigational game maps, and a variety of extradiegetic, spatialized gestures like click, swipe, and tap, which reader/players must deploy to trigger and respond to intradiegetic events and actions.

This chapter focuses on an experimental DF that diversely denaturalizes narrative spatiality: *The Pickle Index* consists of a paperback codex, a set of two hardcover volumes, and a touchscreen app. It can be read through multiple entry points and in various material combinations. Furthermore, its app component uses the format of a digital map to spatialize and animate human connections in the storyworld and to visualize how they serve as trajectories for grotesque pickle recipe exchanges. TPI weaves the reader into its storyworld metaleptically, thus evoking a surrealist, anti-mimetic experience. I argue that TPI stands in a postdigitally critical, satirical, allegorical relationship to the Internet, and that the spatial impossibilities, illogicalities, and physical awkwardness that characterize the reading experience as a whole embody a form of geocriticism that exposes contemporary social media as a carnivalesque threat to the very foundations of democracy.

This essay makes a contribution to a number of theoretical areas within postclassical narratology. From a cognitive-narratological vantage point, my analysis re-evaluates Jan Alber's (2016) unnatural reading strategies and maps them onto Ryan et al.'s (2016) typology of textual spaces. I further translate Ensslin and Bell's (2021) medium-conscious reading strategy of "accepted as an unnatural construction" into a postdigital, cross-media framework. This framework foregrounds the material and embodied situatedness of reading across digital-interactive, ambi-linear print and visual-graphic media as well as across ontological spheres in a transmedial aesthetics of difficulty. It further allows me to read spatial unnaturalness in TPI allegorically and to introduce postdigital dystopicalization as a new concept for medium-specific geocriticism.

Unnatural Spatiality and Digital Fiction

In *Towards a "Natural" Narratology* (1996), Monika Fludernik defines "natural narrative" as "naturally occurring [and], mainly, spontaneous conversational storytelling" (13) which "cognitively correlate[s] with perceptual parameters of human experience" (9). Conversely, "non-natural narratives" do not have a "natural grounding in familiar cognitive parameters or in familiar real-life situations" (11). Thus, the starting point of natural narratology, according to Fludernik, is anthropomorphic experientiality and natural narratives typically yet not exclusively include real-life, everyday storytelling as exemplified by anecdotes, interviews, and observational narratives. Unnatural narratology, by contrast, examines narratives that lie beyond or subvert human experience. What is often neglected by (un)natural narratological theory is that human experience is culture-specific and idiosyncratic, and that notions of what is "natural" and "unnatural" cannot therefore be treated as anthropological universals but only within their specialized societal and cultural environments and paradigms. The concepts of natural and unnatural narration assumed in this essay are deeply anchored within a Western, Anglo-American tradition, yet since I critically engage with the problematic implications of this nomenclature elsewhere (Bell and Ensslin 2018; Ensslin and Bell 2021), I shall omit it here.

Unnatural narratologists distinguish between mimetic, non-mimetic, and anti-mimetic narratives. Mimetic texts "seek to reproduce in fiction typical characters and events from the actual world" (Richardson 2011: 31). Narrative forms that do not represent the actual world are either non-mimetic or anti-mimetic. Non-mimetic structures, which are conventionally found in fantasy, fairy tales, and science fiction, "will follow non-realistic conventions" (Alber et al. 2013: 102), yet nonetheless maintain the "mimetic impulse" of a logically structured and inherently consistent story world. Anti-mimetic narratives, conversely, are blatantly subversive and "strikingly impossible in the real world" (Alber et al. 2013: 102). They draw attention to their "own constructedness, the artificiality of many of [their] techniques, and [their] inherent fictionality" (Richardson 2011: 31). Anti- and non-mimetic representations thus differ in terms of the degree to which they "defamiliariz[e] … the basic elements of narrative" (Richardson 2011: 34), "contravene the presuppositions of nonfictional narratives, violate mimetic expectations and the practices of realism, and defy the conventions of existing, established genres" (Richardson 2016: 3). Distinguishing between non- and anti-mimetic structures is therefore a matter of degree, and the two concepts may better be conceptualized as end poles of a spectrum than in a binary, mutually exclusive relationship. While not all unnatural narratologists accept non-mimetic texts as part of their remit, I shall engage with both non-mimetic and anti-mimetic structures in my analysis of TPI to show how both interlace, thus affording a defamiliarizing, entertaining, and critically thought-provoking reading experience.

In his examination of unnatural spatiality in print narratives and drama, Alber (2016) defines anti-mimetic spaces as "[n]arrative spaces [that] can be physically impossible (if they defy the laws of nature) or logically impossible (if they violate the principle of non-contradiction)" (186). Anti-mimetic spaces may range from situational frames to entire worlds, and they denaturalize our spatial schemata to "fulfill a determinable function" in the narrative (187). These functions are for the reader to decode via a range of reading strategies. These can involve, for example, frame blending (combining previously unconnected cognitive structures, such as the possibility of a unique unit existing in two ontological spaces at the same time), generification (attribution to one or more narrative genres and their conventions), transcendentalization (positing a transcendental realm such as a supernatural or divine presence), subjectification (attribution to a character's or the narrator's psychological condition, such as dreams, hallucinations, or psychopathology), satirization, parody, and/or allegory (evoking an extended metaphor and/or a critical-humoristic stance), and foregrounding of the thematic (reading the unnatural in terms of amplifying a thematic concern, such as postmodern identity fragmentation. For narratives that "can serve as a construction kit or collage that invites free play with its elements" (Alber 2016: 53; see Ryan 2006), as often seen in choose-your-own-adventure novels and hypertext fiction, Alber suggests a "do-it-yourself" strategy. Finally, to come to terms with structures that do not lend themselves to a naturalizing reading, Alber suggests a "Zen way of reading" (2016: 54). This strategy requires an "attentive and stoic" (54) stance that accepts and embraces aesthetic effects of bewilderment and non-comprehension.

In their medium-specific development and transmedial refiguring of Alber's strategies, and particularly the "Zen" approach, Ensslin and Bell (2021) introduce the idea of paying attention to and accepting medium-specific, anti-mimetic "unnatural constructions" (Richardson 2016) as a new reading strategy. This kind of approach is required when considering the affordances of digital media for unnatural narratives. Narrative contradiction, for example, is a staple technique in multilinear hypertexts that allow different pathways through the story, which often lead to mutually contradictory endings. Logical contradiction, such as the possibility of a character dying in one path and surviving in another, is fully conventionalized in digital narratives such as video games. However, the extent to which the logical impossibility of contradiction is also defamiliarizing depends on how anti-mimetically it operates. It also depends on whether readers are either led to naturalize them as possible paths in a variationist yet inherently consistent storyworld or whether the paths are so defamiliarizing and incoherent that they draw attention to their own medium-specific constructedness. In the latter case, which occurs in many Storyspace hyperfictions, for example, readers must adopt not only a Do-It-Yourself approach to patch together one or more possible plotlines, but they also need to develop a Zen-like stance that enables them to reflect critically on the affordances of the medium itself and to accept non-closure, disorientation, and ambiguity as *sine-qua-non* of literary hypertext.

Spatial impossibilities – as measured against real-world mimeticism – are ubiquitous in digital narratives. Video games in particular allow players to escape into dreamlike realms that blatantly defy the law of physics and biology and "allow [them] to crawl, jump, run, fly, and teleport into new worlds of unheard-of form and function" (Nitsche 2008: 2). In fact, as I have argued elsewhere (Ensslin 2015), spatial and gravitational impossibilities and other types of immersive and mechanically challenging non-mimetic structures form an integral part of the imaginative and interactive appeal of blockbuster game design. To progress in a digital narrative, reader/players learn to adapt swiftly to physically and logically impossible spaces. They internalize the software and hardware constraints to often masterly degrees, no matter how much physical and cognitive adaptation they require, and they willingly accept and integrate physical impossibilities and logical incompatibilities into their own cognitive infrastructure.

This readiness to naturalize ludonarrative difficulties and impossibilities is subverted by experimental digital narratives that deploy unnatural spatiality in anti-mimetic ways to defamiliarize and draw attention to metafictional and extrafictional concerns. These techniques can operate on all four levels of textual spatiality (Ryan et al. 2016): mimetic space, spatial context, materially occupied space, and spatial form of text. For example, so-called hypermimetic game worlds (Ensslin and Bell 2021: 93), like the Shropshire-inspired deserted village of Yaughton in The Chinese Room's *Everybody's Gone to the Rapture*, operate in environmentally anti-mimetic ways. The *mimetic space* of the pastoral-inspired mediated world here becomes the leading narrative agent of the story. In its morbidly blinding perfection, it carries the alienating and terrifying aftereffects of an epidemic the cause of which the player must identify. The stiflingly photo-hyperrealistic idyllic space is overlaid with supernatural elements like voices coming from seemingly nowhere, animated light swirls, and human-shaped light effects. The player's challenge is to overcome atmospheric alienation and solve the narrative riddle despite the odds of defamiliarizingly slow and haphazard navigation. At the same time, we are left wondering throughout whether to apply a transcendentalizing strategy, which would attribute the unnatural to some kind of supernatural force, and/or whether generification and attribution to science fiction or fantasy conventions might be equally if not more appropriate.

An example of defamiliarized *spatial context* is Kate Pullinger's ambient app fiction, *Breathe*. Using application programming interfaces (APIs), the app feeds the reader's personal and site-specific spatial and meteorological data into the narrative. Whilst GPS-sensitive apps and cookies are a fully conventionalized experience and integral part of digital culture, Pullinger's work creates a strong sense of defamiliarization as the fictional world of the narrative intrudes metaleptically into the reader's personal space. This happens in an unexpected and uncanny way that exposes surveillance and privacy issues characteristic of algorithmic culture, and thus calls for an allegorical or thematic reading (Alber 2016).

A pertinent example of anti-mimetic *space materially occupied* by a digital text is given by Ryan (this volume). Noah Wardrip-Fruin's 3D Cave Automatic Virtual Environment (CAVE) poem, *Screen*, defamiliarizes by shifting the reader/player's attention from decoding the words on the virtual walls to catching and reattaching them as they fall to the ground with increasing speed. This yields an unsettling "anti-reading experience" (Raley 2006) that foregrounds and problematizes the reader's extradiegetic interaction with the text and makes meaningful semiotic engagement impossible. In projecting memory loss as a thematic concern of the work, Ryan (this volume) implicitly suggests a combined thematic and subjectifying reading strategy (Alber 2016).

Finally, many DFs experiment with defamiliarizing the *spatial form of the text*, accessible through the Graphical User Interface (GUI). So-called palimpsestic writing in digital media stretches across multiple conceptual and/or spatial layers. Jason Nelson's *Dreamaphage*, for example, has a 3D zoomable and clickable interface that symbolizes the interior of a person's mind that has been infested by an imaginary virus. The work layers poetry, narrative, scientific writing, and ludic multimedia as a puzzle to resolve in the search of a cure. Yet it withholds the answer to the riddle and instead transforms the "orienting space" (Punday 2017) of the GUI into a disorienting space (Ensslin and Bell 2021), leaving reader/players looping and zooming without a clear sense of direction. The work thus yields a combination of unnaturalizing and potentially thematic reading strategies, especially when read retro-referentially, against the backdrop of a global pandemic.

In what follows, I will demonstrate how *The Pickle Index* as an experimental, transmedial novel anti-mimetically defamiliarizes all four types of textual spaces. In my analysis, I take a variationist approach that emphasizes how spatial defamiliarization operates via multiple entry points, multiple material manifestations, and multiple temporalities. I expand Alber's (2016) and Ensslin and Bell's (2021) repositories of cognitive and medium-conscious reading strategies by adding key aspects of material engagement and accessibility, and I arrive at an overall allegorizing understanding of the work as a postdigital, dystopicalized (dystopian and spatially denaturalized) critique of social media culture.

The Pickle Index: *Transmediality and Unnatural Spatiality*

The Pickle Index is a transmedial novel *par excellence*: it contains a paperback codex, two hardcover volumes, and a touchscreen app, which have to be read in combination for its full aesthetic effects. In transmedial narratives, storytelling "takes place *across* media" (Gardner 2017: 76), with "integral elements of a fiction [becoming] dispersed systematically across multiple delivery channels for the purpose of creating a unified and coordinated entertainment experience" (Jenkins 2007). Transmedial storytelling thus distributes elements of a narrative across different media rather than simply remediating a story from one medium to the next. Its most popular forms include global blockbuster franchises like Nintendo's *Pokemon* and Disney's *Marvel Universe*, both of which span a variety of media, such as live action and animated film, TV series, comic books, and various types of digital, card, and board games. Their success is supported by lucrative merchandise and a vibrant fan culture, which, in turn, spins the narrative further, beyond commercially produced "canonical" material. Yet the transmedial spectrum reaches way beyond mass conglomerates and includes smaller, standalone experimental mixed-media forms as well. TPI is an example of the latter, and whilst it is commercially traded, with a price tag of between US$ 3 and US$ 28, depending on which item one chooses to buy, its design, distribution, and audience appeal are distinctly nichey.

Previous studies have examined TPI particularly in terms of its multimodal aesthetics. Grzegorz Maziarczik (2019) aligns the work with other contemporary digital-born novels, such as Danny Cannizzaro's and Samantha Gorman's *Pry* and Reif Larsen's *Entrances & Exits*, which employ touchscreen haptics to augment visual aspects of reading and thematize fragmentation as a psychological or pathological concept. Daniel Lynch et al. (2017) place TPI in the tradition of transmedia creative writing dating back to materially experimental works like BS Johnson's book-in-a-box, *The Unfortunates*, and multimodal print novels like Mark Z Danielewski's *House of Leaves*. Lynch et al. (2017) employ the term "iterative multimodal ecologies" to describe the ways in which transmedia writing engages in world building and world expansion through iterative circles, leveraging a variety of semiotic modes and deploying them across platforms so as to challenge readers to construct mental frames of the narrative while moving between symbolical forms and materially situated platforms. In TPI and other transmedia novels, this strategy helps to amplify "a range of character perspectives, world building and 'reader participation'" (Lynch et al. 2017). It "exploit[s] the increasingly porous nature of the book's 'binding'" and foregrounds the effect the reader's choices may have on "who gets to do the representing, who is represented, and what effect the means of representation may have on the story" (ibid). Thus, while some research exists that examines key transmedial aspects of TPI from a mostly semiotic and research-creation perspective, none of these studies analyze the work more closely, using a rigorous postclassical narratological framework. This chapter will address this gap while, at the same time, helping to preserve important digital aspects of TPI that are threatened by obsolescence.

TPI tells the story of a circus clown named Zloty Kornblatt, whose gift of entertaining and enthralling the masses with optimism and humor is perceived as a threat to the dystopian society in which the narrative is set. Having been caught "lacerating personal attacks upon our Madame J [the 'Prime Mother' of the story world's totalitarian regime]" (*News*: 9), Zloty is captured by a parachute strike team and put behind bars. The ensuing core narrative follows a group of friends from Zloty's circus, who set out to rescue him from the Confinement Needle, where he is imprisoned awaiting death by one or more unspeakably torturous execution methods. In a super-humanly difficult and comically clumsy attempt to free Zloty, the friends manage to get themselves captured and end up in the same cell as Zloty, with a panoramic view of the crowd-designed Termination Field where they are destined to die. In a surreal attempt to alter their fate, Zloty seduces and rhetorically distracts the masses gathered around the Field to watch the deadly spectacle, and the friends manage to escape during a short moment of fanatic mass approval and carnivalesque upheaval that precedes the restoration of totalitarianism.

The novel can be read in materially diverse ways and from many points of entry, but as a reader I found starting with the hardcover volumes, *News* and

Snacks, the most conducive to cognitive processing and text world construction. In the front matter, readers learn that:

> The Pickle Index is designed to be read in alternating chapters, first this book ["*News*"] and then the other one, for each day of the story. Each pair of illustrations [featuring at the beginning of each chapter] can be joined to reveal a larger scene.
>
> *(News)*

Following these instructions, readers will experience the plot unfolding from two main political points of view, embodied by the two hardcover volumes: *News* features daily reports from two journalists from the government-friendly *Daily Scrutinizer*: Yevgeny Pinkwater, author of the first chapter "We got him," and Hank Hamper, author of all other reports in *News*, who replaces Pinkwater as Destina's chief mouthpiece in the press after reporting him to the authorities for including "certain unsanctioned iambic patterns in his subordinate clauses, possibly as some sort of rhythmic code to outside agitators" (*News*: 17). *Snacks* is written from the vantage point of Flora Bialy, a citizen of Burford and "Zloty's understudy" (Sudden Oak 2020). Flora issues her daily updates in the form of pickle recipes, thus hiding the politically sensitive, government-critical nature of her reports in an officially sanctioned format that travels through the fictional storyworld's "first, best, and only forum for citizen-to-citizen fermentation-recipe exchange" (*Snacks*: 25–26): the Pickle Index.

A key aspect of TPI's transmedia universe is that its culinary, fictional, social media network, "the Index," reaches across the storyworld and into the reader's own world. The TPI app visualizes, in animated form, how each recipe released by the reader travels between recipients and straight into the reader's intradiegetic mailbox. From there readers can, in turn, forward the recipe to their own extradiegetic mail and social media accounts. Each social node on the abstract, two-dimensional (2D) topographical map is a yellow, 3D cube, labeled with the inhabitant's name and their current number of friends. The cubes turn into green rings as soon as a pickle recipe has arrived. Each recipe's path through the Index is illustrated with an animated dotted line (Figure 1.1).

In what follows, I offer an unnatural transmedial analysis of how TPI exploits, transforms, and ultimately subverts all four types of space, as outlined by Ryan et al. (2016), and renders them pluralistic. The work denaturalizes the mimetic space of the storyworld by evoking objects, events, and concepts that are surreal, abject, and/or physically impossible. It alienates readers whose spatial and material contexts bar them from accessing all physical elements of the novel. It defamiliarizes the spaces materially occupied by the text by challenging readers with its unconventionally spatialized material artifacts; and it subverts the spatio-textual conventions of narrative digital media by rendering

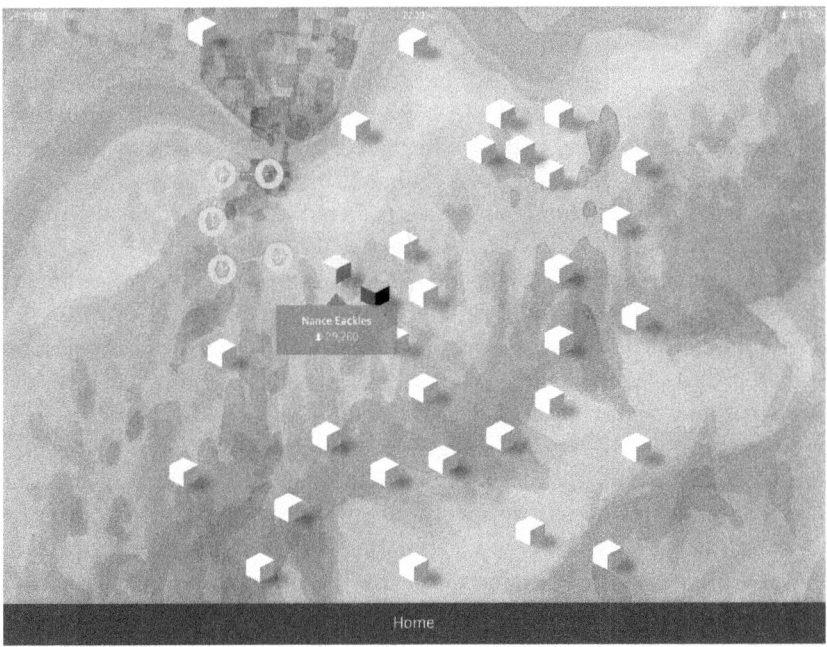

FIGURE 1.1 Map view of the Pickle Index.

the "orienting" navigational and socially networked space of the Pickle Index psychologically and interactionally unusable. Simultaneously, TPI creates an ontologically and socially impossible metaleptic linkage between mimetic space and the extra-mimetic space or spatial context of the reader.

The fictional universe of TPI is a dystopian world that combines mimetic, non-mimetic, and anti-mimetic elements. It mimetically and monomythically relates the capture and imprisonment of Zloty Kornblatt by "our nation's" (*News*: 16) totalitarian regime, the circus crew's subsequent journey from the parochial region of Burford to the capital city of Destina, their adventures, trials and tribulations on the way, their final rescue of Zloty, and finally their joint escape. In alignment with science fiction, cyberpunk, and fantasy, TPI features a host of non-mimetic elements such as futuristic machines ("Disorienting Luge" and "Parasite Time Machine"), fantasy animals commonly used for torturous executions ("swamp raccoons," "ratfish," and "wolf crabs"), biologically impossible characters ("bearded, unwashed toddlers"), and physically impossible human abilities (e.g. circus acrobat Kovacsz's transformation into a box with "the face of a man" [*Snacks*: 63] at Destina's entry checkpoint). Furthermore, TPI explicitly thematizes epistemic modality: its politically subjugated protagonists are self-consciously concerned with the impossibility of life under Madame J's regime, as expressed by Flora's free indirect discourse, "In those quiet mornings [with Zloty], it all seemed possibly possible" (*Snacks*: 21). Thus, readers are textually cued towards epistemic modality and made to reflect on elements and degrees of possible structures, both on a conceptual and formal level.

Most non-mimetic structures in TPI's story world can be fully naturalized by applying generification strategies (Alber 2016), attributing their occurrence to the conventions of science fiction and fantasy. Others, like the many references to impossible food items and how they might be merged into surreal recipes (e.g. "Ear Plugs" made from cornichons and ear holes, "Brined Snouts" made from "elderly hog," roasted fennel and tears or "Friendship Pickles" containing party decorations and friends) for the Index, are verging on the anti-mimetic. Not only are they alien to the extradiegetic world, but the fact that they are sent to the fictionalized reader through the metaleptic social network generates an ontological dilemma that I consider "permanently defamiliarizing," in the sense that they confront "the audience with unsolvable riddles that constantly resist recognition" (Iversen 2016: 459–460). Through extradiegetic system dialogues, readers are encouraged to forward impossible, unpalatable, revolting, or simply inedible intradiegetic recipes to their own extradiegetic networks. The fact that TPI is little known and does not have a fan community to speak of makes this metaleptic communication unlikely if not absurd or inappropriate. It turns the reader's extradiegetic space into an additional mimetic or hypothetical space that leads to an epistemic and ontological clash and renders the story world incompatibly pluralistic.

Spatial context and spaces materially occupied by the text are inextricably interwoven, thus pluralizing transmedial reading in unconventional ways. Whereas the paperback version can be read in a linear way (two-dimensionally via e-reader or three-dimensionally in print), the app releases its day-by-day narrative sections episodically and operationalizes touch and tap as a trigger for recipe dissemination and textual navigation. The hardcover novels, by contrast, are read in an alternating, ambi-linear way: first from the grey *News*, then from the red *Snacks*. The full spread illustrations at the beginning of each chapter work like multiperspectival, complementary puzzles: they can be placed side-by-side vertically or horizontally for a more complete picture, combining Flora's and Hamper's ideological and spatial perspectives. The opening illustrations for Chapters 5 (the plural is intended) even call out to be placed opposite each other to spatialize the hole in the prison wall from the points of view of the intruders and the guards (Figure 1.2). This 3D, embodied spatial requirement defamiliarizes the embodied reading process in a playful, multimodal way, disrupting immersion and leaving the reader puzzled over their augmented gestural role in transmedial spatialized reading.

The work's multiple entry points and navigation options are contingent upon which material edition(s) the reader has access to – by choice or accident. Engaging with all three material components of the text – the hardback volumes, the paperback or e-book omnibus, and the app – costs over US$ 50, and not all editions are available in all regions and at all times (the app can no

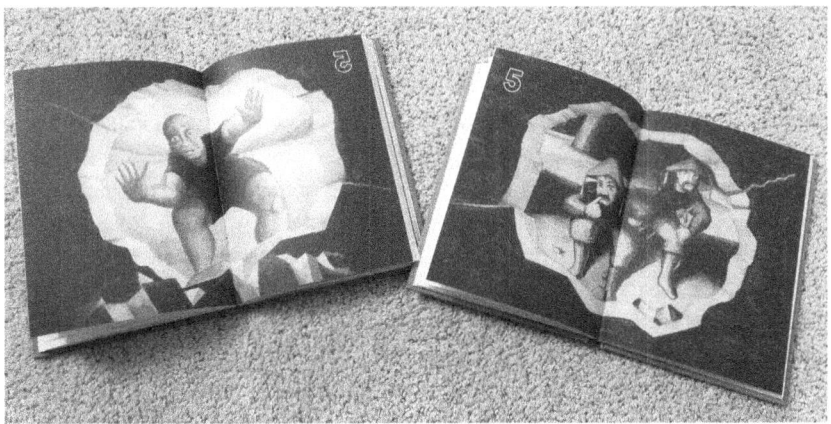

FIGURE 1.2 Complementary, spatialized illustrations in the hardback edition of TPI.

longer be downloaded). It is therefore likely that most TPI readers will have a subjectively incomplete experience of the work, which, in turn, contributes to their contextually spatial defamiliarization.

Similarly, even the most materially enabled reader is bound to struggle with the question of how to navigate the material objects of the text in a way that is intellectually satisfying and emotionally immersive. Switching between hardcover volumes after each of their ten chapters feels awkward, and replacing the experience with the fully sequentialized option in the paperback edition may be perceived as cheating or missing out on key aspects of embodied textuality. Likewise, having to wait for individual chapters to be released on the app challenges reader agency and immersion, adding both epistemic and deontic uncertainty to the reading experience. Thus, the phenomenologically multiplied extradiegetic spatial impossibilities of TPI are just as defamiliarizing if not financially or technologically unfeasible for many.

Finally, in relation to the spatial form of the text, "The Index" is described in the print works of TPI and depicted as an animated map in the app version. The animated dispatch of pickle recipes adds an important temporal dimension to the spatialized narrative experience. It aligns with the episodic receipt of individual chapters for readers of the app version and overlays the high-speed transmission of the fictional world (story time) with the low-speed transmission of the actual world, which is part of the medium-specific discourse time (Chatman 1978). This again creates an experiential clash and leaves readers wondering why they should care to wait for episodic releases if the material is available in alternative material form.

The map of the Index also operates metaleptically, by including a node for the reader ("You"). The social network is depicted with a high degree of cartographic obscurity and abstraction (Figure 1.1), revealing minimal visual details about the storyworld and leaving app-first TPI readers confused about its referentiality. I refer to this textual phenomenon, which draws attention to its medium-specific constructedness (see Section 2) and requires a Zen approach from app-first readers, as "inscrutable mapping" (Locke 2015). Its defamiliarizing effects are augmented by the fact that network participants' names do not match those in the main narrative, suggesting to the reader that they (alias their fictional counterparts) are supposed to have met and "friended" these participants in the fictional world of the text, which again is a logical incompatibility. The film footage and photographs of friends celebrating pickle-centered parties, which are displayed on the TPI website and in emails sent to the reader's actual digital networks, support this intuition. Overall, the invocation and photorealistic depiction of fictional friends via actual representational means permanently defamiliarizes the reading experience by making readers question their own subjectivity and connectedness. Furthermore, bizarre, impossible, and text world specific as the recipes are, the chances of a single reader forwarding any of them to their extradiegetic network are slim, and so the metaleptic effect becomes a key constraint of unnatural spatiality at the formal textual level.

Conclusion

Seen as a multiple spatialized textual ecology, TPI combines, pluralizes, and subverts the entire repository of spatial textuality proposed by Ryan et al. (2016). It implements an array of medium-specific and transmedial devices that formally, materially, contextually, and mimetically exceed what any one of its composite media (print, e-book, graphic design and illustration, live action film, animation, cartography, and touchscreen interactivity) can achieve individually. Simultaneously, it defamiliarizes the spatio-temporal conventions of its composite media with respect to the mimetic story world, the text's spatial form and the context, and the space materially occupied by the text. My overall reading strategies combined aspects of generification (Alber 2016) and accepting medium-specific constructedness (Ensslin and Bell 2021). The latter considers the ways in which the work calls attention to its own medial consciousness and formal experimental character. Further to this, reading the work allegorically, which I consider appropriate and necessary, evokes a critique of digital culture, specifically of social media, surveillance, and cancel culture. The speed at which the rancorous masses gathered around for Zloty's and his friends' execution change their minds and convert to Zloty fandom and back (within a matter of only ten pages) resembles the speed and volatility of meme culture; the Confinement Needle can be read as a satirical distortion of Foucault's *panopticon*; and the absurdities of the Termination Field resonate with the dark sides of the Internet and the speed and brutality at work in cyberbullying, doxxing, and other forms of online ostracism. The (fun) fact that there is a "pickle index" in our actual world – a demographic measure employed in China to track worker migration and urbanization (Ai 2014) – may be further suggestive of an allegorizing satirical reading. Importantly, Horowitz was not aware of this real-world phenomenon before TPI was published (personal correspondence, 04/01/2021), and while he confesses to seeing the resonances between both, he says he was more inspired by the potentially positive, democratizing tendencies of social media, exemplified by the Arab Spring in the early 2010s.

According to Horowitz, the distinctly dystopian elements of TPI are an indirect reference to the "Kafkaesque double-speak" related to the War on Terror and the "ridiculous" and "blatantly absurd" Guantanamo trials set up during the Bush administration (personal correspondence, 04/01/2021). Nonetheless, when viewed from a more contemporary perspective, the work also offers a critical, postdigital statement on the blindness with which society commonly approaches algorithmic exploitation of privacy and the propensity of digital, networked media to overturn democracy and ethical imperatives. Given its print-friendly, cross-platform, ontologically transgressive, and spatially multidimensional character, TPI therefore instantiates postdigital dystopicalization, in the sense of blending dystopian narrative conventions with unnatural spatiality in a pluralistic way.

TPI defamiliarizes transmedial storytelling and cross-media navigation by drawing attention to its own constructedness. Applying this medium-conscious, unnatural reading strategy needs to take into account key material-contextual elements of embodied reading. These elements include the diverse ways in which readers navigate, interact with, and become (dis)oriented by the parameters of their own reading space. Reading space thus transcends the spatial context of the text. It includes the reader's actual embodied, in the sense of haptic and situated interactions with the work – described here as unnaturally awkward. Finally, paying attention to medium-specific constructedness needs to consider how embodied engagement with the work complicates and problematizes the materialities of cross-media reading logistically, financially, and haptically, amplifying and foregrounding questions of equitable access and obsolescence.

Works Cited

Aarseth, Espen. 1997. *Cybertext: Perspectives on Ergodic Literature*. Baltimore, MD: Johns Hopkins University Press.
Ai, Chi-Han. 2014. "Pickle Index of China's Urbanisation," *Urbachina: Sustainable Urbanisation in China*, 2 Sept., https://urbachina.hypotheses.org/.
Alber, Jan. 2016. *Unnatural Narrative: Impossible Worlds in Fiction and Drama*. Lincoln, NE: University of Nebraska Press.
———, Stefan Iversen, Henrik Skov Nielsen and Brian Richardson. 2013. "What Really Is Unnatural Narratology?" *Storyworlds* 5: 101–118.
Bell, Alice and Astrid Ensslin. 2018. "Digital Fiction and Unnatural Narrative," in Z. Dinnen and R. Warhol (eds) *The Edinburgh Companion to Contemporary Narrative Theories*. Edinburgh: Edinburgh University Press, 292–304.

Bogost, Ian. 2007. *Persuasive Games: The Expressive Power of Videogames.* Cambridge, MA: MIT Press.

Bouchardon, Serge. 2014. "Figures of Gestural Manipulation in Digital Fictions," in Alice Bell, Astrid Ensslin, and Hans Kristian Rustad (eds) *Analyzing Digital Fiction.* New York: Routledge, 159–175.

Chatman, Seymour. 1978. *Story and Discourse: Narrative Structure in Fiction and Film.* Ithaca, NY: Cornell UP.

Ensslin, Astrid. 2015. "Video Games as Unnatural Narratives," in Mathias Fuchs (ed) *Diversity of Play.* Lueneburg: Meson Press, 41–72.

——— and Alice Bell. 2021. *Unnatural Narrative and Digital Fiction.* Columbus: Ohio State University Press.

Fludernik, Monika. 1996. *Towards a 'Natural' Narratology.* London: Routledge.

Gardner, Jared. 2017. "Transmedial Narratives in the Age of Mixed Media," *Narrative Culture* 4(1): 76–88.

Hawreliak, Jason. 2019. "On the Procedural Mode," in Astrid Ensslin and Isabel Balteiro (eds) *Approaches to Videogame Discourse: Lexis, Interaction, Textuality.* New York: Bloomsbury, 227–246.

Horowitz, Eli, Russell Quinn and Ian Huebert. 2015. *The Pickle Index*, http://www.thepickleindex.com.

Iversen, Stefan. 2016. "Permanent Defamiliarization as Rhetorical Device; or, How to Let Puppymonkeybaby into Unnatural Narratology," *Style* 50(4): 455–461.

Jenkins, Henry. 2004. "Game Design as Narrative Architecture," electronic book review, Oct. 7, https://electronicbookreview.com/essay/game-design-as-narrative-architecture/.

———. 2007. "Transmedia Storytelling 101," Mar. 21, http://henryjenkins.org/blog/2007/03/transmedia_storytelling_101.html.

Locke, Charley. 2015. "The Pickle Index Is a Delightfully Weird, App-driven Novel Like No Other," *Wired*, Nov. 24, https://www.wired.com/2015/11/the-pickle-index/.

Lynch, Daniel. 2016. "Between the Network and the Narrative: Transmedia Storytelling as a Philosophical Lens for Creative Writers," *New Writing* 13(2): 161–172.

———, Lee McGowan and Donna Hancox. 2017. "Iterative Multimodality: An Exploration of Approaches to Transmedia Writing," *Text* 21(2): 1–12.

Maziarczik, Grzegorz. 2019. "Singularity, Multimodality, Transmediality: Fragmentary Future (s) of the Novel?" in Vanessa Guignery and Wojciech Drąg (eds) *The Poetics of Fragmentation in Contemporary British and American Fiction.* Wilmington, DE: Vernon Press, 149–160.

Nielsen, Henrik, Skov. 2011. "Unnatural Narratology, Impersonal Voices, Real Authors, and Non-Communicative Narration," in Jan Alber and Rudiger Heinze (eds) *Unnatural Narratives, Unnatural Narratology.* Berlin: De Gruyter, 71–88.

Nitsche, Michael. 2008. *Video Game Spaces: Image, Play, and Structure in 3D Worlds.* Cambridge, MA: MIT Press.

Punday, Daniel. 2017. "Space across Narrative Media: Towards an Archeology of Narratology," *Narrative* 25(1): 92–112.

Raley, Rita. 2006. "Editor's Introduction: Writing.3D," *The Iowa Review Web*, https://elmcip.net/node/1445 [No longer accessible].

Richardson, Brian. 2011. "What Is Unnatural Narrative Theory?" in Jan Alber and Rüdiger Heinze (eds) *Unnatural Narratives, Unnatural Narratology.* Berlin: De Gruyter, 23–40.

———. 2015. *Unnatural Narrative: Theory, History, and Practice*. Columbus: Ohio State University Press.
Ryan, Marie-Laure. 2006. *Avatars of Story*. Minnesota: University of Minnesota Press.
———, Kenneth Foote and Maoz Azaryahu. 2016. *Narrating Space / Spatializing Narrative: Where Narrative Theory and Geography Meet*. Columbus: Ohio State University Press.
Sudden Oak. 2020. "End-of-life information for THE PICKLE INDEX and THE NEW WORLD," 13 Nov. 2020, http://www.suddenoak.com/endoflife/.
Zunshine, Lisa. 2008. *Strange Concepts and the Stories They Make Possible*. Baltimore, MD: Johns Hopkins University Press.

2

TAILING REBUS

Plotting a Conspiracy in Digital Space

Brian L. Greenspan

There are millions of stories in the digital city, and this is one that refuses to end. The modern genres of the noir detective novel and police procedural revealed new perspectives on twentieth-century urban settings, foregrounding everyday places that most city dwellers actively avoid. Nearly a century after Sam Spade and Philip Marlowe stalked crime in the fictionalized streets of San Francisco and Los Angeles, novel forms of urban storytelling allow readers to follow in the stealthy footsteps of hard-boiled investigators while exploring new global locales. Site-specific locative media for mobile devices have the potential to enhance the fictional spaces of police procedurals with procedural spaces, putting the reader in the role of the detective to face the dangers and thrills of the mean city streets. Locative media mingle real spaces with fictionalized and mediated spaces, providing the perfect platform for a murder mystery story—providing that it's safe to tell.

This chapter introduces *Tailing Rebus*, a project currently in (suspended) development.[1] Our goal is to adapt a popular detective novel in print for site-specific digital presentation using StoryTrek, a locative media authoring system developed at Carleton University's Hyperlab. The StoryTrek authorware allows users to layer text and rich media onto Google maps, creating extensive and intricately connected spatial stories that respond in real time to the vector and style of the user's physical movement and ever-changing geospatial context (Greenspan 2011a). You experience a StoryTrek narrative simply by walking through an urban or natural environment with your mobile device in hand while the story follows along, tacking and turning in response to your movements. Most locative apps track the user's geophysical location at any given moment, perhaps allowing them to check in at particular hotspots or revealing a virtual prize. As Mark Sample (2014) observes, "such platforms for social

DOI: 10.4324/9781003053880-3

interactivity tell us very little about our network, our interactions, and our places. Location is not compelling.[...S]tories are" (68). StoryTrek includes the narrative element that is missing from most geolocative games and installations by responding not only to where a user is at any given moment, but also how they got there and where they are headed next.

While previous StoryTrek installations involved original, born-digital narratives, in this case we're using the system to adapt Ian Rankin's (2000) novel *Set in Darkness*, the eleventh installment in the Inspector Rebus series, for locative delivery through mobile devices. *Tailing Rebus* aims to expand the reach of this internationally best-selling murder mystery into a medium that is ideal for wayfinding or games, but not typically associated with the delivery of lengthy suspense novels. Following Rankin's lead, our app uses everyday locations in the city of Edinburgh as a map of Scottish nationalism in the era of global capitalism. The facts in the case reveal that detective fiction is not what it used to be, and the culprit is globalization. Fredric Jameson (2010) observes that, as detective fiction migrated from its early locations in the United Kingdom to the United States, the genre lost several defining features. Gone are the "sleepy English towns and villages, [...] cloistered settings and vicarages," along with many of the traditional motives for murder (366). The family dynasties and passions that once motivated crime "have become increasingly irrelevant in the permissiveness of contemporary society, [with] its rootless and restless movement and postregionalism," a new geographical and social mobility enabled by globalization that has allegedly killed the murder mystery. In this flattened global context, Ian Rankin's detective novels are something of an inspired throwback. His renowned Inspector Rebus series unfolds in an Edinburgh that straddles the twenty-first century, recalling all the classic features of the detective story: the cloistered settings, clan systems, and passionate motives—generic features that have supposedly disappeared. Yet, Rankin also manages to situate his highly local "Tartan Noir" aesthetic within a much broader geopolitical context, as his global fan following attests: the Inspector Rebus series has been translated into 26 languages and adapted for radio and television by the BBC.

To this successful transnational and transmedial property, *Tailing Rebus* adds new layers and new medialities. The app opens with a cinematic video of a dark alley, accompanied by a bluesy saxophone riff to help establish the mood and setting, before presenting a map of the city with an arrow to mark the user's location and track their movement through the streets of Edinburgh. Our users will be able to follow Rebus's unfolding story via their smartphones or tablets simply by moving through the city, triggering story segments adapted from the *Set In Darkness* audiobook, and cued to their precise locations. By searching the city for zones that activate digital audio segments and advance the narrative, users enact the novel's underlying quest motif at every turn, while gaining a deeper understanding of the relationship between the story and its setting.

We chose to mobilize *Set in Darkness* in part because of its focus on setting and spatial processes. The novel foregrounds Edinburgh's old Gothic buildings that sit alongside new construction projects driven by the city's boom in urban renewal and development: "'So many building sites,'" as the villain points out, with "'lots of good, deep holes'" in which to bury bodies and secrets (Rankin 2000, 68). Rankin uses architectural landmarks to ground its consideration of historical and contemporary issues such as Scottish nationalism, gentrification, and class and gender politics, a strategy that we remediate. For instance, arriving at Grassmarket in the Old Town triggers a present-day photo of the street, along with a passage from the audiobook that encourages the user to reflect on their own place in Edinburgh's history of class struggle and creative destruction:

> Grassmarket was an odd little world all of its own. Centuries back, they'd held executions here, a fact commemorated by the name of one of the pubs, The Last Drop. Until the 1970s, the area had borne the reputation of being a haven for the destitute and the wandering. But then, gentrification became the model. Small specialist shops opened; the bars were spruced up, and tourists began their hesitant, steep descent down Victoria Street and Candlemaker Row.

In Rankin's handling, such descriptions of urban settings do more than merely add local color to the noir detective genre. As Peter Clandfield (2008) explains, *Set in Darkness* is characteristic of contemporary Scottish "architectural crime novels," in which the narrative connects small-scale crime surrounding private domestic dwellings to the city's monumental urban redevelopment projects, or "architectural crimes" on a national scale (85). As in other Inspector Rebus novels:

> [t]he blocks and schemes of the era of monumental redevelopment can stand not only as metonyms for Scottish socioeconomic misfortunes in the postimperial, postindustrial era, but also as haunting reminders of the uncanny resurgence of crime and other ills in the very places that were supposed to design them out of existence.
>
> *(Clandfield 2008, 82)*

Our goal is to activate the narrative's geopolitical critique by anchoring its descriptions of the effects of the city's changing architectural plan to the material city itself. Audio-visual assets layered onto the city map deepen the reader's immersive experience, while revealing how past and present intersect dialectically in Rankin's narrative. The photographic layers provide snapshots of the user's location at various points in the city's development, condensing the "allegorical impulse" that Craig Owens (1980) identifies variously with ruins, photography, and contemporary site-specific art installations into a single, convergent mobile experience. In combining printed text, streaming audio, digital photographs, and physical architecture, *Tailing Rebus* transforms Rebus's story into a literal rebus,[2] a "writing composed of concrete images" that reflects "allegory's hopeless confusion of all aesthetic mediums," exemplifying "the reciprocity which allegory proposes between the visual and the verbal," between visual and sonic language, between images and concrete things (Owens 1980, 74–75). For Owens, "the site-specific work becomes an emblem of transience, the ephemerality of all phenomena; it is the memento mori of the twentieth century" (71)—a fitting description of *Set In Darkness*, a millennial murder mystery that reflects constantly on its own historicity.

In fact, most locative media installations could be described as postmodern allegories in this sense, since the textual assets they distribute across geophysical space are connected through the sequence of the user's access, in paratactic "strategies of accumulation" that represent "the epitome of counter-narrative" (Owens 1980, 72). Yet, *Tailing Rebus* goes further by situating the fictional locations of *Set In Darkness* in proximity to their geophysical referents while also retaining the overall sequence of Rankin's narrative, a syntactic dimension that is unusually pronounced for a locative installation. Our adaptation uses Edinburgh's street syntax and landmarks to guide users toward certain preferred story paths, while StoryTrek's chapter feature allows them to "level up" and advance the story in set directions upon reaching certain zones of the city. Each revelation of new information and of new paths to follow is augmented with additional layers of digital images from various points in the city's history that resonate paradigmatically within this spatialized, postmodern allegory of transience and contingency.

In his influential discussion of fictional discourse, John R. Searle (1975) argues that the detective fiction genre constrains the representation of spatial referents to a higher standard of accuracy than other aspects of the narrative:

> if Sherlock Holmes and Watson go from Baker Street to Paddington Station by a route which is geographically impossible, we will know that Conan Doyle blundered even though he has not blundered if there never was a veteran of the Afghan campaign answering to the description of John Watson, M.D.
>
> *(331)*

However, such "nonfictional commitments" (Searle 1975, 331) are far less rigid in Rankin's detective fiction, which thematizes the differences between historical referents and the state of Edinburgh's cityscape at the turn of the millennium. Our app adds more cartographic layers still, pinning the original narrative to referents in the material city as they are (or will be) experienced by a contemporary user at any given future instance. This geolocative indexing reinforces the referential fidelity of the narrative when it unfolds near historical landmarks, while foregrounding its fictionality at those parts of the story situated in more rapidly developing urban zones, where recent changes to the cityscape are more evident. Although we have strived to make our locative adaptation as faithful as possible to Rankin's original story, its ever-changing spatial context can only undermine its referential accuracy in ways that will be less evident to readers of the printed novel, increasing the app's fictionality while threatening its geolocative accuracy.

A multimedia and multimodal text, our adaptation combines fictional spaces with sonic spaces (comprising spoken word, audio flashbacks, and incidental music) and mediated visual spaces (photographs and video) connected to the central story, all of which share screen space with a Google map that sets the stage and guides the user, who must also negotiate the non-diegetic spaces of the mobile interface and associated browser dashboard in order to navigate both the app and the actual city. Like all location-specific narratives, ours foregrounds the interactions of these various spaces with what Marie-Laure Ryan (2021) calls *the spatial context of the text*, "the physical space where the material support of the text is located, and from where the story can be accessed" (9). The text's multiple spatial contexts can arguably be extended to include its widely distributed sites of prior and ongoing production. Different individuals and teams worked at various times on adaptation, story editing, voice acting, soundtrack composition and performance, video production, locative plotting, and site-testing from Edinburgh, Belfast, Ottawa, and St. John's, while media assets are streamed from the commercial server located nearest to the end user, wherever in the world they may be accessing the story.

Some argue that interactive hypertext fictions, which are typically presented as texts that you must click through to read, are unappealing to the average reader because they fragment the story and increase the cognitive demand of reading. In an empirical study of hypertext fiction, James Pope (2010) found that when confronted with such a literary story, readers imported interpretive habits learned not from reading novels, but from playing videogames or surfing the web. These readers were understandably frustrated when the hyperfiction's narrative and interface conventions didn't align with their expectations of websites and games. Pope concluded that, despite the view "that there is pleasure to be derived from the almost limitless indeterminacy" and readerly co-creation involved in digital hyperfiction, "the lack of clear narrative structural markers [in many interactive fictions can…] block full enjoyment of the reading experience" (82). Other studies (e.g. Chaouli 2005; Dobson and Miall 1998; Ryan 2006) likewise point to the navigational challenges of hyperfiction, its disorienting effects, and its constant disruption of readerly immersion and pleasure by intrusive links and interfaces.

The navigational challenges that can disrupt the immersive experience of desktop hyperfictions are actually a feature of many locative stories and games, which rarely take full immersion as their goal, but rather unfold simultaneously in both fictional and real-world settings, transcoding disorientation or navigational barriers like random jumps, drifting, or backtracking into a meaningful form of input (Greenspan 2011b, 9–10). Early locative installations often deliberately misled users in order to heighten their disorientation, sparking comparisons with Situationist psychogeographies and *dérives*, tactics for disrupting the consumer spectacle. Locative media today, though not exactly commonplace, do seem less disruptive than they once did, thanks in part to the popularity of apps like Foursquare and Pokémon GO (Wilken 2012). *Tailing Rebus* acknowledges the growing adoption of mobile and locative media within everyday life, and aims to leverage that familiarity in a relatively seamless and readerly locative adaptation of Rankin's novel that turns away from disorienting jump cuts, *détournements*, and other disruptive formal features. We have aimed to retain both the popular appeal of the original print novel and its utopian commitment to radical politics and a better future, even while introducing site-specific affordances and forms of engagement that alter its mediality and spatio-temporal dimension.

Ironically, the very growth in popularity of locative media poses additional narrative challenges for the detective genre in particular. Jameson (2010) notes that "the introduction of cell phones radically transformed the constructional problems involved in plotting a mystery or adventure film, as well as in tracing calls and wiretapping as such […]" (363). That today's smart phones are always on and connected to data and GPS networks, making everyone subject to constant surveillance, might explain why Rankin has been so reluctant to include mobiles in his novels. Whereas GPS and digital surveillance figure prominently in popular detective conspiracy series such as *24* or *The Wire*, Inspector Rebus relies on old-school surveillance methods. During a 2018 live interview in Ottawa, Rankin pointed out that in his new Rebus novel, *In a House of Lies*, a character had to locate one of the last three public telephone boxes in Edinburgh to make a call that couldn't easily be hacked. Rebus does, however, enlist the help of younger colleagues in negotiating digital networks and social media, suggesting that even he can't resist the lure of the digital forever.

If the ubiquity of mobile devices disrupts the conventional narrative strategies of detective fiction, locative media have the potential to remediate and intensify those conventions. As Jameson (2016) observes, Raymond Chandler's private detective Philip Marlowe gathers information by visiting "either those places you don't look at or those you can't": either the public waiting rooms and elevators that comprise "the mass, collective side of our society […] the dimension of the interchangeable, the inauthentic," or the private estates, clubs, clinics, and gambling ships of secretive elite society (7–8). The private detective describes these invisible spaces without ever drawing them into a coherent totality; rather, the primary separation of urban Americans

> is projected out on to space itself: no matter how crowded the street in question, the various solitudes never really merge into a collective

experience, there is always distance between them. Each dingy office is separated from the next [...].

(Jameson 2016, 11)

Chandler's narratives close this social distance by mapping geographic space onto the social order, so that the Southern Californian landscape confers "a kind of completeness" or ideological closure on the social system (Jameson 2016, 50).

The *Tailing Rebus* app renders similar geographical mappings in the most literal fashion, even as the secret act of listening to a story while navigating a crowded urban site intensifies the user's sense of solitude, offering firsthand access to the experience of the gumshoe detective. Moreover, the app's virtual assets direct attention to places in the city that might otherwise go unnoticed, through narrative descriptions and photographs of interior locations that are physically inaccessible. Although each instance of *Tailing Rebus* tracks only the primary user, it alters the "social accessibility" of the city in ways similar to locative apps designed to track multiple users at once. As Darryl A. Pieber (2020) argues, such multiuser apps not only "render parts of the city visible or invisible to some or all of its inhabitants," but also "can render the inhabitants of the city visible or invisible" in ways that "reinforce existing racisms and other prejudices" (2020)—a problematic effect for actual sociality, but one that potentially enhances the spatialized social typology of the classic detective fiction (Jameson 2016, 43 et passim).

Our adaptation requires its user to explore the city while literally following the story, like a sleuth tailing a suspect, foregrounding the original novel's spatial settings and meditations on Edinburgh's geographic history. Like other augmented reality apps, *Tailing Rebus* adds spatial layers onto the city, accentuating certain features while filtering out others. But instead of augmenting reality, our goal is to strip it away in order to reveal to our users how diminished reality is in the twenty-first century. This approach transforms Rankin's narrative into what Elana Gomel (1995) calls an *ontological detective story*, "in which the world where the action takes place [itself] becomes an object of investigation, a mystery to be solved, a secret to be uncovered" (345). For Gomel, the dynamic of revelation and apocalypse in the ontological detective story is closely connected to the utopian impulse: "The world of mystery is, as a rule, a world of darkness, violence and evil, ripe for the cleansing of an apocalypse and a subsequent utopian transformation [...] predicated on the successful disclosure of some momentous secret," a transformation that "puts an end to the frighteningly unpredictable narrative of history," implying "that the world ultimately makes sense; that underneath the irrationality of human suffering lies a perfectly rational pattern" (346, 352).

Tailing Rebus enacts this apocalyptic dynamic by inviting users on a quest to find the secret locations that reveal fragments of Edinburgh's history, clues to a historical pattern of violence, privilege, disenfranchisement, and deceit, leading ultimately to the solution of the mystery. This larger historical arc is closely tied to the more immediate and practical temporalities, rooted in the embodied experience of the city, that guided our process of adaptation and development. Since the complete audio book version of *Set in Darkness* takes 14 hours to complete, we had to radically edit the narration to adapt it to a walkable experience. The process of editing the novel was iterative, and involved multiple site tests to determine the average time a user on foot would need to move between the story's various locations. Large portions of the original text had to be literally left off the map, while still leaving enough plot and character points to move the mystery along and enough local color to echo the user's whereabouts within Edinburgh at any given time. We also had to ensure that the user would reach key locations in the city that are integral to the plot, including the crime scene at Queensbury House, St. Leonards Police Station, and Rebus's favorite local watering hole, the inconspicuous Oxford Bar, all the while maintaining a coherent storyline. Our field tests revealed that these three locations alone take about 49 minutes to walk, not including time for listening to the audio clips or popping into the pub for neeps and tatties. Notably, we had to omit several character-driven subplots surrounding the police station as well as the important proto-feminist story of Rebus's younger colleague, Detective Sergeant Siobhan Clark. Our initial fears of bowdlerizing Rankin's novel gave way with the realization that our adaptation was not just a new version of the original story, but a portal through which users can create their own versions. Lai-Tze Fan (2017) notes

> the quality of contingency that users bring to different narratives composed through *StoryTrek*. […] What can be said of the individual experience of reading a *StoryTrek* narrative is that it utilizes users' agency to create contingent paths and also contingent meaning. In this way, dynamic narratives are formed, each of which serves as a copy with a difference […].
>
> *(16)*

The greatest challenge of the project has involved adapting the serial form of the popular detective novel to the open sandbox of a map-driven story, remediating the detective narrative's serial temporality in a spatial medium with a different relation to closure, and which allows for different forms of indeterminacy. In Rankin's novel, the discovery of a body in the Scottish Parliament at Holyrood leads Inspector Rebus to uncover a national conspiracy that solving the murder will not dispel, and which resonates beyond the text's conclusion. For Philip M. Wegner (2014), the indeterminacy and deferral of closure that are characteristic of conspiracy narratives only reinforces a conservative politics:

> […] there are in fact two different forms of 'death' that are at play in these conspiracy narratives. The first is […] the intolerable death of the critical

> investigator that ends the challenge to the conspiracy, a death [...] at one with the end of history itself.[...] However, there is a second form of death that is also possible, and occasionally realized in conspiracy narratives: this would be the death of the conspiracy itself, with its investigator successfully bringing it to the light of day, [....].
>
> *(139–140)*

Crucially, Wegner argues that the serial form of contemporary detective novels and television shows dictates that the mystery never ends and that neither the detective nor the conspiracy ever dies. Audiences are thus left suspended in a "half-life" between two deferred deaths, that of the detective and that of the conspiracy, thereby deferring the apocalyptic revelation and radical politics that would usher in a transformed, utopian world. This dynamic of deferral also haunts our users who enact the flatfoot's quest at every turn, tailing Rebus as he tails fictional suspects, and advancing the story by finding the next X that marks the spot. With each new discovery, the mystery continues; there are always more hotspots to uncover just around the corner, repeating in quick succession the detective genre's series of false "revelations," like the false endings of each novel in the series that keeps Rebus, the conspiracy, and paranoia alive, while endlessly deferring any political commitment to a transformed world.

And yet, by remediating Rebus's adventures in the form of a spatial hypertext, our app modulates the detective serial's temporality and dynamic of deferral, offering local discoveries at every turn that signify beyond the temporal setting of the story and the user's present day. The more our users explore the app and the city, the more they encounter both present-day locations and historical avatars that echo more loudly than the mystery's somewhat disappointing ending. Eleanor Bell (2008) likewise locates Rankin's ethical project in a deferral of closure that reaches beyond the detective serial form, and scales up to the level of global geopolitics:

> Central to Rankin's fiction [...] is [a] strong sense of Scotland in transition, a movement into twenty-first century global uncertainty and what might be thought of as a more postnational vision of the nation. In this way Rankin extends the notion of crime as a continual, disruptive, unknown force to the national level, implying that the nation is also in a process of continual evolution, one also full of mystery and lacking assurance.
>
> *(54)*

Bell adds, quoting Rankin himself, that "if the role of crime-fiction writers is to explain the world in some way, then 'being such a (relatively) small and (relatively) self-contained country, Scotland can work as a microcosm for the wider world'" (60–61). Our app enacts this spatial dialectic at the level of the interface, mediating Edinburgh's past and present through spaces that are at once fictional, virtual, and actual. It situates our users both locally within the city and in relation to Global Positioning Systems, freeing them from a half-life suspended between the death of the detective serial and the death of the conspiracy.

While *Tailing Rebus* does not bring closure to either Rankin's story or its fictional conspiracy, allowing readers to navigate that conspiracy through an actual city map updates the experience of the global conspiracy narrative, or what Jameson (1988) calls "the poor person's cognitive mapping," which itself stands in as "a degraded figure of the total logic of late capital, a desperate attempt to represent the latter's system" (356). Neither does our app provide access to any information that might help solve Scotland's larger mystery and bring about a transformed world here and now. In the final estimate, all it can do is transform local sites of national relevance into access points for global information networks that ultimately remain beyond the user's comprehension and beyond the nation-state itself, standing in for the totality of a new geopolitical order just over the horizon, a map of the world that has yet to be drawn.

Coda: Locative Under Lockdown

As a locative media project that blends virtual networks with embodied interactions in physical space, *Tailing Rebus* offers its users the potential to engage in new forms of mobile, embodied, and collective storytelling at a moment in history that discourages just such behaviors. As of this writing, the project—while not yet a cold case—remains suspended in a half-life between too many deaths. Our final user tests, originally scheduled to take place in the streets of Edinburgh in early 2020, were interrupted by the global pandemic that made locative exploration both impossible and, somehow, less crucial. With real fatalities lurking in each and every corner of the city, the virtual deaths that we encoded suddenly appeared distasteful. Mobility, the privilege of the police detective and the measure of twenty-first-century global citizenship, has become the principle vector of infection. Only now, as vast segments of the global population work, shop, and socialize through virtual platforms without leaving the safety of their own houses, does the real cost of networked solitude strike home.

Geolocative data have meanwhile assumed a new visibility, as governments openly embrace surveillance technologies to limit the mobility of individual subjects in the hope of curbing infection rates, and users the world over download contact tracing apps to their mobile phones, the nodes and edges of our social networks redefined as victims and vectors. The new urgency of geospatial data has also led to their politicization, as revealed in the firing and politically motivated investigation of scientists who refuse to manipulate geospatial data to misrepresent the safety of physical spaces (Luscombe 2020). These urgent new syntagms take precedence over interpretive paradigms: in his assessment of the current crisis, Slavoj Žižek (2020) urges us to resist the "premodern" temptation of seeking some "deeper meaning" in the pandemic, as though to prove that "[w]e matter in some profound way" to the universe (13). Žižek would disable the very allegorical register upon which *Tailing Rebus*—as hybridized rebus, site-specific disinterment, arbitrary supplement, intermittent paradigm, and concrete ruin—depends as it invites our users to discover analogs between the fictional spaces of the story and the material reality of the city.

And yet, what better medium for allegorizing this new generalized awareness of our urban surrounds, replete with viral hotspots, potentially infectious fomites, and the constant threat of social contact? As Jameson (2019) argues, while the plague in Albert Camus's eponymous novel has conventionally been read as a dualistic *allegoresis* of Germany's wartime occupation of France, it can also be understood as "genuine allegory [that] does not seek the 'meaning' of a work, but rather functions to reveal its structure of multiple meanings" (30). Contemporary texts in particular exhibit "perpetual dissolution and recombination in such a way that durable structures cannot be formed" (Jameson 2019, 347), endlessly displacing and "nullifying" their content. Jameson reads this unstable form of postmodern allegory as both a symptom of global capitalism's continual displacement of forces of production and a recognition of the historical contingency of narrative realism, which is grounded in "the adding in of meaningless details [...] in order to certify the 'realism' of the literary document," but "which vanishes with each new generation; and each realism which succeeds, competes with, and overcomes the preceding one, now unmasked as mere literature and 'fiction'" (349). *Tailing Rebus* is allegorical in this postmodern sense, even while it resists allegory's disintegration of narrative "agent, action, and setting" into "an anonymous spatial background, an anyplace" (Jameson 2019, 356). On the contrary, our adaptation multiplies the story's spatial settings, connecting Rankin's fictional spaces to historically specific images of those spaces, alongside their constantly transforming referent sites in the actual city. *Tailing Rebus* reveals the contingency of reference and fictionality themselves through spatially arranged episodes that promise a potentially boundless seriality, placed into an unstable interplay of paradigmatic links to the city's past, syntagmatic links to global data networks, and a material specificity that each and every situated user cannot but experience differently.

If current prohibitions against merging our "various solitudes [...] into a collective experience" only reinforce the atmosphere of the noir detective story, then the currently heightened atmosphere of suspicion that hovers over urban spaces may well lead our users to understand this police procedural that tracks their every movement as an allegory of social monitoring and surveillance. The pandemic has forced us into the net of geolocative tracing algorithms, raising fears of state-sanctioned privacy violations that escalate quickly into conspiracy theories, as individuals attempt to grapple with the global scale of the crisis. These are the spatial contexts into which our story about hidden crimes, neglected bodies, and clandestine surveillance through the city streets will eventually be released. I have elsewhere explored how locative media foreground the complex interactions of technical network protocols (e.g. TCP/IP, DNS, HTML, WPAN) with spatial, legal, and social-cultural protocols in ways that raise critical questions about the implications of ubiquitous mobile access for the Deleuzian "control society" (Greenspan 2021). Even if Žižek is right to warn against reducing containment measures and population tracing "to the usual paradigm of surveillance and control propagated by thinkers like Foucault" (2020, 76), the pandemic has added new layers of social control in the form of rapidly evolving protocols surrounding public health and social distancing, which future users of our app will doubtless connect to the story's themes. Until that time, if our locative project can be said to do anything while in its suspended state, it at least reveals that mobile devices and digital networks continue to derive any potential significance they may hold from their users' real, embodied interactions with material spatial contexts.

Notes

1 *Tailing Rebus* was developed with my intrepid co-conspirators Andrew Pepper, Dominique Jeannerod, Sarah Thorne, and Kazimir Stubitsch. We are grateful to Ian Rankin and Orion Books for their ongoing support of this project and for financial support from Carleton University, Queen's University Belfast, and the UK Arts and Humanities Research Council.
2 This is not to consider Rebus as a traditional personification of the rebus, which would be paradoxical. As Jameson (2019) proposes, "personification is itself the allegorical figure of reification," that very nominalist fixing of concepts which the allegorical impulse resists, and for which he would substitute "classes in formation, perhaps, where everything static about traditional personification is replaced with the process of personifying and of identifying agencies to come" (384–385).

Works Cited

Bell, Eleanor. 2008. "Ian Rankin and the Ethics of Crime Fiction." *Clues* 26(2): 53–63.
Chaouli, Michel. 2005. "How Interactive Can Fiction Be?" *Critical Inquiry* 31(3): 599–617.
Clandfield, Peter. 2008. "Denise Mina, Ian Rankin, Paul Johnston, and the Architectural Crime Novel." *Clues* 26(2): 79–91.
Dobson, Teresa M. and David S. Miall. 1998. "Orienting the Reader? A Study of Literary Hypertexts." Presented at the VIth Biannual IGEL Conference, Utrecht, The Netherlands, August 26–29. https://www.researchgate.net/publication/2515890_Orienting_the_reader_ A_study_of_literary_hypertexts.
Fan, Lai-Tze. 2017. "Writing While Wandering: Material and Spatial Contingency in Locative Media Narratives." *Convergence* 23(1): 5–19.
Golem, Elana. 1995. "Mystery, Apocalypse and Utopia: The Case of the Ontological Detective Story." *Science Fiction Studies* 22(3): 343–356.
Greenspan, Brian. 2011a. "Songlines in the Streets: Story Mapping with Itinerant Hypernarrative." In *New Narratives: Stories and Storytelling in the Digital Age*, edited by Ruth Page and Bronwen Thomas, 153–169. Lincoln: University of Nebraska Press.

Greenspan, Brian. 2011b. "The New Place of Reading: Locative Media and the Future of Narrative." *Digital Humanities Quarterly* 5(3). http://www.digitalhumanities.org/dhq/vol/5/3/000103/000103.html.

Jameson, Fredric. 1988. "Cognitive Mapping." In *Marxism and the Interpretation of Culture*, edited by Cary Nelson and Lawrence Grossberg, 347–357. Urbana: University of Illinois Press.

Jameson, Fredric. 2010. "Realism and Utopia in *The Wire*." *Criticism* 52(3–4): 359–372.

Jameson, Fredric. 2016. *Raymond Chandler: The Detections of Totality*. New York: Verso.

Jameson, Fredric. 2019. *Allegory and Ideology*. London: Verso.

Luscombe, Richard. 2020. "Florida Scientist Says She Was Fired for Refusing to Change Covid-19 Data 'to Support Reopen Plan.'" *The Guardian*, May 20. https://www.theguardian.com/us-news/2020/may/20/florida-scientist-dr-rebekah-jones-fired-refusing-change-covid-19-data-reopen-plan.

Owens, Craig. 1980. "The Allegorical Impulse: Toward a Theory of Postmodernism." *October* 12 (Spring): 67–86.

Pieber, Darryl A. 2020. "Filtered In/Filtered Out: Locative Media Apps and Social Accessibility in Urban Spaces." *Studies in Communication Sciences* 21.1: 1–13.

Pope, James. 2010. "Where Do We Go From Here? Readers' Responses to Interactive Fiction." *Convergence* 16(1): 75–94.

Rankin, Ian. 2000. *Set In Darkness: An Inspector Rebus Novel*. London: Orion.

Rankin, Ian. 2018. *In a House of Lies: An Inspector Rebus Novel*. Orion: London.

Rankin, Ian and Alan Neal. 2018. "In a House of Lies: One on One with Ian Rankin." Oct. 25. Christ Church Cathedral, Ottawa.

Ryan, Marie-Laure. 2006. *Avatars of Story*. Electronic Mediations 17. Minneapolis: University of Minnesota Press.

Ryan, Marie-Laure. 2021. "Four Types of Textual Space and Their Manifestations in Digital Narrative." In *Digital Space*, edited by Dan Punday, pp. 1–19. New York: Routledge.

Sample, Mark. 2014. "Location Is Not Compelling (Until It Is Haunted)." In *The Mobile Story: Narrative Practices with Locative Technologies*, edited by Jason Farman, 68–78. New York: Routledge.

Searle, John R. 1975. "The Logical Status of Fictional Discourse." *New Literary History* 6(2): 319–332.

Wegner, Philip M. 2014. *Shockwaves of Possibility: Essays on Science Fiction, Globalization, and Utopia*. Ralahine Utopian Studies 15. Oxford: Peter Lang.

Wilken, Rowan. 2012. "Locative Media: From Specialized Preoccupation to Mainstream Fascination." *Convergence* 18(3): 243–247.

Žižek, Slavoj. 2020. *Pandemic!: COVID-19 Shakes the World*. New York: Polity Press.

3
VIRTUAL WANDERING

Embodied Spatial Narrativity in Walking Simulators

Gregory Whistance-Smith

Introduction

Recent years have seen the emergence of a new videogame genre termed "walking simulators" where players explore a virtual environment in first-person perspective, piecing together a story as they traverse a world. These works emphasize narrative and the exploration of a setting instead of the kinetic or strategic challenges found in most videogames, and they often tackle literary themes such as modes of perception in *The Witness* (Thekla Inc. 2016), sexuality in *Gone Home* (The Fullbright Company 2013), and the nature of narrators in *The Stanley Parable* (Galactic Cafe 2013). While many walking simulators use verbal and written communication in the form of voiceovers and texts integrated into their worlds, the genre is defined by the experience of wandering through an evocative space rich with meaning, where progression through the environment parallels the progression (or the progressive uncovering) of the narrative (Jenkins 2004; Manovich 2001, 245). By using a designed environment as a narrative medium, walking simulators remediate the spatial narrativity inherent in architecture, installation art, and designed landscapes, using techniques of spatial expression that are unique to these domains (Jenkins 2004; Ryan et al. 2016). These techniques are rooted in the embodied nature of spatial experience, where the human body's perceptual biases and affordances for movement shape our engagement with the world; as Merleau-Ponty notes, "the body is our general medium for having the world" (2005, 169). While a player may be sitting at a computer monitor with their hands on a game controller or a keyboard and mouse, their engagement with the virtual environment beyond the screen reflects their "phenomenological bedrock" of a lifetime engaging with physical spaces (Gualeni 2019, 162). By using a built environment to

DOI: 10.4324/9781003053880-4

deliver a narrative in a more elusive and total way than other videogame genres, walking simulators are best viewed through a multimodal lens that addresses the uniquely spatial modes of expression that they incorporate.

How do structures of embodied spatial experience inform the ways that readers engage with walking simulators and interpret their narratives? This article proposes an approach for analyzing walking simulators' expressive worlds using theories of embodied cognition, an emerging multidisciplinary field which argues that cognition is grounded in the body's interactions with its environment. I will begin by arguing for a restrictive definition of "walking simulator" that includes the genre-defining works while excluding ones that feature a different form of virtual embodiment (and thus a different form of engagement). Following this, I will discuss three core questions: how is the player (virtually) embodied? How is the virtual environment structured? And how do players' interactions with a space evoke embodied meaning? For each of these questions, I will introduce theories of embodied cognition that are particularly suited to addressing them. The article will conclude with short spatial analyses of three walking simulators to demonstrate how these theories can be used in practice, while capturing some of the breadth and dynamism of this new narrative genre. It should be acknowledged that while the spaces of these works serve as highly evocative frames that contribute to and contextualize their narratives, in most cases the explicit details of the story are conveyed orally and textually. This is true to the nature of space as a mode, which – far more often than not – serves as the meaningful ground for the figures that capture our attention. This exploration of walking simulators was developed out of a larger study into expressive space in videogames, and a reader desiring a more in-depth argument for the theories and approach presented here is invited to read Whistance-Smith (2022).

Defining Walking Simulators

While the term "walking simulator" appears rather neutral or perhaps a little comic at first glance, it began as a derogatory one directed towards games which lacked the game mechanics (read: gun violence) that players had come to expect from certain types of videogames (see Clark 2017; Kill Screen Staff 2016). Games featuring navigable three-dimensional environments presented in a first-person perspective are overwhelmingly first-person shooters (FPS), where the player's primary engagement with the virtual world is through the barrel of a gun (and sometimes the blade of a knife). Over the course of its history, this genre experimented with integrating narratives into its worlds, with many celebrated examples such as *Half-Life* (Valve 1998) and *System Shock 2* (Irrational Games and Looking Glass Studios 1999); however, it took over a decade for a growing number of small developers to release narrative works that built on these examples while removing the combat altogether. After the first major genre-defining works were released – *Dear Esther* (The Chinese Room 2012) and *The Stanley Parable* being two notable examples – a flood of new works by amateur creators and more seasoned developers has followed. This reflects the presence of freely available game engines such as Source, Unity, and Unreal that make it comparatively easy to develop walking simulators; individuals can now construct expansive narrative environments that they can self-publish online on sites such as itch.io. This democratization is doubly significant when one considers that expressive physical environments have historically been limited to the most expensive architectural works – religious buildings, palaces, gardens – severely limiting who was permitted to create narratively charged spaces. From this angle, walking simulators (and other genres of videogame) bring spatial expression to the masses in an unprecedented way.

"Walking simulator" emerged as a genre defined by an absence, and the label has since taken on a life of its own through fan classification on online storefronts (itch.io, Steam, etc.) and as a useful marketing term to alert players looking for this kind of narrative experience. The result has been a more open view of the genre that this article contests. One of the few scholarly papers discussing the form, Carbo-Mascarell's "Walking Simulators: The Digitisation of an Aesthetic Practice" situates them "as continuations of the Romantic tradition of walking as an aesthetic" and conducts literary analyses of three works using the psychogeographic practice of the *dérive* (2016, 1). While her analyses are richly descriptive accounts of these works that befit the notion of the *dérive*, they lack the fixity of the approach advanced here. Carbo-Mascarell notes that debates around terminology go beyond the scope of her paper, but nevertheless defines walking simulators as "games with an immersive use of exploration as a core mechanic utilised for environmental storytelling purposes" (2016, 2). While acceptable on the surface, this definition departs from the initial "first-person-without-shooting" and defines the genre according to the form of player activity instead of defining it according to both player activity and the mode of virtual embodiment. The first-person perspective is a highly distinctive view into a virtual environment, one that limits and directs the player's virtually-embodied actions in particular ways (Stockburger 2006, 146–150); allowing the genre to encompass works that feature other forms of virtual embodiment, such as a third-person view of an avatar, widens the classification in a way that weakens comparisons between works. Vitally, it also distances these experiences from their physical counterparts: the first-person view of the walker wandering a building, garden, city, or landscape, where the direction of one's gaze is free to diverge from that of one's locomotion. Coming from a phenomenological perspective, Leder (1990) has discussed how our first-person view of the world has the curious effect of making our body recede from awareness and take on an "absent" quality, one which remains a defining quality in first-person videogames (and is not present in works with a visible avatar). Given these considerations, this article defines a walking simulator as a first-person videogame where the major activity is uncovering a narrative through engagement with a setting, and where engagement mainly consists of navigating an environment and interacting with the objects (and less commonly, characters) within it. Walking simulators offer a unique spatial-semiotic mode of narrative expression that this article seeks to unpack.

Virtual Spaces and Embodied Meaning

Walking simulators use a virtual environment to deliver a narrative in a far purer way than many other videogame genres; here there is simply the player, a space to calmly traverse and interpret, and a story to bear witness to. This sparseness is a welcome change from feature-packed videogames that seek to be all things to all players, and it also allows for a more focused look at how an expressive environment can contribute to a narrative experience. Space, here, is understood as a unique mode in a multimodal ensemble, existing alongside text, sound, and image, and it can be analyzed apart from a work's other modalities in order to see whether the spatial experience harmonizes with them or meaningfully juxtaposes them (Hawreliak 2018; Kress and Van Leeuwen 2001). As multimodal works, walking simulators communicate textually through their user interfaces and the written texts in their worlds, aurally through voice-overs of non-player characters (NPCs) or narrators, visually through images in the world, and spatially through the player's central experience of traversing the environment. Since these other modes have received much more attention elsewhere, the discussion here will focus on the embodied spatial dimension and how it contextualizes and situates these other modes within a cohesive narrative experience. Spatial expression is concerned with sharing meaning through designed environments: buildings, landscapes, installation artworks, and now virtual spaces. "Meaning" here is understood as non-propositional and embodied, it "arises from our feeling of qualities, sensory patterns, movements, changes, and emotional contours" (Johnson 2007, 70). Designed spaces are doubly meaningful: first, for the embodied experience of inhabiting them, and second, for how they can symbolically point to other things. These two aspects can take many forms, and a short inventory of spatial semiotic strategies will be discussed at the end of this section.

All spatial expression is rooted in the dynamic relationship between body and environment that is directly addressed by the theories and findings of embodied cognition. This emerging field spans philosophy, cognitive science, psychology, and linguistics (among others), and it has explored the role of the body in shaping and constraining human experience and understanding (Clark 2008; Gibson 1979; Johnson 2007; Lakoff and Johnson 1999; Shapiro 2011). Significant insights coming out of embodied cognition include Gibson's theory of affordances for analyzing body-environment interactions (1979), Noë's argument that perception is a form of action (2004), Kirsh's argument that cognition is embedded in the environments it takes place within (1995), and Lakoff and Johnson's work on the central role of conceptual metaphor in bridging concrete, embodied experience with abstract understanding (1999). The dynamic relationship between brain, body, and environment is foundational; as Johnson claims: "Change your brain, your body, or your environments in non-trivial ways, and you will change how you experience your world, what things are meaningful to you, and even who you are" (2007, 1–2). Tools extend the human body and mind in its interactions with the world and designed environments reshape the world a body inhabits. Seen as a new technology, walking simulators now allow for bespoke narrative environments *en masse*.

The following sections address three major questions regarding walking simulators while introducing the theories that make up the analytical framework: how is the player virtually embodied? How is the virtual environment structured? And how do interactions with a space evoke embodied meaning? Five theories from embodied cognition will help address these questions: affordances, image schemas, conceptual metaphor, priming, and framing. These theories run a spectrum from the physical interactions of affordances to the mental structures of frames, with metaphor providing a key bridge between these realms. Used in concert, they address the multifaceted nature of spatial experience and can help us unpack how environments can be designed as evocative narrative spaces.

How Is the Player Embodied?

Walking simulators embody their players in extremely similar ways, befitting a genre whose title claims to simulate a particular embodied activity. Players are provided with a first-person view of the virtual environment and allowed to freely look in all directions, and they can walk through the world in ways that parallel how one would traverse a real space (walls are barriers, stairs and ladders can be climbed, etc.). This speaks to the first theory, Gibson's (1979) theory of affordances for action between an organism and its environment. Gibson argues that environments *afford* particular interactions to particular organisms: water affords splashing, rocks afford throwing, and a solid surface at knee-height affords sitting. An affordance is a relationship between an entity and the environmental element it can interact with, so the same space has different affordances for differently embodied organisms: birds can perch on small branches while humans cannot. Our countless experiences of traversing built environments provide us with a strong intuitive sense of where spaces encourage us to walk and where access is discouraged or prevented. Elaborating, Johnson notes that:

> You may enter here, but not there. You must walk up these steps, or down this stairway, to gain access. You may, or may not, open this door or window. You must move along this narrow corridor. … All of these

experiences of restricted or free access involve structured forceful interactions. Even when were merely see a building, before ever entering it, we *feel* its affordances for how it will forcefully shape our engagement with it.

(2015, 44)

In the context of walking simulators, the theory of affordances can help us map the forms of motion and interaction that are possible for players engaging with the virtual environment. As noted above, the two primary forms of interaction are looking and walking (on PCs using the mouse to look and WASD keys to walk, and on game controllers using one analog stick for walking and one for looking), and many walking simulators also include additional abilities conventionalized in first-person shooters, such as running, jumping, and crouching. The ability to interact with objects is also present in some works, be this simply pressing switches in the environment or actually picking up and inspecting objects strewn around the world. The first-person perspective can also be seen as a significant affordance, as it determines how the player perceives the space. Environments can be perceived allocentrically from without (think of a bird's-eye view) or egocentrically from within (think of a first-person view); these two perspectives mirror the two types of spatial descriptions explored by De Certeau (1984, 118–122), maps (allocentric) and tours (egocentric). By providing a first-person perspective, walking simulators ensure their virtual environments are experienced egocentrically in much the same way as buildings: in perceptual fragments that are combined into a sense of the whole by physical movement through them (Dade-Robertson 2011, 115). A space can be expressive by how it shapes this rhythm of moving through it, and through how the affordances of the world help signify the paths through the world. Affordances also speak to the different relationships that a player can have to a virtual environment: if the environment is challenging to traverse, then it becomes something of an adversary in the experience and the player is no longer simply wandering a space; this is the case in *NaissanceE* (Limasse Five 2014). Equally, if an environment is structured around puzzles that restrict access to spaces, as in *The Witness*, then the affordances for solving puzzles have a significant impact on the player's spatial experience.

How Is the Virtual Environment Structured?

Spatial experience is a holistic phenomenon: we first encounter a place as "a qualitative, 'total' phenomenon, which we cannot reduce to any of its properties" (Norberg-Schulz 1980, 8). Giving the example of a walk in nature, Johnson notes that: "Before you perceive *this* or *that* tree, bush, rock, pond, stream, tree trunk, or deer path, you are caught up in the pervading spring-light-bathing-the-valley quality of the *entire situation*" (2007, 73; emphasis in original). This quality that pervades a space is often termed its "atmosphere," and it speaks to how qualitatively rich spaces are experienced as true "places" (the difference between a "space" and a "place" is quickly captured in the difference between a house and a home). Since their environments are a key point of interest, all well-regarded walking simulators feature worlds enveloped by distinctive and compelling atmospheres, from the alienating megastructure of *NaissanceE* to the desolate island of *Dear Esther*. An atmosphere literally and figuratively colours the actions and events that take place within it, and this brings us to the next theory, framing.

The notion of framing has taken on different meanings in fields such as sociology, communications, and psychology (Borah 2011), and its inclusion here reflects the embodied cognitive view. Put simply, frames are cognitive structures that we rely on to make sense of the world and reason about it. Lakoff further explains that:

> The neural circuitry needed to create frame structures is relatively simple, and so frames tend to structure a huge amount of our thought. Each frame has roles … relations between the roles, and scenarios carried out by those playing the roles. … A hospital, for example, has roles like doctors, nurses, patients, operating rooms, X-ray machines, and so on, with scenarios like checking in, being examined, having an operation, being visited, and so on.
>
> *(2008, 22)*

This gives frames an important role in spatial communication, since the structure of a built environment often reflects the activities it was designed for and helps an individual quickly select a frame for understanding it (Miller 2010, 50). Just consider the desks in a classroom, the tables in a restaurant, or the screen and seating of a movie theatre. Once we determine which frame best fits the qualitative unity (gestalt) of a place we find ourselves in, that frame shapes our behaviour within it as well as how we interpret and understand the environment (Goffman 1974; Lakoff 2008, 22). Spaces with ambiguous design elements can be particularly evocative, as they forestall the quick selection of a frame and encourage visitors to project various frames onto the space to see which ones are the most appropriate. This reflects how frames define the part-whole relationships of a situation, "provid[ing] an overall conceptual structure defining the semantic relationships among whole 'fields' of related concepts" (Lakoff and Johnson 1999, 116) such as the menus, ordering, waiters, and furniture that make up a "restaurant" frame. Since the atmosphere of a built environment is often tightly linked to how it is inhabited – and thus to its frame – a place's atmosphere "gives us a world that we can inhabit – not just a physical world, but a social and cultural world with its defining values" (Johnson 2015, 46). The virtual worlds of walking simulators can be analyzed for which frames they evoke and for how their atmospheres frame the events taking place (often through their soundscapes as much as through visual ambiance). Pertinent here is a strategy Domsch notes in melodrama where the qualities of an environment, such as gloomy weather, reflect the mood of a character; a technique "known to literary scholars as 'Seelenlandschaft (*soul-landscape*),'" (2019, 111); *Dear Esther* is a potent example. Finally, it is important to note that the virtual spaces of walking simulators serve as powerful frames that contextualize the textual and acoustic narrative elements "taking place" within them.

Frames concern virtual spaces at the scale of their overall configurations; the theory of priming addresses individual evocative elements. A prime is a charged stimulus that triggers particular cognitions and frames, impacting a person's affect and how they understand the situation they are in (Goldhagen 2017, 59). Stated differently, "priming research centers on the temporary activation of an individual's mental representations by the environment and the effect of this activation on various psychological phenomena" (Bargh and Chartrand 2014, 314). Hearing a siren will likely prime thoughts of emergency while seeing animal tracks will prime thoughts of which species made them. Walking simulators often make heavy use of priming when they seek to embed narratives in their worlds through evocative traces such as footprints, discarded objects, ambiguous markings, lone buildings in natural settings, and objects strangely out of place, such as the streetlamps in *The Beginner's Guide* (Everything Unlimited Ltd. 2015). Fernández-Vara (2011) terms this approach "indexical storytelling" for how these traces indexically point to narratively significant events that took place prior to the player's traversal of the environment, inviting them to generate stories from the traces they observe. The primes noted so far have been visual ones; however, music and sound effects can also be used as potent primes that shape the space's narrativity.

How Do Spatial Interactions Evoke Embodied Meaning?

The most significant claims in embodied cognition argue against mind/body dualism, proposing ways that embodied experience underpins abstract reasoning and helping to explain how particular spatial experiences can evoke abstract concepts. Affordances highlight the limited ways that organisms can interact with their environments, and this results in a routine character to most human motion: breathing, walking, and visual scanning are some of the motions that permeate daily life. Through repetition, these motions define cognitive structures and patterns termed "image schema" or "cogs" (short for "cognitive primitives") which "structure visual perception, motor action, and mental images, and ... are used in the semantics of natural language" (Lakoff 2012, 775). These include concepts such as CONTAINER, CYCLE, VERTICALITY, and CENTER-PERIPHERY, and Johnson notes that:

> [I]mage schemas are an important part of what makes it possible for our bodily experiences to have meaning for us ... For example, humans will

share certain general understandings of what it means for something to be located within a container, and they will understand at least part of this without having to reflect upon it or think about it. Seeing a container, manipulating one, or hearing or reading the word *in* will activate a CONTAINER image schema in our understanding of a particular scene.

(2007, 139; emphasis in original)

While the exact nature of image schemas is still debated, their existence is firmly established (Hampe 2006). Against views that see them as simply skeletal conceptual structures, Johnson (2006) argues that image schemas can hold affects associated with them, such as the containment provided by a room feeling claustrophobic or living on the periphery of a city contributing to a feeling of marginalization.

For walking simulators, PATH schemas will always figure prominently in the player's experience, as navigating the world is the central action; as noted earlier, narrative progression is often directly linked to progression along a path. Two major ways of structuring narrative environments are possible, with endless gradations between them: processions, where players move along a single orchestrated route, and landscapes, where players are free to wander a network of paths (or an unrestricted area) and contemplate evocative elements scattered across the world. Processional spaces are structured using the SOURCE-PATH-GOAL schema that defines a clear beginning and end to the journey through the world, allowing for more orchestrated narrative experiences; Kromhout and Forceville (2013) have analyzed how this image schema structures both stories about journeys and movement in videogames where the player has a destination. Landscapes support the idea of indexical storytelling noted earlier, as they allow players to encounter narrative fragments in any order and piece them together in their own minds instead of through a predetermined order based on progression through the space. Bonner discusses these two environmental designs as "architectural determinism" (processions) and "architectural possibilism" (landscapes), noting how "the linear fluid promenade architecturale" can be interwoven "with the open, nonlinear, networked concept of the hôtel particulier" to create highly dynamic virtual spaces (Bonner 2019, 232). This also speaks to scale: a work that is defined by one of these approaches at the macro scale is free to include the other within it, such as areas for open wandering at points along a clearly defined path (as is the case in *Dear Esther*).

Beyond PATHS, other image schemas like CENTER-PERIPHERY that structure relationships between important places in the world can also create spatial meaning. Given its deeply meaningful asymmetry in human experience, the VERTICALITY (up/down) image schema often achieves this; ascending a mountain has spiritual implications worldwide, and descending deep into a structure may evoke a sense of getting to the heart of a mystery. The relative vertical positioning of places within the gameworld may also speak to a meaningful hierarchy between them. Finally, any spatial narratives that toy with repetition and have players end the experience where they started make use of Cycle through their recurrence. These are just a few of the possible image schemas that walking simulators may use to structure their gameplay and narratives, and individual works can be defined by which image schemas are given central importance.

Conceptual metaphor theory is the final part of this article's framework, revealing how embodied action underpins abstract reasoning. This watershed theory from cognitive linguistics argues that metaphor is a pervasive cognitive process of "understanding and experiencing one kind of thing in terms of another" (Lakoff and Johnson 2003, 5), allowing patterns learned in concrete experience to structure abstract thought. For example, theories can be understood as buildings, as things which are constructed and have foundations (Lakoff and Johnson 2003, 52), and the process of understanding an idea can be experienced as one of grasping an object in one's hand (Lakoff and Johnson 1999, 45). Conceptual metaphor takes place on two levels: first, primary metaphors arise from regular links (neural coactivations) between subjective judgements and sensorimotor experiences, such as Important is Big, Knowing is Seeing, and Affection is Warmth (Johnson 2007, 179; Lakoff and Johnson 1999, 50–51); and second, higher-level conceptual metaphors are constructed by combining primary metaphors with other frames. These constitute the mapping of one frame onto another, where a sensorimotor "source" frame (e.g., the feeling of grasping) is used to structure an abstract "target" one (e.g., the feeling of understanding an idea). Giving the example of the metaphor A Purposeful Life Is A Journey, Lakoff and Johnson note that it includes the primary metaphors: "Purposes Are Destinations [and] Actions Are Motions," and the fact that "A long trip to a series of destinations is a journey"; these result in the mappings "A Person Living A Life Is A Traveler[,] Life Goals Are Destinations[, and] A Life Plan Is An Itinerary" (Lakoff and Johnson 1999, 61). This example highlights the power that metaphors have to frame our understanding of a situation: believing that A Purposeful Life Is A Journey may push someone to travel more, especially compared with an equally tangible metaphor like A Purposeful Life Is Building A Home, which may instead push them to develop deeper roots in their community.

Importantly for this spatial analysis, environments can be designed to be metaphorically evocative and meaningful. Goldhagen (2017, 255–256) provides the example of the Sydney Opera House, whose iconic shape invites viewers to understand it in terms of sails, seashells, and beaks. Buildings can also embody metaphorical associations through their use of materials and the general articulation of their forms; a large brutalist concrete building evokes vastly different things than a small wooden one. At the scale of a landscape, peculiar landforms can evoke metaphoric readings (many mountains are named after the images they evoke), as can highly patterned landscapes which suggest some kind of cosmic ordering through their forms.

Spatial Communication Strategies

Having discussed the theories that this article will use to analyze the spaces of walking simulators, we can now briefly touch on the major ways that the spatial mode can meaningfully shape the narrative of a walking simulator alongside its acoustic and textual elements. The first dimension is movement: as the theory of affordances highlights, environments can communicate through shaping bodily motion and action within them. A space might be experienced as hostile by limiting movement and having many confusing dead-ends, while another may feel tranquil due to the ease of traversing it and the picturesque views along the way. The second dimension is the structure of the world itself: what are the spatial patterns (image schemas) that structure the relationships between important places in the virtual space? A tall tower looming over a town or landscape will no doubt prime cognitions of authority and perhaps domination. The final dimension is associative: spaces can prime frames and metaphors for understanding them, which go on to shape players' experiences and understanding of them. The atmosphere conveyed through faintly coloured light may evoke particular affects, while the simulated materials of the virtual buildings communicate the state of the world, be it new and clean or old and decaying. The tactility of the world's materials may also evoke associations, be it harshness from rough rock surfaces, or peace and calm from a smooth lake surface or a grassy field gently moving in the breeze. Together, these three dimensions touch on the major forms of spatial communication present in the worlds of walking simulators and the roles that expressive spaces can play in these narrative works.

Analyzing Walking Simulators

The remainder of this article demonstrates this embodied approach to analyzing spatial expression in walking simulators through short analyses of three representative works: *Dear Esther, The Stanley Parable*, and *Genius Loci* (Bourhis 2016). These analyses aim to reveal both the wide range of spatial semiotic strategies that are possible and the richness of this emergent genre.

Dear Esther

The first work, *Dear Esther*, helped inspire this genre through its tight pairing of setting and narration. The game was first released in 2008 as a free Source engine mod, but this analysis is based on the enhanced 2017 Landmark Edition. Set on a desolate Hebridean island off the coast of Scotland, players learn about the history of the island and the personal tragedy experienced by the unstable protagonist as they journey across the landscape to a radio tower flickering in the distance. Reaching places along this journey triggers voiceover narrations concerning the unnamed protagonist, the titular Esther, a character named Donnelly who wrote a history of the island, and a man named Jakobson who was the first to shepherd on the island. Players begin near a decaying lighthouse and journey across barren hills, past ruined ships and houses, through bioluminescent caves, and finally along a moonlit beach and up windswept cliffs to the radio tower. Over the course of the player's journey, it becomes clear from the narrator's fragmented ramblings that Esther was killed in a car accident potentially caused by drunk driving, and that a character named Paul was responsible. The narrator's musings become increasingly impassioned and confused over the course of the journey, and he mixes up his own story with those of the other characters, challenging players to discern what took place and whether he may be the Paul he speaks of. The work never provides definitive closure to these questions, but it does provide a dramatic end: after reaching the radio tower, the player loses control over the protagonist, and watches a first-person view of him climbing the radio tower and jumping off. Right as he would have hit the ground, the camera swoops up and flies along the shoreline and off into the horizon, briefly casting the shadow of a bird midflight. Befitting a work that helped launch a genre, *Dear Esther*'s narrative could not have been delivered in an equally compelling way in any other medium than the spatial one it chose.

Beginning with players' affordances for movement, *Dear Esther* strips these down to the very core: walking and looking. The walking speed is quite limited, forcing players to slow down and take in the scenery and the narrator's musings as they traverse the landscape. Heavy winds and steep paths slow the player's movement, creating a sense of heaviness to their virtual body that resonates with the narrator's weariness. These simple affordances are used to shape the path through the world: since the player cannot jump, even low walls or tree trunks can serve as obstacles, and in a few instances the player must fall down a small ledge to progress, pushing them onwards and preventing them from turning back. At one critical point in the caves, the work expertly toys with players' sense of affordances: the only way forward is along a precarious ledge, and having already crossed a slightly wider one moments earlier, it appears possible to do so again. But as the player attempts this, they invariably slip and fall into a deep watery pit, triggering a hallucination of the motorway where the car accident took place. The player's initial motivation to safely traverse the space makes the unexpected fall much more impactful. Beyond the ability to look in all directions, players can also zoom their view by clicking and holding the mouse button and a flashlight will automatically turn on when entering dark spaces. These two affordances allow players to inspect details in the environment and to enter the dark and decaying abandoned buildings on the island, inspecting the narratively significant objects within. At the macro scale, players' movement through the world follows the Source-Path-Goal image schema with the radio tower serving as the ultimate destination; the narrator speaks of his journey on a few occasions and states that some kind of rebirth is waiting for him at the tower. The VERTICALITY image schema is equally prominent, as the rhythm of the journey often involves ascents and descents, such as the many narrow paths which switch back along steep cliff faces and the winding interconnected tunnels of the bioluminescent caves. The work has players become acquainted with the island and explore its inner depths before ascending a tower at its highest point.

As with many later works in the genre, *Dear Esther* makes full use of indexical storytelling by filling its world with evocative spatial primes, some of which are contextualized by the narrator. Early on, he notes that the white lines cut into the cliffs were created by people who were dying or severely ill, serving to call for aid or to warn outsiders to avoid the island for a generation until anyone with diseases had perished. Many surfaces have phosphorescent drawings of circuit diagrams, chemical compounds, and organisms painted on them (with empty cans of paint nearby), and late in the work the narrator sparsely contextualizes these with lines like "My life reduced to an electrical diagram." Areas later in the journey also have lines of Biblical scripture painted on the rock concerning Paul's journey to Damascus, implying some form of allegory with the Paul the narrator speaks of. Other primes include a copy of the Bible sitting next to a book on chemistry in a circle of standing stones, Donnelly's book on the history of the island and ultrasound photos (perhaps implying that Esther was pregnant) in the house the narrator has been living in, and ghostly figures which can sometimes be seen further ahead along the path and who disappear before the player reaches them. These primes all invite narrative speculation on the part of the player and invite readings which try to make sense of them alongside the sparse hints in the narration. They also serve to ground some parts of what the unstable narrator is talking about, confirming that at least some of what he is saying is "real."

Through both the design of its space and the musings of the narrator, *Dear Esther* frames its world as one of desolation, decay, and despair. There are no trees to be found here, only barren rock, windswept scrub brush, and beaches covered in debris, from bits of plastic to shipwrecks of all sorts. The island's few man-made structures – with the exception of the pristine radio tower – are in various states of ruin and filled with filthy debris. The first two segments of the journey take place during a pinkish dusk, where the fading light resonances with the desolate atmosphere; the third sharply contrasts this, where the blue-green glow of the bioluminescent caves frame them as otherworldly and the trek through them as a mental journey as much as a physical one; and the final area takes the player along a moonlit shoreline dotted with candles, with the narrator recalling a moon floating above the location of the car accident. Music and sound effects also serve as important frames for establishing the island's atmosphere, but the cadence of the narrator and his evocative language is the strongest frame around the experience of this virtual space. At many points throughout *Dear Esther*, he metaphorically connects his tired famished body to the barren landscape, such as calling the caves his guts and noting that they are where the kidney stones he suffered from first formed. At the very start of the work, he discusses feeling as though he gave birth to the island, and this immediately frames the exterior landscape as a means of understanding his internal state; this island is a "soul-landscape" in the truest sense.

Dear Esther uses its journey across the island to externalize the mental anguish and traumas of its protagonist, inviting players to develop their own narrative closure out of the evocative pairing of the narrator's prose with the elements of the landscape. The compelling power of this pairing helped inspire the many works that now constitute the genre, and later ones have explored different ways of infusing their spaces with narrative elements.

The Stanley Parable

Three years after *Dear Esther*, another watershed walking simulator was also released as a free Source engine mod, *The Stanley Parable*. It received a commercial remake in 2013, and this version is the one analyzed here. This darkly comedic work frames the player as an office worker happily content to carry out the orders he receives at his desk, until one day the orders cease and he leaves his room to discover his office devoid of inhabitants. The overeager narrator sets the scene by explaining Stanley's strange predicament, but his role becomes suspect as he starts commenting on Stanley's actions before they have taken place, such as which door he walks through when confronted with two options. This early scene introduces the work's central conflict: since the player is free to choose their own path in space, they can go against the wishes of the narrator and leave him increasingly frustrated and angry at their "disobedience" of his desire to progress the story, making him an unnatural narrator *par excellence* (Ensslin 2015). In contrast to *Dear Esther*'s linear journey, *The Stanley Parable* is a branching structure of narrative routes which directly correspond to the paths players take through the world; the game's wiki notes 19 different endings, all of which result in the narrator restarting the game or the player having to manually restart it themselves ("Endings," n.d.). Yet as the work makes explicit in one of its routes, choice here is entirely illusory since all of these paths have been determined for the player in advance, and restarting the game allows the player to exhaustively experience all of them. This space that initially has a sense of architectural possibilism becomes one of architectural determinism as players chart its various and finite paths. *The Stanley Parable* uses spatial interaction to create a conflict between player and narrator, and beyond that between player and game designer. While many corners of the videogame industry try to create endlessly compelling worlds that offer their players meaningful choices, *The Stanley Parable* scoffs at this even being possible, wryly declaring the inherent finitude of virtual environments through the existential experience it offers players.

After watching an introductory cutscene that shows Stanley at his desk, players are given control over him, having affordances for walking, crouching, looking around, and clicking to interact with the occasional object or button. In contrast to *Dear Esther*, the walking speed here is quite fast and frantic, fitting the anxious state that Stanley is surely experiencing in the surreal situation he finds himself in. A number of image schemas help to structure the work, and CYCLE is first among them. All narrative meaning in *The Stanley Parable* arises out of repetition: every time the player finds an "ending" to the game it resets to the beginning or simply waits for the player to reset the game (or quit it), never providing the closure of automatically being returned to a main menu or having the game close itself. Some of these resets are explicit punishment from the narrator for not following his instructions, and the "Confusion Ending" route involves the narrator resetting the game numerous times, opening new paths for the player with each reset, until eventually this ending is reached and the game is properly reset. It is through CYCLES of play that possibilism shrinks into determinism, and a space that felt ready to be explored takes on an increasingly claustrophobic character. CONTAINMENT is another prominent schema, due in part to this and in part to the fact that the player never leaves the building and is never provided with views to the outside (some endings do involve limited views outside). Many interior spaces do have windows, yet these are a blindingly bright white that prevents any views out and emphasizes that Stanley (and by extension the player) are trapped in this determined space. Existential CONTAINMENT is also emphasized through occasional encounters with spaces that evoke infinity by looping back upon themselves, and by the infinite textual loop on the loading screen "...the end is never the end is never the end..." Finally, like all walking simulators the PATH schema is also prominent, and its meaning here lies in the contrast between the single path that the narrator wants the player to follow and the many ones on offer. The "Confusion Ending" noted earlier features one of the game's more memorable elements, a bright yellow line painted on the floor called "The Stanley Parable Adventure Line" which is supposed to help carry the player through the building in a path that is ideal for the narrator's storytelling. The line becomes more erratic over the course of the resets and the narrator eventually gives up on it as a result. This ending also features a room which emphasizes the illusion of choice that different paths offer: the narrator debates which of two doors Stanley should take (mirroring the iconic room early in the game), and once he settles on one, opens it, and the player proceeds through, it becomes clear that both doors access the same space (a room with a large screen outlining the steps of the ending that the player has been playing). Together, these image schemas serve to structure both the virtual space and the narrative meanings that players read out of their experiences exploring it.

The Stanley Parable's world situates its narrative in instantly recognizable frames: mundane office spaces, executive suites, industrial warehouses, panopticons, art galleries, and pastoral fields are all present. These spaces are loaded with associations for players and let them quickly grasp the setting and their character's place within it. Discovering the panopticon surveillance room with a view to your own desk works as the "big reveal" that the narrator is all too eager for, and the sparse white art gallery in another route effectively communicates its extra-diegetic position relative to the rest of the game's world (helped by the fact that it exhibits and contextualizes elements from the game itself). Moving on to spatial metaphors, on a few occasions *The Stanley Parable* frames its world as a stage set by taking players from "finished" spaces to ones that appear under construction, in one route showing them spaces that were not textured and that simply have the default orange grid of the Source engine wrapping their geometry. This stage set metaphor speaks to the central conflict where the player is trying (and failing) to escape the bounds of reality set by the narrator, and it resonates with works such as *The Truman Show* (Weir 1998) where the protagonist is trying to escape from a form of spatial narrative confinement. Spatial metaphor is also used in a route where the world begins to glitch as a direct result of "narrative contradictions," with the glitched world communicating a broken story. Finally, *The Stanley Parable* does not make much use of evocative objects to prime the player, and it even mocks this tendency in other games. In one route the player walks past a fern in a large planter, and the narrator quickly tells them to turn around and inspect it since this fern will be important to the story later (which of course it is not).

The Stanley Parable uses space to allow for a central conflict between protagonist and narrator, and by extension between player and designer. By placing CYCLES at the heart of the work, it lets players experience the virtual environment compress around them as they exhaust its limited predetermined paths. Through this, the work constitutes a compelling argument against certain approaches to videogame storytelling while presenting a compelling – though irreplicable – one of its own.

Genius Loci

Genius Loci is a vignette compared to the prior two works, though no less compelling for it. Through a short dizzying walk, it invites players to contemplate how different places can exist at the same point in space across time. By engaging with this truth about the world through a walking simulator, *Genius Loci* allows players to experience this disorienting reality instead of simply thinking about it. Affordances are limited to walking and looking, and there is no use of language beyond the title (whose contemporary meaning is "sense of place"), forcing the design of the space to deliver the narrative singlehandedly. Players begin in a dark hallway, with stairs leading up to a rectangular room containing a Greco-Roman statue and a ceiling open to the sky. Approaching the statue and looking at it triggers the surrounding space fading away, leaving the player looking at the statue now surrounded by ruined columns where the walls had been, and a rolling landscape with a Modernist house in the distance. The player is unable to enter the house, but when they head to the ravine at its rear, the foundation of the house is shown to have Italianate arches embedded within it. Staring through the arch makes the wall vanish, and the player finds themselves at the bottom of an archeological dig site with a framework above them. Climbing out of the dig reveals an evocative semi-circular structure, half constructed, and players must stare at a tree in order to once again change the time period. The trees in the world now lose their leaves and a trench blocking their path to the tunnel is now filled in. The Modern house is nowhere to be seen, and the structure is now a completed tunnel with hills overtop it. Continued wanderings in this slice of the world take the player back to other parts of the dig site, the upper floors of the Modern house, and also a dense apartment building where all the views out show skyscrapers filling the spaces that were empty in other time periods. Eventually, the player ends up on the roof of the house, and ascending a final staircase they see a paper crane perched on a ledge. Staring at it triggers the final time-shift and a melancholic song, leaving them in a wasteland where the general height of the ground is the same as the roof they had been standing on. The narrative here is conveyed entirely through the spatial primes and frames of this disorienting procession, and *Genius Loci* highlights the kind of themes that a purely spatial narrative can hope to engage with.

Beginning with its use of frames, *Genius Loci* presents its world in a grainy black and white, establishing a serious tone and forcing players to consider the forms of its places instead of getting caught up in their textures or colours. Beauty here can only be found in the stark contrast of light and dark. The experience has a soundscape of droning hums and what sounds like aircraft that carries between the time periods, and it creates a sense of activity, perhaps priming thoughts of conflict or war in spaces that would otherwise be marked by their stillness. The fact that all these different places exist in the same slice of the world is conveyed through an outline of a cube that is visible at the edges of the world across all periods, and the distinctive architectural styles directly prime the time periods that they were prominent in. Beyond style, the qualities of some of the architectural forms are evocative on their own: the tunnel is formally ambiguous and may just as well be the entrance to an aircraft hangar or bomb shelter, and the dense apartment experienced late in the journey creates a sense of compression and claustrophobia as one moves through it. The game understands that players will be drawn to smaller objects and certain locations in the world, and these serve as time-shift triggers that reward their curiosity. In order, these primes are the Greco-Roman statue, the Italianate arch, a tree which loses its leaves in the shift, a model of Saturn hanging from the ceiling of the tunnel, a staircase leading nowhere, which shifts time as the player goes up it, two small balls on a plinth, which trigger a time-shift when started at where the ground falls away, a crow looking out the window of the house, what appears to be a mirror above the fireplace in the dense apartment, a cage-like grid of small metal bars atop a tall column in the dig site, and finally the paper crane. These forms all invite speculation as to their meaning, and the paper crane in the wasteland carries a metaphoric association to the atomic bombing of Hiroshima, where it is a prominent element at the memorial site. The VERTICALITY of the ground height slowly rising across the ages also evokes the slow accumulation of history and of things turning to ruin and then dust. Paired with the melancholic song, the final scene of empty, rolling dunes makes it clear that this work laments this slow march of history towards desolation.

Genius Loci is an excellent demonstration of the sort of evocative, open-ended narrative speculation that purely spatial works can hope to inspire in their players. The story here lacks the fixity of ones that pair space with oral and textual modes, and it is completely devoid of characters, seriously limiting the kinds of themes it can engage with. But these limitations notwithstanding, it remains a compelling spatial scaffold for contemplating the historically contingent reality of place.

Conclusion

This article sought to argue that embodied cognitive theories are valuable tools for analyzing the spatial experiences afforded by walking simulators. It began by introducing the genre and arguing for a restrictive definition that covered both the spatial narrative approach and the type of virtual embodiment, and proceeded to discuss three key questions to ask of any work: how is the player embodied? How is the virtual environment structured? And how do its spatial interactions evoke embodied meaning? These questions served as a framework for introducing the five theories used to analyze the spaces of walking simulators – affordances, framing, priming, image schemas, and conceptual metaphor – and this section concluded with an inventory of the many ways that space can communicate meaning, and thus the necessity of a broad approach which incorporates a range of theories. The article concluded with analyses of three walking simulators, highlighting the most salient aspects of their spatial experiences and discussing how these supported the delivery of their narratives. The walking simulator is an exciting new genre still in its infancy, and its tight pairing of spatial experiences with narratives delivered orally and textually requires new tools for analysis like the ones proposed here. The steady stream of new walking simulators has only increased, and it is likely that this genre will make a smooth transition into virtual reality, and perhaps into locative augmented reality works that take their players on physical walks through memorable settings using the same techniques as their virtual cousins. In any case, as a comparatively easy-to-develop, democratic form rooted in freely available game engines, walking simulators will surely continue to surprise their players as new authors continue to push the possibilities of the form in the spirit of the genre's originators.

Works Cited

Bargh, John A., and Tanya L. Chartrand. 2014. "The Mind in the Middle: A Practical Guide to Priming and Automaticity Research." In *Handbook of Research Methods in Social and Personality Psychology*, 2nd ed., edited by Harry T. Reis and Charles M. Judd, 311–344. Cambridge: Cambridge University Press.

Bonner, Marc. 2019. "Piercing all Layers of the Anthroposphere: On Spatialization and Architectural Possibilism in Hitman." In *Architectonics of Game Spaces: The Spatial Logic of the Virtual and Its Meaning for the Real*, edited by Andri Gerber and Ulrich Götz, 215–232. Bielefeld, Germany: transcript Verlag.

Borah, Porismita. 2011. "Conceptual Issues in Framing Theory: A Systematic Examination of a Decade's Literature." *Journal of Communication* 61: 246–263.

Bourhis, Gaël. 2016. *Genius Loci*. Paris: Self Published (itch.io).

Carbo-Mascarell, Rosa. 2016. "Walking Simulators: The Digitisation of an Aesthetic Practice." In *Proceedings of the First International Joint Conference of DiGRA and FDG 2016*. Dundee, Scotland: Digital Games Research Association and Society for the Advancement of the Science of Digital Games.

Clark, Andy. 2008. *Supersizing the Mind: Embodiment, Action, and Cognitive Extension*. Oxford: Oxford University Press.

Clark, Nicole. 2016. "A Brief History of the 'Walking Simulator,' Gaming's Most Detested Genre." *Salon*, November 11, 2017. https://www.salon.com/2017/11/11/a-brief-history-of-the-walking-simulator-gamings-most-detested-genre/.

Dade-Robertson, Martyn. 2011. *The Architecture of Information: Architecture, Interaction Design and the Patterning of Digital Information*. New York: Routledge.

De Certeau, Michel. 1984. *The Practice of Everyday Life*. Los Angeles: University of California Press.

Domsch, Sebastian. 2019. "Space and Narrative in Computer Games." In *Ludotopia: Spaces, Places, and Territories in Computer Games*, edited by Espen Aarseth and Stephan Günzel, 103–123. Bielefeld, Germany: transcript Verlag.

"Endings." n.d. *The Stanley Parable Wiki*. Accessed January 27, 2021. https://thestanleyparable.fandom.com/wiki/Endings.

Enslin, Astrid. 2015. "Video Games as Unnatural Narratives." In *Diversity of Play*, edited by Mathias Fuchs, 41–72. Lüneburg: Meson Press.

Everything Unlimited Ltd. 2015. *The Beginner's Guide* (videogame). Austin, TX: Everything Unlimited Ltd.

Fernández-Vara, Clara. 2011. "Game Spaces Speak Volumes: Indexical Storytelling." In *Proceedings of the DiGRA 2011 Conference: Think Design Play*. Hilversum, The Netherlands.

Galactic Cafe. 2013. *The Stanley Parable*. Austin, TX: Galactic Cafe.

Gibson, James J. 1979. *The Ecological Approach to Visual Perception*. Boston: Houghton Mifflin.

Goffman, Erving. 1974. *Frame Analysis: An Essay on the Organization of Experience*. New York: Harper & Row.

Goldhagen, Sarah Williams. 2017. *Welcome to Your World: How the Built Environment Shapes Our Lives*. New York: Harper Collins.

Gualeni, Stefano. 2019. "Virtual World Weariness: On Delaying the Experiential Erosion of Digital Environments." In *Architectonics of Game Spaces: The Spatial Logic of the Virtual and Its Meaning for the Real*, edited by Andri Gerber and Ulrich Götz, 153–165. Bielefeld, Germany: transcript Verlag.

Hampe, Beate. 2006. *From Perception to Meaning: Image Schemas in Cognitive Linguistics*. Berlin: Mouton de Gruyter.

Hawreliak, Jason. 2018. *Multimodal Semiotics and Rhetoric in Videogames*. New York: Routledge.

Irrational Games and Looking Glass Studios. 1999. *System Shock 2*. Redwood City, CA: Electronic Arts.

Jenkins, Henry. 2004. "Game Design as Narrative Architecture." In *First Person: New Media as Story, Performance, and Game*, edited by Noah Wardrip-Fruin and Pat Harrigan, 118–130. Cambridge, MA: MIT Press.

Johnson, Mark. 2006. "The Philosophical Significance of Image Schemas." In *From Perception to Meaning: Image Schemas in Cognitive Linguistics*, edited by Beate Hampe, 15–33. Berlin: Mouton de Gruyter.

———. 2007. *The Meaning of the Body: Aesthetics of Human Understanding*. Chicago, IL: University of Chicago Press.

———. 2015. "The Embodied Meaning of Architecture." In *Mind in Architecture: Neuroscience, Embodiment, and the Future of Design*, edited by Sarah Robinson and Juhani Pallasmaa, 33–50. Cambridge, MA: MIT Press.

Kill Screen Staff. 2016. "Is It Time to Stop Using the Term 'Walking Simulator'?" *Kill Screen*, September 30, 2016. https://killscreen.com/previously/articles/time-stop-using-term-walking-simulator/.

Kirsh, David. 1995. "The Intelligent Use of Space." *Artificial Intelligence* 73: 31–68.

Kress, Gunter, and Theo Van Leeuwen. 2001. *Multimodal Discourse: The Modes and Media of Contemporary Communication*. New York: Oxford University Press.

Kromhout, Roelf, and Charles Forceville. 2013. "Source–Path–Goal Structure in the Videogames 'Half-Life 2', 'Heavy Rain', and 'Grim Fandango'." *Metaphor and the Social World* 3 (1): 100–116.

Lakoff, George. 2008. *The Political Mind: Why You Can't Understand 21st-Century Politics with an 18th-Century Brain*. New York: Viking.

———. 2012. "Explaining Embodied Cognition Results." *Topics in Cognitive Science* 4: 773–785.

Lakoff, George, and Mark Johnson. 1999. *Philosophy in the Flesh: The Embodied Mind and Its Challenge to Western Thought*. New York: Basic Books.

———. 2003. *Metaphors We Live By*. Chicago, IL: University of Chicago Press.

Leder, Drew. 1990. *The Absent Body*. Chicago, IL: University of Chicago Press.

Limasse Five. 2014. *NaissancE*. France: Limasse Five.

Manovich, Lev. 2001. *The Language of New Media*. Cambridge, MA: MIT Press.

Merleau-Ponty, Maurice. 2005. *Phenomenology of Perception*. London: Routledge.

Miller, Daniel. 2010. *Stuff*. Cambridge: Polity Press.

Noë, Alva. 2004. *Action in Perception*. Cambridge, MA: MIT Press.

Norberg-Schulz, Christian. 1980. *Genius Loci: Towards a Phenomenology of Architecture*. London: Academy Editions.

Ryan, Marie-Laure, Kenneth Foote, and Maoz Azaryahu. 2016. *Narrating Space / Spatializing Narrative: Where Narrative Theory and Geography Meet*. Columbus: Ohio State University Press.

Shapiro, Lawrence. 2011. *Embodied Cognition*. New York: Routledge.

Stockburger, Axel. 2006. "The Rendered Arena: Modalities of Space in Video and Computer Games." PhD diss., University of the Arts, London.
The Chinese Room. 2012. *Dear Esther*. Brighton, UK: The Chinese Room.
The Fullbright Company. 2013. *Gone Home*. Portland, OR: The Fullbright Company.
Thekla Inc. 2016. *The Witness*. Berkeley, CA: Thekla Inc.
Valve. 1998. *Half-Life*. Bellevue, WA: Valve.
Weir, Peter, director. 1998. *The Truman Show*. Hollywood: Paramount Pictures.
Whistance-Smith, Gregory. 2022. *Expressive Space: Embodying Meaning in Video Game Environments*. Berlin: De Gruyter.

4
MAPPING IMAGINARY SPACES
From Database to Folk Cartography

Paul Wake

> Make notes and draw a map as you explore –
> *The Warlock of Firetop Mountain*

In *Narrative Space/Spatializing Narrative*, Marie-Laure Ryan, Kenneth Foote and Maoz Azaryahu set out four types of space: "Narrative space" (the environment in which characters live and move); "contextual space" (the space in which storytellers, texts and audiences are situated); the "space taken by the text" (the material book, for example); and the "spatial form of the text" (the text's narrative organization). These spaces are, they tell us, "somewhat interrelated" (2016, 3). Picking up on Gabriel Zoran's tantalizing note that there is a "lack of ontological clarity" in the total space of a text, a space he describes as a "direct continuation of the reconstructed world in the text, but also as a continuation of the real space of the reader, of the external field of reference, the act of narration, and possibly more" (1984, 332), my concern is to think through this interrelation in detail. This thinking through, or thinking with, is staged through an analysis of three reader-made maps of Steve Jackson and Ian Livingstone's *The Warlock of Firetop Mountain* (Puffin Books, 1982). Applying insights from geography, narrative theory, new materialism and interface studies, I ask how a focus on the activity of mapmaking and on the objects with which maps are made might allow us to connect these interrelated spaces. How, I ask, might we understand mapping as a process that expresses a continuity between rather than the separation of technology, user and world? More precisely, my analysis of cartographic responses to Jackson and Livingstone's influential text reveals that these mapping practices, practices I term folk cartography, function as orienting devices that both guide readers through textual topographies and

DOI: 10.4324/9781003053880-5

situate them within a constellation of actors that establishes the interrelation or integration of the reader to the text's narrative, contextual, material and organizational spaces. Mapmaking, I suggest, involves readers in a process of orientation as integration.

The questions with which I begin signal a departure from previous work on the mapping of fictional spaces, in large part in shifting the discussion from cognitive (see, for example, Herman, 2009; Wolf, 2012; Ryan, 2016; Easterlin, 2018) to graphic maps. While there have been a number of important studies of graphic maps of fictional spaces, these discussions generally describe material maps as extensions of cognitive processes that support the comprehension of the narrative spaces within which characters live and move. Franco Moretti, in his *Atlas of the European Novel*, describes the map as "a connection made visible" (1998, 3), an idea that is revisited in *Graphs, Maps, Trees* in the suggestion that maps "may bring hidden patterns to the surface" (2005, 54). Anne-Kathrin Weber and Lorenz Hurni argue that maps provide "analytical insight into the spatial structure of a story" addressing the "uncertainty inherent in fictional spaces" (2011, 293, 298). And, starting from similar principles, David Cooper, Christopher Donaldson and Patricia Murrieta-Flores suggest in the introduction to *Literary Mapping in the Digital Age* that mapping "enriches the reader's appreciation of literary texts" (2016, 1). Ryan, Foote and Azaryahu's findings in *Narrative Space/Spatializing Narrative* generally support this emphasis on mapping as comprehension – "people read for the plot not the map" they tell us – but their suggestion that "we construct mental models of narrative space only as far as we find cognitive advantage – only as far as is needed to achieve immersion in the storyworld and understanding of the action" (2016, 100) helpfully shifts attention from approaches that validate maps in terms of their interpretative force towards their potential to support immersion. As Ryan goes on to suggest in "Narrative Mapping as Cognitive Activity and as Active Participation in Storyworlds": "When the creation of narrative maps constitutes a mode of active participation in storyworlds, the question of the ability of these maps to yield relevant interpretations becomes largely irrelevant" (2018, 246). The construction of graphic maps of fictional texts then would appear to support both comprehension and immersion, reflection and action.

Given the prominent role of space in discussions and definitions of video games and digital media (see, for example, Aarseth, 1997, 2001; Nitsche, 2008; Murray, 2017; Aarseth and Günzel, 2019), it comes as little surprise that maps and mapmaking have drawn significant comment. In his discussion of video game spaces, Daniel Punday makes the useful distinction between primary spaces, "those of action," and orienting spaces that "provide a context" (2019, 59). While orienting spaces (such as in-game maps and menus) are not described as "secondary" (avoiding, deliberately I assume, the temptation of the more obvious pairing), Punday's use of "primary" to describe the most immediate setting of a story's action nonetheless privileges this space over the more distant (perhaps extra-textual) frames through which those actions are apprehended. The necessary exploration of the division of action/context, present in Punday's discussion of the ways in which spaces are "staged" (2019, 63), finds expression in work that explores the integration of cartography into gameplay in a way that effectively combines the user interface and the user experience. Toups et al. (2019, 2020) identify an emerging tendency in video games to integrate mapmaking and gameplay, distinguishing between "read-only map interfaces," which afford only consumption, and what they call "game cartography interfaces," which enable modification and which, they argue, allow designers to use in-game maps to promote "high-level play activities" (2019, 5). Sybille Lammes demonstrates the political significance of such play activities through a discussion of cartography in *Age of Empires III* (Ensemble Studios, 2005) and Sid Meier's *Civilization IV* (Firaxis Games, 2005), arguing that game maps "allow gamers to appropriate spatial practices and make sense of them in their own way, hybridizing notions of objective place and subjective space" (2008, 94) in ways that allow players to engage with, disrupt and replicate discourses of power. Toups et al. and Lammes's work is connected by a concern with player agency – Toups et al. talk of "creativity" (2020, 8), Lammes of "playful domains" (2008, 94) – and the sense that players are implicated by and imbricated in their cartographic practices. Continuing the line of thinking and concerned with the co-constituting agencies of readers, players, texts and tools, my aim in this chapter is to think of maps not as epistemological artefacts (as means of knowing), but rather as a part of an active ontological process, an act of worlding arising from what Sara Ahmed calls "the messiness of the experiential" (2007, 214).

To use Genette's terminology, my reading of these paratextual materials – *what else are maps of texts but guides to those texts?* – shifts from the peritextual, the maps materially appended to the text, to the epitextual materials that circulate freely outside (I use the term cautiously and temporarily) the texts themselves (Genette, 1997). Introduced in *Palimpsestes* (1982) and mapped out in detail in *Seuils* (1987), Genette's introduction to the paratext is at once highly prescriptive in its terminology, dealing in "levels," "inside/outside" and "authority" – paratexts are, Genette tells us, "always subordinate" (1997, 12) to the texts they serve – while being cautiously but constantly aware of the fluidity of the distinctions by which it proceeds. Given Genette's focus on the marginal and the peripheral, it is entirely fitting that, on the first page of his book, he places J. Hillis Miller's discussion of "para" – "a double antithetical prefix signifying at once proximity and distance, similarity and difference, interiority and exteriority" (1997, 1) – in the subordinate position of the footnote. This move, surely a knowing one given his later description of the authorial note as "a disorder [of the text] that, like some others, may have its proper use" (1997, 328), establishes the mutable tone of *Paratexts*. It is this sense of the intrarelation of text and paratext that I take up in my reading of maps that is necessarily a reading of mapmakers, texts, objects. The argument that follows, then, effects something of a folding-in of epitextual and peritextual while further diverging from Genette's use of the term through the inclusion of reader-made paratexts in recognition that, now more than ever, fans "cease to be simply an audience for popular texts; instead they become active participants in the construction and circulation of textual meaning" (Henry Jenkins, quoted in Gray, 2010, 145). The reader-made maps I discuss, epitexts that bridge the inside and the outside of textual spaces, act as "threshold objects" (Murray, 2017, 156) connecting the reader and storyworld, the epitextual and the peritextual and the text and the social space. Specifically, my interest is in the networks – a word that does not appear in the English translation of *Paratexts* – that act at and constitute the thresholds between these different actants. Here I am borrowing from Bruno Latour (1996, 2005), from whom I take the sense of the network as a concept describing the temporary constellations, associations and connections of things; mutable groupings defined by the interaction among the actants – human or non-human – that act and react to one another and ultimately "do something" (Latour, 2005, 54).

The connection of paratexts, those "liminal devices and conventions, both within and outside the book, that form part of the complex mediation between book, author, publisher and reader" (1997, x) and maps is readily drawn. As J.B. Harley puts it in *The History of Cartography*, graphic maps act as "mediators between an inner mental world and an outer physical world," offering "fundamental tools helping the human mind make sense of its universe at various scales" (1987, 1). This account of maps as mediators speaks directly to Genette's account of the paratext. Pursuing this parallel, pushing it further than it will perhaps stand, replacing Harley's "mental world" with "reader" and "physical world" with "book" proves instructive, suggesting a distinction between "inner" (a property of the reader) and "outer" (the exteriority of the book) that ultimately Genette's text cannot sustain.

Mapping Fictional Spaces: **The Warlock of Firetop Mountain**

Written as an introduction to tabletop roleplaying games, Steve Jackson and Ian Livingstone's Fighting Fantasy gamebook *The Warlock of Firetop Mountain* takes the form of a print hypertext, requiring the reader, addressed in the second person, to make a series of choices that determine the reading order of the book's numbered passages. The book, in which player-adventurers negotiate a monster-filled maze in search of treasure, proved wildly popular, selling over two million copies, topping the best-seller lists and bringing tabletop roleplaying gaming, then in its infancy, to the attention of a global audience (Pramas, 2007; Green, 2014). This popularity led to a series of adaptations across multiple media, including a third-person computer adventure game for the ZX Spectrum (Mottershead and Brattel, 1984), a boardgame (Jackson, 1986), a tabletop roleplaying game (Wallis, 2003), an action-RPG for the Nintendo DS (Big

Blue Bubble, 2009), a coloring book (Snowbooks, 2016), an audio drama (Fox and Smith, 2017) and most recently, an isometric adventure for the Nintendo Switch (Tin Man Games, 2018). While the focus of this chapter is on the reader-made maps of Jackson and Livingstone's book, my thinking is informed throughout by the possibilities suggested by the story's many manifestations. The gamebook is not a past artefact, ready for excavation to help us appreciate the present and future, but a present text whose existence threads its way through, revealing connections to, a series of media – bringing together pencils, paper, pixels, print, card, plastic, paint, imagination, crayons, hands and eyes. This kind of media archaeology, "excavating the past in order to understand the present and the future" (Parikka, 2), was at work as these texts were being created, allowing reviewers of the computer game, a thinly veiled clone of Crystal Computing's *Halls of the Things* (Mottershead, Brattel and Horsley, 1983), to describe the Fighting Fantasy gamebooks as "computer flow diagrams in book form" (Crash, 1984, 12).

The navigation of space is significant in all of these adaptations – even staying within the lines of the coloring book and the "zero space" of the audio drama draw attention to the interrelation of multiple overlapping zones of engagement. In the gamebook we see this in the spatial challenges faced by the reader ("you") and the unnamed adventurer (also "you") who engage in an act of double navigation, negotiating both the lexia of its material database (Manovich, 2001) and the topography of the storyworld, which takes the form of a maze, constructed from those lexia. Unsurprisingly, the book's authors emphasize the need for mapmaking. The villagers living at the foot of the Firetop mountain encourage you (the reader as adventurer) to "keep a good map of your wanderings" (1982, 21) fearing that you will otherwise end up hopelessly lost. This instruction is repeated (epitextually) in the book's preface: "Make notes and draw a map as you explore – this map will be invaluable in future adventures and enable you to progress rapidly through to unexplored sections" (1982, 17), and again (peritexually, and belatedly) in *Warlock*, the official magazine of the Fighting Fantasy series: "As you will soon discover after entering the Warlock's dungeon…. Keeping a map of your adventure is an important step towards completing your quest successfully" (Jackson and Livingstone, 1984, 10).

This advice is typical of that offered to players of text-based adventure games. The manual accompanying Philip Mitchell and Veronika Megler's *The Hobbit* (Beam Software, ZX Spectrum, 1982), for example, directs players to the map of Middle Earth in Tolkien's book, noting that "It is a good idea to draw a map of the way the different locations connect to each other, should you need to go back or if you should get lost" (Beam Software, 1982, 3). Players of *ZORK I* were warned that "[s]ome puzzles are almost impossible to solve without completely mapping the area" (InfoComm, 1984, 13). Mapmaking remained a key aspect of gameplay in early animated adventure games such as Roberta William's *King's Quest* where the player is told, "You can easily lose your way in the large kingdom of Daventry. It is to your advantage to draw a map during your travels" (Sierra On-Line, 1984, 22), an instruction accompanied by examples of possible mapping techniques, while in *Space Quest*, another of Sierra On-Line's games, the "Beginning Adventurer" is advised "Draw a map that includes each place you visit, objects found, dangerous areas, any and every landmark you see along the way" (Sierra On-Line, 1986, 7).

These paratextual injunctions to mapmaking initiate a blurring of reader and character that will be continued in the story proper – "A thrilling fantasy adventure in which YOU are the hero" (1982, front cover) – which, in common with many text adventure games, requires readers to recognize themselves as the subject of its second person address. The alignment of reader and character is achieved through the careful deployment of situational markers. Take, for example, the following sequence from early in *The Warlock of Firetop Mountain*:

79
The passageway ends in front of you in a dead end. If you wish to search for secret passageways, turn to **137**. If not, return to the crossroads at **267**.

267
You now stand at a crossroads.
To go north Turn to **312**
To go south Turn to **246**
To go west Turn to **79**
To go east Turn to **349**

349
You walk a few metres down the passage and find yourself at a dead end. You may either return to the crossroads (turn to **267**) or investigate the end of the passage (turn to **30**).

The passages above follow the tripartite structure typical of text-based adventure games. Connecting the temporal and the spatial (time and motion), these passages move from the past, making prior action the condition of present seeing – "The passageway ends" – to the present – "You now stand" – and finally gestures towards possible futures – "You may…" This tripartite structure, which recalls Augustine's account of time in terms of memory, perception and expectation (1961), aligns the reader and character through a temporality that is "articulated through a narrative mode" (Ricoeur, 1984, 52). Moreover, embedded in these passages are a similar set of spatial markers organized around the vision of the narrative's second-person protagonist in the present moment: "in front of you," "You now stand" and tellingly "You walk a few metres down the passage *and find yourself*" (emphasis mine).

As a story, *The Warlock of Firetop Mountain* requires readers to recognize themselves as the addressees of its second-person address (translating the external "you" into an internal "I") in order to affect their location to the topographies of its storyworld. As a game with a clearly defined goal – finding the Warlock's treasure – the book requires a further, perhaps contradictory, act of translation: this time from the limited perspective of the intradiegetic narratee to the seemingly omniscient perspective of the extradiegetic third-person narrator. In other words, gameplay in *The Warlock of Firetop Mountain*, concerned with the navigation of its fantastic spaces, entails the movement from a position of uncertainty "standing at the crossroads" (Jackson and Livingstone, 1982, entry 37) to certainty "master of the domain" (Jackson and Livingstone, 1982, entry 40). This movement, best understood in terms of perspective, entails a shift from a space that is shaped by, and for the player-protagonist, an "oriented" or "lived" space (Merleau-Ponty, 2012, 293–294) to an "external," "objective" space characterized by its pure exteriority.

Success in the gamebook might then be seen to effect the removal of the reader, implicated/imbricated in the topographies of the storyworld, to an external location – spatially and temporally distinct from the Warlock's maze. This notion of success might well be understood in terms of the production of maps on recognizable north-south-east-west grids. Just such a space was provided for readers in the first issue of *Warlock: The Fighting Fantasy Magazine* (Figure 4.1). Advising readers that "[m]aps can be drawn out on plain paper, but squared graph paper is by far the most convenient" (Jackson and Livingstone, 1984, 10), the authors of "How to Map" provide a sheet of graph paper on which readers are advised to work in pencil rather than pen – "it is highly unlikely you will map the dungeon correctly" – a suggestion that, combined with the formality of the grid, indicates the co-existence of two possibilities. The first is

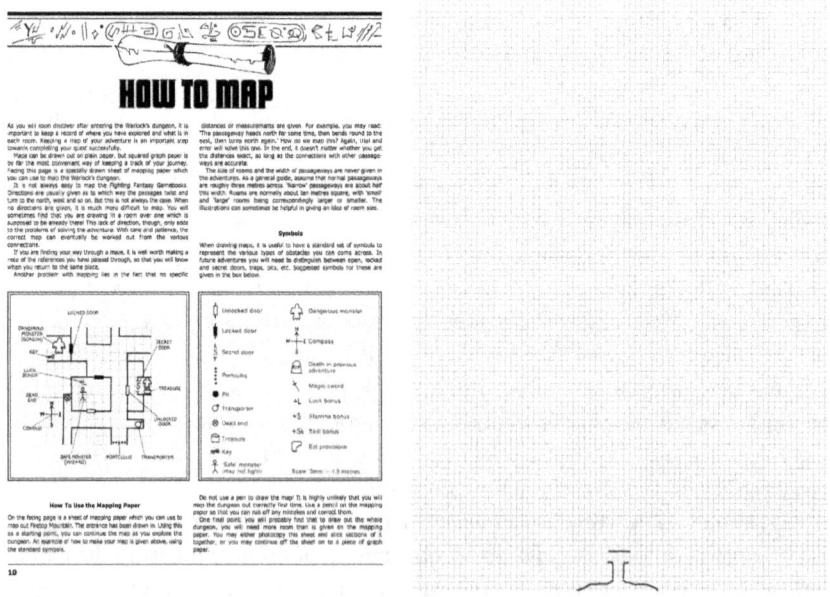

FIGURE 4.1 'How to Map.' Steve Jackson and Ian Livingstone, *Warlock* (1984).

the "correct" gridded solution map that will emerge on the completion of the game, a map well described in terms of the knowledge of an order of places and which, detached from the individual and put into circulation, becomes, as de Certeau puts it, "a projection that is a way of keeping aloof" (1988, 92–93). The second, towards the map as a work in progress, a story map whose creation represents the unfolding of an individual's movement through the narrative space.

In the years since its publication, readers of *The Warlock of Firetop Mountain* have responded to the text's cartographic invitation by turning the experience of movement through the text, "tours" to use de Certeau's terms, into "maps" (1988, 119). A significant number of these maps survive, circulated in online communities and retained in private and, to a far lesser extent, public archives. In what follows, I look at two distinct cartographic practices that emerged in response to the text: "database maps" and "folk maps."

Database Maps: DNA and Solution

Broadly speaking, the database map is a diagram of a text's formal properties, accounting for the relative position – which may be spatial or temporal – of narrative elements (see Ryan, 2006, 142–144; Ryan, Foote, and Azaryahu, 2016, 48). The first of the two maps (Figure 4.2) is an excerpt of

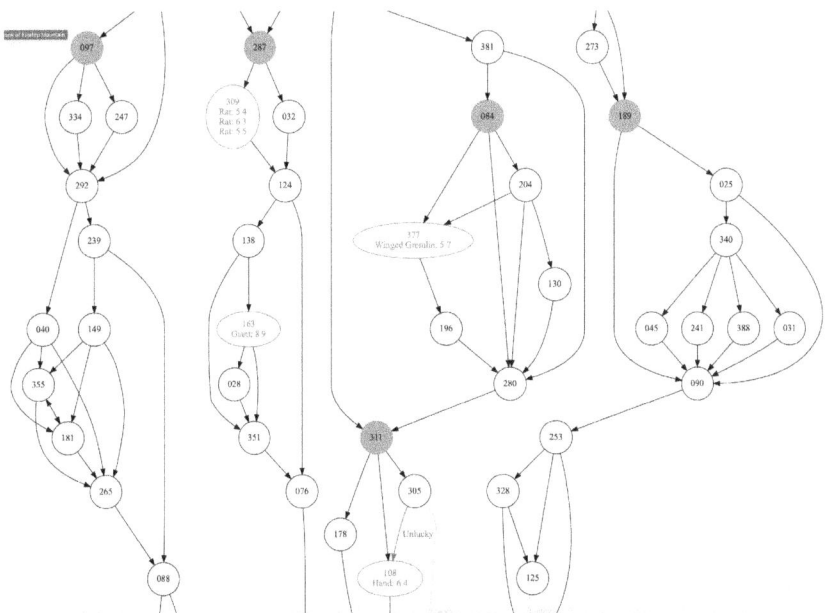

FIGURE 4.2 SVG database map. Simon Osborne, *The Outspaced Shrine* (n.d.).

78 Paul Wake

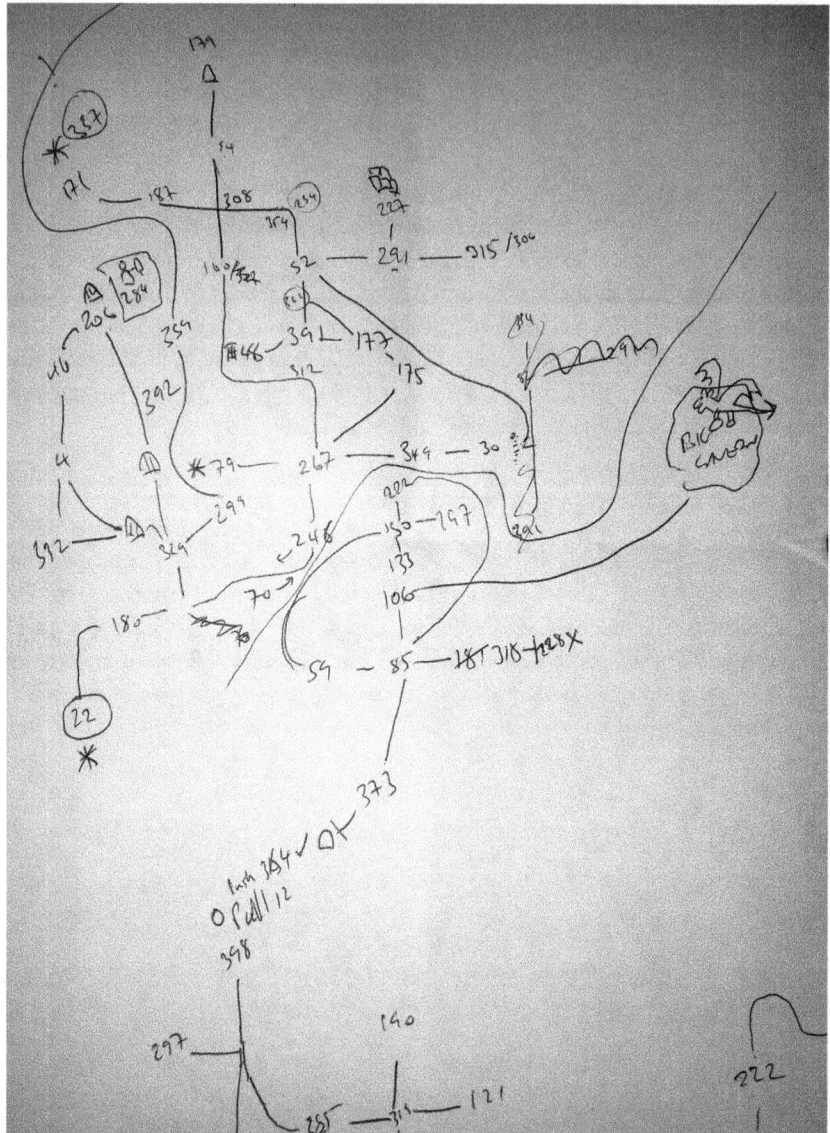

FIGURE 4.3 *The Warlock of Firetop Mountain* solution map. Tim Hatton (2018).

a database map of *The Warlock of Firetop Mountain* rendered in Scalable Vector Graphics and published online. This map represents the entire text, indicating the connections (and the direction of travel) between the different lexia, each of which is numbered. SVG maps of this type have been described as DNA sequences, in that they lay bare the underlying structures out of which individual readings rather than solutions of the book emerge (McGuire, 2013).

The second map (Figure 4.3), a "solution," is presented here as a subset of the database. While hand drawn, this map is close in form to the SVG database map in indicating the paths between the text's lexia in abstract form. In other words, both offer a spatial representation of the text's structure rather than of the physical space of the storyworld. In this, they resemble the linear cartograms of underground rail systems, in which "geometric accuracy is less important that linkages, adjacency, and relative position" (Monmonier, 1996, 34). As readers of the *Warlock* "How to Map" article are informed, "it doesn't matter whether you get the distances exact, so long as the connections to other passageways are accurate" (Jackson and Livingstone, 1984, 10). Where the two maps diverge is in the extent of the mapped space – the solution map which presents one of several possible routes through the text, offers an abbreviated sequence of the book's 400 lexia (around 150 are needed to "complete" the game).

A comparison of the two maps makes it evident that success, where success equates to the mastery of the text, relies on pattern matching. In having a fixed solution, the book resembles a puzzle as much as a game (a distinction that gamebooks begin to unravel). While the Fighting Fantasy books' combat system affords a dynamic aspect that prevents them from having an entirely fixed path, a feature that distinguishes the series from the popular Choose Your Own Adventure books (Bantam, 1979–1998), it becomes clear that the negotiation of space (both of the storyworld and the material book) is the *object* of the game. Here, work on endings in fiction (Brooks, 1992; Kermode, 2000) and goals in games (Caillois, 1961; Avedon and Sutton-Smith, 1971; Suits, 2014) begins to align. "Winning is the 'end' of the game," as David Parlett puts it, "in both senses of the word, as termination and as object" (2018, 3). In other words, reading and playing are connected by a shared drive – Peter Brooks writes of the death instinct – towards endings that will confer meaning.

Folk Maps: Private and the Communal Cartography

While database maps detail fixed and communicable patterns, folk maps, typically hand drawn, are expressions of unique encounters with the geography of a text's storyworld. The map below (Figure 4.4), a hand-drawn map of an imaginary place, is typical of player-created maps of text-based adventure games, both analogue and digital. Such maps, which evince an intimate connection to their makers, are examples of what I am calling "folk cartography," a term that recalls the history of folk art, which was, as Holger Cahill wrote in the catalog to the Museum of Modern Art's 1932 American Folk Art exhibition, "an expression of the common people, made by them and intended for their use and enjoyment" (1932, 6). Cahill's definition helpfully foregrounds the process of making, personal pleasure and ownership in folk art. As personal documents, such maps record personal encounters with the texts they describe. Replacing

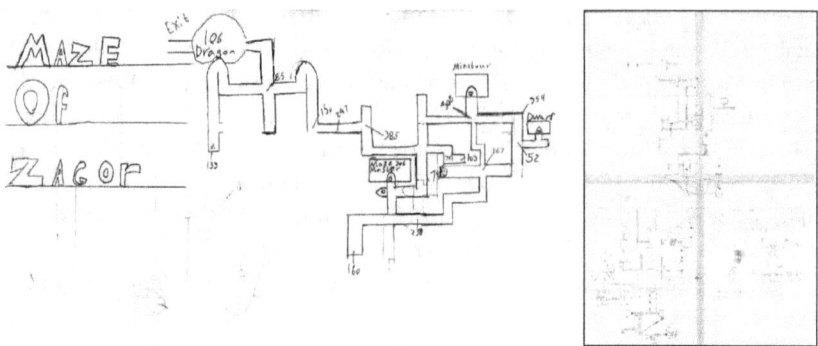

FIGURE 4.4 Folk map of *The Warlock of Firetop Mountain*. Hans Gustafsson (2013).

the bookmark, which functions so neatly to store the location of paused reading of the linear print codex, or the "save game" that emerged alongside digital adventure games, maps of print gamebooks detail "the player's specific trajectory that must be preserved to allow the finishing of the player's own story" (Salter, 2014, 41). Connecting games and their player-cartographers, these maps are "private" paratexts, the creation of which is central to and a vital expression of the gameplay experience. As such, it is no surprise that discussions of strategy guides and walk-throughs (public paratexts) tend to be framed as acts of last resort. "Please don't pick up a pen at the first sign of a problem," wrote Keith Campbell in *Computer & Video Games*, "You will only get a full sense of achievement from a completed adventure if you have solved every problem yourself" (1983, 131). As Mia Consalvo remarks in *Cheating*, for many the "overuse of the paratext strips away too much of the game experience" (2007, 45). The question underlying such a sentiment is whose paratext is used? The private or the communal?

As John Michael Vlach has noted, definitions of folk art are riven by "confusion over whether folk art should be seen as unique, individualistic, and singular or ordinary, communal, and unexceptional" (1992, 21). This division lies at the heart of my description of these maps as folk cartography, a term I use to suggest that they are both as acts of individual expression and acts that emerge from and speak of the intrarelation of a network of participants and materials. Folk art, then, returns us to the madness of maps that emerge through the interaction of a range of material actors. Denis Wood writes of maps as made objects in *The Power of Maps*:

> Freed from the tyranny of the eye (the map never was a vision of reality), the map can be returned to … *the hand* (that makes it) … *the mind* (that reasons with it) … *the mouth* (that speaks with it). Freed from the pretense

of objectivity that reduced it to the passivity of observation, the map can be restored to the *instrumentality* of the body as a whole. Freed from being a thing to ... *look at*, it can become something .... *you make*.

(1993, 182–183)

Wood's evocation of the body in the production of maps and his use of the continuing present tense in the description of this process of production is helpful. As indeed is his larger project of identifying the power relations inherent in mapmaking that exist between the different agencies involved, agencies that include not only map makers and map users, but also the mapped entities which have always included more than physical geography. Where the completed map has "disengaged itself from the itineraries that were the condition of its possibility" (de Certeau, 1988, 120), the map, in process, is active. In this way these networked maps, assemblages of material actors, remind us that the scopic and gnostic drives that de Certeau attaches to the view of the world as text are rooted in an ontotheology that seeks to hold the material and temporal at a distance (itineraries are, of course, accounts of movement through both time and space).

There is, then, more at play than the human in the making of maps. The body, in all the aspects that Wood observes, might more properly be situated as one actor among a network of material actors, alongside the pen, the eraser, the die, the paper, the table. Considered in this way, mapmaking happens in response to the invitation of paper. The book's unturned pages and the mapping paper's blank spaces represent not so much *terra incognita* as what Alfred Hiatt has called *terra nondum cognita*, the "'not yet' land that will be found, and that has already been claimed" (2008, 175). Just as the text's "*spots of indeterminacy*" (Ingarden, 1973, 246) are open invitations to the reader, the white space and abrasive properties of mapping paper act in concert with the soft graphite of the pencil as "inducer-producers" (Bennett, 2010, 39) of cartographic activity.

The objects out of which maps are constructed are, then, not so much "threshold objects that take you in and lead you out of the experience" (Murray, 2017, 134) as they are part of a network of material actors. Rather than negotiating entrance and exit across a hard border (Murray writes of the screen), the map-as-network complicates the appealingly straightforward (in Genette's words, "purely spatial") distinction between epitextual and peritextual paratexts. This co-constitutive relation – which is well described in terms of Barad's intra-action – sees agencies emerge through and from networked action. Indeed, Daniel Reynolds, drawing on Barad's work, usefully describes the relations that transpire between users and media as "intrafaces" (2019, 123). Moreover, as Latour (2005) suggests in his influential account of Actor Network Theory, these constellations are mutable, in his words "provisional," their various actors forming networks that are temporary and often unstable. In fact, these maps are perhaps best described as aspects of what Murray calls "participatory environments," as items that become "real through use" (2017, 138). In this sense the materiality of these maps is performative – acting and provoking action (Drucker, 2013).

Conclusions

To return to the questions with which I began: how might this focus on the activity of mapmaking allow us to understand the possible connections of actual and imagined spaces? Do these maps present a unified way of understanding the mapmaking activity, or indeed, of the player-reader's relation to the storyworlds they map? In one sense, no, at least in as much as maps are both static in the most ordinary sense of cartography, while also being dynamic, responsive and embodied. Maps are both fixed (retrospective, solution to puzzle) but also processual, temporal and subject to revision. They are interfaces, intertexts, paratexts, intratexts, threshold devices and texts themselves. Nonetheless, this thinking about maps, which are characterized here both as records of past action and as records of action (in action), gestures towards their significance as guides (maps) to the experience of games in the recent past and towards the possible directions (signposts, road maps) of games in the present and future.

In relation to the first point, this account of game maps indicates the nature of (game)play as an emergent and individually realized activity. Responding to "unfinished" (Lunenfeld, 2020) texts, these maps document both the hybrid interfaces – keyboard, screen, pencil, paper – of early adventure games and provide historically situated records of the player experience. The preservation and study of these paratextual materials is essential in accounting for a once-central aspect of the player experience that is at risk of being lost through both platform obsolescence and the rapid evolution of player practices and competencies (Newman, 2011, 2012; Stuckey, 2014). While these materials, seen as personal, as craft rather than art, have tended to be neglected, efforts to preserve this work are underway. There are, for example, two artist-curated archives: the Hand Drawn Map Association established by Kris Harzinski in Philadelphia and the Play Generated Map and Document Archive (PlaGMaDA), established by Tim Hutchins and housed at The Strong National Museum of Play in Rochester, New York.

Alongside the preservation of gaming's rich and rapidly developing history, an understanding of the mapping, most clearly evident in earlier forms but nonetheless embedded within contemporary and emergent forms, offers a model for understanding present and the potential future practices. The potential for writers, designers, publishers and players to explore the potential of the assembly of networks comprised of players, texts and objects (be they controllers, threshold objects or props) has been explored across a range of media (and in doing so often brings together different media). Explorations of this territory are readily found in games, both analogue and digital. Prominent examples include Jordy Adan's roll-and-write *Cartographers: A Roll Player Tale* (Thunderworks Games, 2019), tile-laying games such as Klaus-Jürgen Wrede's *Carcassonne* (Hans im Glück, 2000) and story-exploration games such as Ludovic Roudy and Bruno Sautter's *The 7th Continent* (Serious Poulp, 2019). Video games have made similar use of these such as Sid Meier's *Pirates!* (MicroProse, 1987), which was packaged with a cloth map that allowed players to navigate the game's world (combining this information with in-game mapping), and the more recent *Etrian Odyssey*, in which players maintain and update their maps with stylus and touch screen. More frequently perhaps, video games explore the creative spaces that emerge through the parallel impulses of cartographic extraction and entanglement by folding together primary and orienting spaces through the situation of their (orienting) maps within the (primary) story-world. In games such as *Zelda: Breath of the Wild* (Nintendo, 2017), maps exist both within the story world (in narrative terms, they are diegetic) and as elements of the orienting interface (now extradiegetic). Forging links (pun intended) between player-cartographers and cartographer-characters, the game connects its ludic and narrative elements and the spaces occupied by the player. Complicating the distinction between these spaces, in-game maps foreground mapmaking as an activity that involves a network of objects: Link's tablet-like Sheikah Slate and the accompanying pins, markers and stamps, and alongside these in-game objects, the screen buttons, bumpers, triggers and analog sticks of Nintendo's Joy-Con™.

I have presented here two ways of understanding reader-created maps of fictional space: database maps and folk cartography, both of which have two aspects. The first, the database map, is a spatial representation of the text, presented as a series of coordinates that indicate relative position (combining the spatial and the temporal). The solution map, a subset of this database map, represents a single realization of the encounter with this database. The alignment of these two maps, one the property of the text, the other of the reader, might be taken as indicative of successful navigation. The second pairing, which I placed under the heading of folk cartography, recognizes the creativity of the individual reader-player while drawing attention to the network of actors involved in the process of that creative endeavor. It is for this reason that I draw attention to the tension inherent in definitions of folk art, a form regarded as both highly individualistic and as a form of community practice and representation. Of course, the distinctions I draw between these different maps are temporary at best. Their defining qualities are not mutually exclusive, nor do they necessarily align perfectly with any one of the types of map that I have described. As an activity, then, the mapping of fictional spaces has at its core two defining and seemingly antithetical impulses: extraction and entanglement. By extraction I mean to refer to the goal-oriented pattern matching by which readers and players recognize texts as complete, a state of affairs that is accomplished from a position that is beyond the borders of the storyworld. By entanglement, which as Chloé Germaine Buckley tells us, "is not a simple relationship of being caught up in something from which it is difficult to extricate oneself" (2021, 276), I mean the "messy" connections that allow readers and players to immerse themselves within a storyworld. By way of closing, then, mapmaking initiates a series of relationships, placing players within networks of objects that form and reform, decentering the imaginative world of the text and exploring the fluidity of the constellation of author, text, reader and world.

Works Cited

Aarseth, Espen. 1997. *Cybertext: Perspectives on Ergodic Literature*. Baltimore, MD: The Johns Hopkins University Press.
Aarseth, Espen. 2001. "Allegories of Space: The Question of Spatiality in Computer Games." In *CyberText Yearbook 2000*, edited by Markuu Eskelinen and Raine Koskimaa, 152–171. Jyvaskyla: Research Centre for Contemporary Culture.
Aarseth, Espen and Stephan Günzel, eds. 2019. *Ludotopia: Spaces, Places, and Territories in Computer Games*. Bielefeld: Transcript Verlag.
Adan, Jordy. 2019. *Cartographers: A Roll Player Tale*. Boardgame: Thunderworks Games.
Ahmed, Sara. 2007. "Multiculturalism and the Promise of Happiness." *New Formations* 63: 121–137.
Atlus. 2007. *Etrian Odyssey*. Atlus. Nintendo DS.
Augustine. 1961. *Confessions*. Translated by R. S. Pine-Coffin. Harmondsworth: Penguin.
Avedon, Elliot M. and Brian Sutton-Smith. 1971. *The Study of Games*. New York: John Wiley & Sons.
Barad, Karen. 2007. *Meeting the Universe Halfway: Quantum Physics and the Entanglement of Matter and Meaning*. Durham, NC: Duke University Press.
Beam Software. 1982. *The Hobbit*. Manual. London: Melbourne House.
Bennett, Jane. 2010. *Vibrant Matter: A Political Ecology of Things*. Durham, NC and London: Duke University Press.
Big Blue Bubble. 2009. *Fighting Fantasy: The Warlock of Firetop Mountain*. Nintendo DS: Aspyr Media, Inc.
Brooks, Peter. 1992. *Reading for the Plot: Design and Intention in Narrative*. Cambridge, MA: Harvard University Press.
Cahill, Holger. 1932. "American Folk Art." In *American Folk Art: The Art of the Common Man in America, 1750–1900*, 3–28. New York: Museum of Modern Art.
Caillois, Roger. 1961. *Man, Play, and Games*. Translated by Meyer Barash. Urbana and Chicago: University of Illinois Press.
Campbell, Keith. 1983. "Adventure." *Computer & Video Games* 2 (8): 130–131.
Consalvo, Mia. 2007. *Cheating: Gaining Advantage in Videogames*. Cambridge, MA: MIT Press.
Cooper, David, Christopher Donaldson and Patricia Murrieta-Flores. 2016. *Literary Mapping in the Digital Age*. London: Routledge.
Crash. 1984. "The Warlock of Firetop Mountain." *Crash: Micro Games Action* 1: 12.
de Certeau, Michel. 1988. *The Practice of Everyday Life*. Translated by Steven F. Rendall. Berkeley: University of California Press.

Drucker, Johanna. 2013. "Performative Materiality and Theoretical Approaches to Interface." *Digital Humanities Quarterly* 7 (1). http://www.digitalhumanities.org//dhq/vol/7/1/000143/000143.html.
Easterlin, Nancy. 2018. "'The New Geography,' Material Science, and Narratology's Space-time Dichotomy: Notes toward a Geographical Narratology." *Frontiers of Narrative Studies* 4 (2): 197–214.
Fox, Richard and David Smith, dir. 2017. *The Warlock of Firetop Mountain*. Barnet. FoxYason Music Productions. Compact disc.
Genette, Gérard. 1997. *Paratexts: Thresholds of Interpretation*. Translated by Jane E. Lewin. Cambridge: Cambridge University Press.
Germaine Buckley, Chloé. 2021. "Unhuman Entanglement: Ontoethics and Frances Hardinge's Gothic Fiction." In *Young Adult Gothic Fiction: Monstrous Selves/Monstrous Others*, edited by M. Smith K. and Moruzi, 274–295. Cardiff: University of Wales Press.
Gray, Jonathan. 2010. *Show Sold Separately: Promos, Spoilers, and Other Media Paratexts*. New York: New York University Press.
Green, Jonathan. 2014. *You Are the Hero: A History of Fighting Fantasy Gamebooks*. Haddenham: Snowbooks Ltd.
Gustafsson, Hans. 2013. "Map of *The Warlock of Firetop Mountain*." Image. https://boardgamegeek.com/image/1695244/ff-geek.
Harley, J. B. and David Woodward, eds. 1987. *The History of Cartography*. Volume 1. Chicago, IL: University of Chicago Press.
Hatton, Tim. 2018. "Map of The Warlock of Firetop Mountain." Image. https://twitter.com/timhatton/status/951556924553736192/photo/1.
Herman, David. 2009. *Basic Elements of Narrative*. Oxford: Wiley-Blackwell.
Hiatt, Alfred. 2008. *Terra Incognita: Mapping the Antipodes before 1600*. Chicago, IL: University of Chicago Press.
Infocomm Inc. 1984. *ZORK I: Instruction Manual*. Cambridge, MA: Infocomm Inc. http://infodoc.plover.net/manuals/zork1.pdf.
Ingarden, Roman. 1973. *The Literary Work of Art*. Translated by George G. Grabowicz. Evanston: Northwestern University Press.
Jackson, Steve. 1986. *The Warlock of Firetop Mountain*. Boardgame: Games Workshop.
Jackson, Steve and Ian Livingstone. 1982. *The Warlock of Firetop Mountain*. London: Puffin Books.
Jackson, Steve and Ian Livingstone. 1984. "How to Map." *Warlock: The Fighting Fantasy Magazine* 1: 10–11.
Jackson, Steve, Ian Livingstone and Russ Nicholson. 2016. *The Warlock of Firetop Mountain: Official Colouring Book*. Haddenham: Snowbooks Ltd.
Kermode, Frank. 2000. *The Sense of an Ending: Studies in the Theory of Fiction*. Oxford: Oxford University Press.
Lammes, Sybille. 2008. "Playing the World: Computer Games, Cartography and Spatial Stories." *Aether: The Journal of Media Geography* 3: 84–96.
Latour, Bruno. 1996. "On Actor-network Theory: A Few Clarifications." *Soziale Welt* 47 (4): 369–381.
Latour, Bruno. 2005. *Reassembling the Social: An Introduction to Actor-Network-Theory*. Oxford: Oxford University Press.
Lunenfeld, Peter. 2020. *The Digital Dialectic: New Essays on New Media*. Cambridge, MA: The MIT Press.

Manovich, Lev. 2001. *The Language of New Media*. Cambridge, MA: The MIT Press.
McGuire, Warren. 2013. "Fighting Fantasy SVGs." *The World of Fighting Fantasy*. http://worldoffightingfantasy.blogspot.com/2013/11/fighting-fantasy-svgs.html.
Merleau-Ponty, Maurice. 2012. *Phenomenology of Perception*. Translated by Donald A. Landes. London: Routledge.
MicroProse. 1987. *Sid Meier's Pirates!* MicroProse: Commodore 64.
Monmonier, Mark. 1996. *How to Lie with Maps*. Chicago, IL and London: The University of Chicago Press.
Moretti, Franco. 1998. *Atlas of the European Novel: 1800–1900*. London: Verso.
Moretti, Franco. 2005. *Graphs, Maps, Trees: Abstract Models for Literary History*. London: Verso.
Mottershead, Neil and Simon Brattel. 1984. *The Warlock of Firetop Mountain*. ZX Spectrum: Puffin Personal Computing.
Mottershead, Neil, Simon Brattel and Martin S. Horsley. 1983. *Halls of the Things*. ZX Spectrum: Crystal Computing.
Murray, Janet. 2017. *Hamlet on the Holodeck: The Future of Narrative in Cyberspace*. Updated Edition. Cambridge, MA: MIT Press.
Newman, James. 2011. "(not) Playing Games: Player-Produced Walkthroughs as Archival Documents of Digital Gameplay." *The International Journal of Digital Curation* 6 (2): 109–127.
Newman, James. 2012. *Best Before: Videogames, Supersession and Obsolescence*. London: Routledge.
Nintendo. 2017. *The Legend of Zelda: Breath of the Wild*. Nintendo: Nintendo Switch.
Nitsche, Michael. 2008. *Video Game Spaces: Image, Play, and Structure in 3D Game Worlds*. Cambridge, MA: MIT Press.
Osborne, Simon. n.d. "Fighting Fantasy #1: *The Warlock of Firetop Mountain*." Image. http://outspaced.fightingfantasy.net/SVG_Flowcharts/ff01.svgz.
Parikka, Jussi. 2012. *What is Media Archaeology?* Cambridge: Polity Press.
Parlett, David. 2018. *Parlett's History of Board Games*. Brattleboro, VT: Echo Point Books & Media.
Pramas, Chris. 2007. "The Warlock of Firetop Mountain." In *Hobby Games: The 100 Best*, edited by James Lowder, 362–364. Seattle: Green Ronin Publishing.
Punday, Daniel. 2019. *Playing at Narratology: Digital Media as Narrative Theory*. Columbus: Ohio State University Press.
Reynolds, Daniel. 2019. *Media in Mind*. Oxford: Oxford University Press.
Ricoeur, Paul. 1984. *Time and Narrative*. Translated by Kathleen McLaughlin and David Pallauer. Chicago: Chicago University Press.
Roudy, Ludovic and Bruno Sautter. 2019. *The 7th Continent*. Boardgame: Serious Poulp.
Ryan, Marie-Laure. 2006. *Avatars of Story*. Minneapolis: University of Minnesota Press.
Ryan, Marie-Laure. 2016. *Narrative as Virtual Reality 2: Immersion and Interactivity in Literature and Electronic Media*. Baltimore, MD: Johns Hopkins University Press.
Ryan, Marie-Laure. 2018. "Narrative Mapping as Cognitive Activity and as Active Participation in Storyworlds." *Frontiers of Narrative Studies* 4 (2): 232–247.
Ryan, Marie-Laure, Kenneth Foote and Maoz Azaryahu. 2016. *Narrating Space/Spatializing Narrative: Where Narrative Theory and Geography Meet*. Columbus: Ohio State University Press.

Salter, Anastasia. 2014. *What is Your Quest? From Adventure Games to Interactive Books*. Iowa City: University of Iowa Press.

Sierra On-Line. 1984. *King's Quest: Quest for the Crown*. User Manual. Boca Raton, FL: IBM Corp.

Sierra On-Line. 1986. *Space Quest: Chapter One - The Sarien Encounter*. User Manual. Coarsegold: Sierra On-line.

Stuckey, Helen. 2014. "Exhibiting *The Hobbit*: A Tale of Memories and Microcomputers." *Kinephanos: Journal of Media Studies and Popular Culture*: 90–104.

Suits, Bernard. 2014. *The Grasshopper: Games, Life and Utopia*. Peterborough, ON: Broadview Press.

Tin Man Games. 2018. *The Warlock of Firetop Mountain*. Nintendo Switch: Tin Man Games.

Toups, Z.O., Nicholas LaLone, Sultan A. Alharthi, Hitesh Nidhi Sharma and Andrew M. Webb. 2019. "Making Maps Available for Play: Analyzing the Design of Game Cartography Interfaces." *ACM Transactions on Computer-Human Interaction* 9 (4), Article 30.

Toups, Z. O., Nicholas LaLone, Katta Spiel and Bill Hamilton. 2020. "Paper to Pixels: A Chronicle of Map Interfaces in Games." *Proceedings of the 2020 ACM Designing Interactive Systems Conference*. New York, NY: Association for Computing Machinery: 1433–1451. https://dl.acm.org/doi/proceedings/10.1145/3357236

Vlach, John Michael. 1992. "'Properly Speaking': The Need for Plain Talk about Folk Art." In *Folk Art and Art Worlds*, edited by John Michael Vlach and Simon J. Bronner, 13–26. Logan: Utah State University Press.

Wallis, Jamie. 2003. *Steve Jackson and Ian Livingstone's The Warlock of Firetop Mountain*. Newbury: Greywood Publishing. Roleplaying Game.

Weber, Anne-Kathrin and Lorenz Hurni. 2011. "Mapping Literature: Visualisation of Spatial Uncertainty in Fiction." *Cartographic Journal* 48 (4): 293–308.

Wolf, Mark J. P. 2012. *Building Imaginary Worlds: The Theory and History of Subcreation*. New York: Routledge.

Wrede, Klaus-Jürgen. 2000. *Carcassonne*. Boardgame: Hans im Glück Verlag.

Wood, Denis. 1993. *The Power of Maps*. London: Routledge.

Zoran, Gabriel. 1984. "Towards a Theory of Space in Narrative." *Poetics Today* 5 (2): 309–335.

5
FROM SCREEN TO SILICON

Reverse Engineering the Computational Infrastructure of Nick Montfort's *Round*

Lai-Tze Fan

When engaging with a digital device—whether pressing keys, streaming a video, or swiping through photographs—the screen is where the attention of most users stops. A user's undivided attention on the screen interface is arguably the sole focus of many commercialized devices, catalyzed by practices in black box design, which are used by many technological industries. In black box design, user perception and examination are limited to an object or system's explicit input and output functions, meaning that internal functions are unavailable for analysis and that users are discouraged from knowing what's going on beneath the hood—or, in the case of computational devices, behind the screens.

Further promoting a surface-level understanding of digital devices, the design of computer input increasingly moves away from external forms such as keyboards, mouses, and buttons, and increasingly moves toward so-called instant, seamless, and "intuitive" forms of interaction that allow users to focus on one flat screen interface instead. For example, the last 10–15 years in commodified computational design and the emergence of an ubiquitous "Internet of Things" has seen several shifts toward "intuitive" interfaces: facial and fingerprint recognition are common alternatives to typed passwords, accessories with Bluetooth connection are opted over wired technologies, and voice control and dictation AI are starting to limit the need to physically type on a keyboard or to move a mouse.

These changes attest to turn-of-the-millennium concepts in media theory that predicted and identified the privileging of screen content and information over materiality, including N. Katherine Hayles' "embodied virtuality" (1999), Jay David Bolter and Richard Grusin's illusion of "immediacy" (1999), and Lev Manovich's "aesthetic of seamlessness" (136). Each term explains that

DOI: 10.4324/9781003053880-6

computational interfaces, especially through screens, are designed to ever-improve the "natural" experience of device interaction.

Culturally, opaque design choices are mirrored by the use of abstract language in production, marketing, and popular culture with which digital devices are often described. Perhaps the most common example is "the cloud," sometimes called "cloud computing"—an overly abstract term that relays data to the status of ephemeral and transient "bits and bytes" that we imagine to float overhead, as if data has no body. In fact, cloud computing is only possible because of very real hardware, cable infrastructure, and energy in the form of natural resources (Fan 2021). Talking about digital media in abstract ways only exacerbates the idea that computers are beyond knowledge and that they are even magical; indeed, Lori Emerson argues that Apple products are "constantly touted as 'magical' or as something that allows us to perform 'magic tricks'" (11).

As a result of these practices of design and abstract language, many everyday users have an equally surface-level understanding of the political, industrial, and sociocultural implications of technocapitalism on a global scale, including the true complexities of computational infrastructures. Here, the term "infrastructure" is not limited to individual device design, but rather refers to a global-scale technocapital infrastructure, thereby encompassing factors in post-industrial capitalism, political economy, globalization, natural resources and their origins, and the exploitation of laborers worldwide that collectively keep the technocapital wheel turning.

Little of our everyday experiences with commercialized devices reveal the multinational technology corporations that produce them. Further, little of everyday interactions with screen content brings attention to their supporting hardware, which users—as consumers—are not encouraged to think about until they are broken or out of date, at which time they are expected to be replaced. *But where in the world do digital devices come from? How—and by whom—are they produced? What happens to them when they are no longer of cultural value to us?* These kinds of quotidian questions begin to open up discussions that this chapter will address, primarily by discussing ways in which we can understand computational infrastructure to be multifarious, networked and interdependent, and crossing borders and boundaries.

This chapter explores how users can be encouraged to think about hardware operations that occur when using digital devices as well as the material, labor, and environmental processes of producing, repurposing, and disposing device hardware. I seek to re-think the ways in which we talk about and imagine computational infrastructure, especially by troubling the linear trajectory that is exhibited by the classic capital circuit model—Production, Distribution, and Consumption—here specifically to account for the conditions of technocapitalism. I draw upon Kate Crawford's *Anatomy of an AI System* and Benjamin H. Bratton's concept of The Stack as examples of visually and theoretically modelling computational infrastructures that represent their networked and non-linear systems more transparently.

I will use a similar non-linear *storytelling* approach, arguing that critical and creative storytelling about computational infrastructures can further our understanding of their systems, processes, and nuances by pairing these complexities with a narration of my own user experience with my device. I will narrate stages of my experience with a laptop, coupling these experiences with information about which hardware are responsible for which processes as well as how these hardware components operate, what natural materials they are made of, where these materials come from, and how they are repurposed or disposed after the device is thrown away. Calling this method "behind-the-screens storytelling" or BTS storytelling for short, this narration represents the capital circuit, expanding it to include the vital stages that precede Production—Excavation and Refinement—and that follow Consumption—Repurposing and Disposal.[1]

As a method of narration, BTS storytelling encourages users to be aware of the complex systems of computational infrastructures without which digital devices simply could not exist. Thinking about digital devices in narrational terms, then—in terms of cause and effect—I will trace computer operations back to the parts of the network that fulfill these requests, the parts of the computer that perform these operations, and the dark histories and even darker futures of those devices.

I demonstrate BTS storytelling in action through a case study that exhibits strong critical consideration of a user's experience as well as hardware and infrastructure: Nick Montfort's generative computational poem *Round* (2013) describes some of the functions of its own operative software and hardware. In choosing *Round*, however, I explicitly note that it is not the objective of Montfort nor of his creative work to address—and that he is not in a position of blame for not addressing—the exploitative aspects of technocapitalism that *Round*, through multiple associative steps, ultimately points to. I choose *Round* for its acute awareness of the relationship among screen content, software, and hardware, and for its success in drawing more attention to these relationships compared to other works that I could have examined.

The stages of computational infrastructure explored in BTS storytelling are non-linear. Due to the incredible detail of each of these stages, I will only focus on four hardware components and three types of natural resources. I begin with the *Immediate Experience* of running *Round* on my laptop, discussing the phenomenological effects that this has on specific laptop hardware components that are named in *Round* as well as the network structures and systems that support my laptop's functions. After describing the *Hardware Operations* of my laptop components, I trace these components in pre-capital circuit stages to the natural materials that they are made of, and further back, to the *Excavation and Refinement* of these natural materials through exploitative, inhumane labor.

Finally, I explore what occurs in the post-capital circuit, discussing the *Repurposing and Disposal* processes of specific hardware components. In this way, this chapter shows that critical forms of storytelling can help users trace their own personal experiences with screens and on-screen content all the way back to their material resources, which have Earthly roots.

Methods in Modelling Computational Infrastructure

In the last two decades, but more prominently since the 2010s, attempts in critical and cultural studies have sought to better understand and communicate the interconnected, globalized, and capitalist systems of technological infrastructures. For instance, in media archaeology, which focuses on alternative and often material histories of media, analytical methods are used to examine relationships among media technologies and the sociocultural systems to which they belong and which they help to shape (Parikka 2015; Mattern 2017). In science and technology studies and critical design studies, the works of Anne Balsamo (2011) and Daniela K. Rosner (2018) have demonstrated new approaches toward the discursive and humanities-minded reverse engineering of technological design.

In my analysis of computational hardware in this chapter, I draw upon Balsamo's methodology of "hermeneutic reverse engineering" from *Designing Culture: The Technological Imagination at Work* (2011). In this approach, science, technology, engineering, and mathematics (STEM)-based reverse engineering methods are used to trace production processes back to design stages; these are combined with ideological interpretation, analysis, and critique to study the sociocultural significance of technological artifacts.

Closely aligned in sociological studies of technology, visual methods have emerged that seek to model and communicate computational infrastructures to scholars and members of the public who are interested in technological society and culture. For instance, Benjamin H. Bratton's (2015) concept and model of The Stack is a planetary-scale model of computational infrastructure that is composed of six intertwined and co-dependent layers: Earth, Cloud, City, Address, Interface, and User. The Stack originates from Bratton's observation that "computation does not just denote machinery" (xvii), yet that "we lack adequate vocabularies to properly engage the operations of planetary-scale computation" (xvii). In response, he offers a more robust conceptual model and language to represent a planetary-level "megastructure" that governs our digital lives to the degree that he describes the relationship as one of sovereignty. In addition to Bratton's discursive exploration of The Stack, it is also offered as a diagram in his work *The Stack: On Software and Sovereignty* (2015), a geometric figure that "shows a vertical-sectional relationship [among] possible positions occupying all six layers at once. It demonstrates that while positions on layers are held simultaneously, each layer governs that position semiautonomously"

(67). In being able to see the structure of computational infrastructure in this way, The Stack allows users to imagine the intertwined dynamics of each layer. These dynamics are additionally expressed by Bratton in this way:

> *Users,* human or nonhuman, are cohered in relation to *Interfaces,* which provide synthetic images of the *Addressed* landscapes an networks of the whole, from the physical and virtual envelopes of the *City,* to the geographic archipelagoes of the *Cloud* and the autophagic consumption of *Earth's* minerals, electrons, and climates that power all of the above.
>
> *(12)*

Of particular note in this chapter is Kate Crawford and Vladan Joler's *Anatomy of an AI System* (2018), also called "An anatomical case study of the Amazon echo as a [sic] artificial intelligence system made of human labor." A visualized flowchart that represents specific parts of computation infrastructure and tracing the geological, industrial, political, and human (ethical) components that make up the Amazon Echo intelligent virtual assistant, the *Anatomy* project allows users to trace their origin point (as the "human operator" of the Amazon Echo) backward to the many branches from which the Echo originates and upon which it depends. Crawford and Joler break down different hardware and software components and their ties to human power and labor. The structure of the *Anatomy* is composed of three adjacent columns that feed into each other:

1. Initial or pre-production geological processes: elements, mines, smelters/refiners, component manufacturers, assemblers, distributors.
2. Quantification processes: AI training, data preparation and labeling, infrastructure (industry planning and organization), Internet platform/services, Internet infrastructure, domestic infrastructure (local planning and organization), human operator/user.
3. Post-consumption geological processes: disposing, recovering, shipping, collecting, abandoned devices.

While Crawford and Joler's focus is specifically on the Amazon Echo, the *Anatomy* project serves as a modelling method that is capable of providing a fractal understanding of the fact that computational infrastructure and its assemblages can go further and further back, to more and more branches, to factors that are increasingly miniscule but always necessary. Different adaptations of the *Anatomy* project could arguably be used to map post-industrial capitalism in general.

I focus on these examples of modelling computational infrastructure for their contributions toward re-imagining the capital circuit. Through Bratton's Stack model that runs in connected vertical planes and Crawford and Joler's flowchart process, both succeed in making a case for dismantling the capital circuit, disrupting its projected linearity from the stages of Production to Distribution to Consumption. This dismantling is revealed to be necessary, as both treat the circuit as incomplete: Bratton shows how much more complicated and networked computational infrastructure truly is. Crawford and Joler unearth the dirty origins and unethical ends of technological resources, components, and labor.

In particular, Crawford and Joler succeed in illuminating the stages of Excavation, Refinement, Repurposing, and Disposal that are too often ignored in discussions of technological and creative industries that offer commodified goods. They visualize through the *Anatomy* project the ways in which these industries are dependent upon what comes before Production and after Consumption, including produced computer components, raw and refined resources, and laboring and exploited human subjects.

Therefore, in describing the same computational infrastructure as Bratton and Crawford and Joler, what I am doing differently and what BTS storytelling does differently is to include a focus on the user's relationship to and knowledge of infrastructure. Also, while it is important to model the infrastructure of computational devices as well as their historical and speculative transformations, it is equally as important to focus on how deterrents and encouragements to users' awareness of that infrastructure may adapt and transform. This bilateral perspective is what BTS storytelling affords: a specific structure and method to tell multiple stories as they exist together at once.

Ultimately, BTS storytelling describes a *process* between infrastructure and humans, a process with its own far-reaching origins. This necessitates tracing as far back as I can go, which is by no coincidence as far back as Bratton and Crawford and Joler also go: to the Earth itself.

The Immediate Experience

I am a reader in Toronto, Canada. I am also a computer user, sitting before a laptop that does not have any programs running. I open my Internet browser and type in the Uniform Resource Locator (URL) "http://round.newbinarypress.com" to access Nick Montfort's generative poem *Round*. Now I have become a client too, seeking a website hosted by the online publishing house *New Binary Press*, with the Internet Protocol (IP) address 78.153.218.40. While the press and its Editors are located in Cork, Ireland, the IP address reveals that *New Binary Press*'s data and web servers, hosted by ISP Blacknight Hosting, are located at the Carlow Data Center in Carlow, Ireland, which is about 170 kilometers from Cork.

I can imagine the trajectory of the data as it is transferred across three cities, from its managers in Cork, the servers in Carlow, and sent to me across the Atlantic Ocean to Toronto. This data is represented as ephemeral content that is uploaded into and downloaded from "the cloud." Abstracts abound: online content has also been described in relation to the flow of water and as a super highway of information.

The Immediate covers the experience of the user (who, in the case of *Round*, is also a reader) and the events that occur within the user's knowledge or which are prompted on a content level with a user's interaction with the screen and networks (including by connecting their device and IP with servers, hosts, and other users). The user's experience and engagement are highlighted through the narrative, which articulates what's happening with content on their screen as well as what is happening to the device in their hands and before their eyes.

The reverse engineering of the Immediate involves addressing the complex nature of cloud computing in terms of the storage, supply, and delivery of networked data as well as the discussion of the software processes that generate screen content and then execute programs and commands. This is in direct response to the phenomenon of abstracting content, which Alan Liu argues has demonstrably increased over the history of media development. Especially in computational media, there occurs "the separation of content from material instantiation or formal representation" (58). In working to illuminate that this abstraction occurs at all, the Immediate layer focuses on the ways that the user receives abstracted version of computational content and the fact that they are not prompted to think about computational form and materiality. Therefore, the Immediate is characterized as sensory, textual, interactive, communicative, and seemingly instantaneous.[2]

Hardware Operations

The next layer, Hardware Operations, is much more complex and therefore a longer story than the Immediate Experience. It tells the story of what is BTS while still physically and materially present for the user: this layer presents the hardware of the device and the reverse engineering of those components into their natural materials. Just because the components are physically present does not mean that they can be observed or analyzed by a user; physically deconstructing a device—by taking apart its shell, examining the disparate parts—can better help us understand their functions and how they come together to create an operative device. However, taking apart one's device risks voiding its warranty with many Big Tech companies (in line with the software equivalent of jailbreaking). Also, many commodified personal devices can only be taken apart with company-specific screwdrivers, physically preventing users from looking under the hood. In these ways, users are actively discouraged from critically inquiring into their devices' material contexts and conditions, and these conditions remain unseen so long as policies and design protocols act as further obstacles. Users end up becoming dependent upon authorized vendors and repair technicians.[3] The Hardware Operations stage is characterized by materiality, technocapitalism, and resource dependency.

This section focuses on individual hardware components that must work together to allow the computer to operate; in the case of *Round*, these components primarily consist of the computer processing units (CPU), the transistor, the fan, and the heatsink. In this chapter, I will not cover other essential components such as the physical screen, the graphic processing unit (GPU), the power supply, the printed circuit board, screen, and random-access memory (RAM), focusing only on the parts and processes that Montfort gestures to in his accompanying "A Note on *Round*" (n.p.).

Having the website load successfully is only the start of running *Round*. The content of the poem is not in the source text, but rather the content is the product of calculations that are performed by my **COMPUTER PROCESSOR**. Montfort explains in "A Note on *Round*" that "*Round* computes the digits of π, pausing after each digit is computed. (Each time *Round* is loaded, it begins at 3, continues to 1, continues to 4, and so on)" (n.p.). That is: *Round* does not store the numerical sequence of π in its code; it runs a program that calculates those digits every time it is loaded.

COMPUTER PROCESSORS or CPUs execute and enable all instructions behind the computer screen. Contemporary computers commonly have CPUs that take the shape of a single chip, which are called microprocessors. It is the CPU that calculates the next digit of π using the additional scripts in the code, jsbn.js and jsbn2.js. These scripts, called JavaScript Big Number 1 and 2 and written by computer scientist Tom Wu, are able to process "the large-integer arithmetic that *Round* performs" (n.p.). The CPU performs these functions by communicating with the computer's memory (RAM), which executes all programs, and also with the energy from the computer's power supply—either a battery or an external source.

The first words of *Round* appear:

"form in/tends in/tense verse crease to tense form tense vent verse tone verse form crease form vent tends to crease to tends form form vent form crease tone verse tense"

Only one line has been produced and it's been two minutes. I try not to fidget, knowing that I will have to wait longer and longer as further calculations are made.

"crease vent vent tends in/verse tone into verse form verse verse form tone tense in tense vent crease cerse tone tends verse tends tends tense verse crease form"

On and on the poem will go. I wonder what digits the numbers correspond to and try to remember the digits of π. 3.14159265358979—and that's as far as I can get, but this means that 3 = form, 1 = in, 4 = tends, 5 = tense, and 9 = verse. As the poem continues, I realize that the number 0 may be represented as a line break in the text. A quick search confirms my hypothesis. What is my computer doing to generate these words and to create these patterns? How are the separate components working together to produce poetry?

The **TRANSISTOR** of the CPU acts as an amplifier of electric currents (to send stronger or weaker currents) and a switch (to start and stop current flows). It is the transistor that allows the CPU to send its electronic signals within itself as well as allowing the CPU to connect to the rest of the hardware, much like the electric pulse of a heart allows it to pump blood to a body.

In order to control currents, transistors have to regulate the flow of electrons, and this ability is literally inscribed into their physical production. Transistors are made out of silicon wafers that are "doped," which means that a gas of a select element's "impurities" is applied to the wafer; when absorbed, those elemental impurities change the wafer's makeup and affect its behavior. As layer after layer is applied—boron, arsenic, and aluminum or copper—the resulting layers look like a cross-section of the Earth's crust (CPU Shack n.p.; Kaplan and White 2003).

The text continues, and around the 10-minute mark, something starts to change in my laptop. The words of the poem begin to appear more slowly and I am suddenly aware of my laptop **FAN**'s hum as its volume begins to rise. Normally, the fan is very quiet even when I am streaming movies. At 12 minutes, the fan is unavoidably loud. I realize that if I were listening to music or watching a video, I would have to increase the volume to be able to hear comfortably. As an experiment, I run *Round* again while taking a video call, which speeds up the onset of the fan's noisiness considerably, now starting at 3 minutes.

I read Montfort's explanation about what is happening:

> As *Round* runs, the production of text will slow down as more and more steps are necessary to determine the next digit of π. Your computer will also slow down on other tasks and will physically heat up. Your computer's fan will work harder as your processor labors to compete these computations.
>
> *(n.p.)*

The harder a computer works, the more frequently electricity passes through copper wires throughout the computer, as electrons run around and create friction that generates heat.

As the fan whirs, I can feel the body of my laptop heat up beneath my resting palms. Along the top length of the laptop, along the keyboard where the two halves of the laptop connect, the computer is getting so hot that I become concerned. How can I cool down my laptop? Should I point a fan at it? An icepack? Should I close *Round*?

Heat reduction is a necessary part of computer maintenance to prevent the machine from overheating and either crashing, shutting itself down, or being permanently damaged. An overheated battery will considerably shorten its lifespan. Overheating a CPU, GPU, or motherboard can reduce their operative functions. If any resin—found in resistors and an integrated circuit, for instance—melts or even catches fire, those parts of the computer or the entire machine must be replaced (Gordon 2018).

Passive forms of heat reduction, such as cold storage environments, are no longer used to manage modern computers.[4] The norm of computer heat reduction is through active forms of ventilation such as fans and heatsinks, and by having enough free space for hot air to blow out of the device through vents (Burke n.p.).

Computer **FANS**, working in tandem with the heatsink, are composed of a motor, a bearing (the frame around the perimeter of the fan), silicon steel plates, magnetic stripes, and copper wire. It is difficult to gage at what temperature the laptop fan goes into overdrive, but a safe maximum temperature is about 35°Celcius (95°Fahrenheit). As *Round* runs, the fan will work harder to prevent the internal temperature, especially of the CPU, from rising much above this. If the CPU reaches a temperature of 80–100°C (176–212°F), the computer will shut down.

The fans work to support the main method of computer heat reduction: **HEATSINKS** draw heat away from internal parts of the computer, as they are made of either or both conductive metal and polymers. Polymers are used in heatsinks to conduct heat away because they are more efficient insulators of heat and cold than conductive metals. By thermodynamic design, heatsinks minimalize air resistance and maximize surface area to conduct heat away from the surfaces of the CPU, the power supply unit (PSU), and the GPU, transferring it out the back or the top of the computer case ("What is a Heatsink?" n.p.).

The heatsink works when a fan blows external cool air across its surface, while also moving the machine's internal hot air along the heatsink's clustered maze of polymers or copper or aluminum pipes. This movement allows the heatsink's conductive materials to absorb the heat away from the CPU and, with the fan's help, escort the hot air out of the machine. As *Round* continues to run, the fan will more quickly blow air at the heatsink ("What is a Heatsink?" n.p.).

Refrain: Excavation; Refinement

This Refrain is so named because it can be returned to later during the discussion of the process of Repurposing natural resources for re-refinement.

The elements of each hardware component may be further broken down into their assembly (products from components), manufacturing (materials into components), and earthly materials, origins, and Excavation (raw materials into Refined materials), including the transportation infrastructure in place that ships these materials from global location to location. In examining these aspects, we may ask: how are these components made and from what materials are they made? Where are the manufacturers and who is doing this labor? What elements do the materials come from? Where are the refineries that processes elements and who is doing the work of refining and smelting them? Where are the mines from which these raw materials are excavated and who are the miners? The Excavation and Refinement stages are characterized by materiality, technocapitalism, resource dependency, exploitation, and invisible and erased labor.

For the stages of manufacturing and assembly, I can be more specific: the Intel CPU microprocessor chip of my Mac laptop was made in either the USA, China, Ireland, or Israel, as these are the manufacturing locations identified by the official Intel corporation. The assembly of the CPU occurred in either Malaysia, China, Costa Rica, or Vietnam ("Intel Global Manufacturing Facts"; "Helping Maintain Industry").

Below is a list of the raw materials commonly found in the CPU, transistor, fan, and heatsink:

- CPU: silicon, aluminum, copper, arsenic, phosphorous, germanium, boron, antimony, hydroflouric acid, and photoresist polymers.
- Transistor: silicon, boron, phosphorous, arsenic, aluminum, and copper.
- Fan: silicon, copper, plastic (refined oils from fossil fuels), stainless steel, chrome steel, and ceramic.
- Heatsink: copper, aluminum, polymers, silicon, boron, zinc, silver, and gallium.

Due to the incredible detail of the origins of each of these materials respectively, I will only focus on three, which are each fundamental to electronic engineering and which make up a major percentage of materials used in computation: silicon, aluminum, and copper.

Silicon

After oxygen, the second most common element on earth is silicon. Over two-thirds of it is mined in China, but it is also excavated from other neighboring countries such as India, Russia, and Norway. According to the British Royal Society of Chemistry, silicon, like many other raw materials, "does not occur uncombined in nature" ("Silicon" n.p.). Rather, it is found as silicon dioxide (silica) and as silicates (which can be refined into asbestos, granite, clay, mica, and other materials) (n.p.).

As only high-purity silicon can be used to produce semiconductors in electronics, the raw materials undergo a refining process: trichlorosilane (a combination of silica and hydrogen chloride) is smelted in a chemical solution and then made solid again in a purification process called recrystallization (Royal Society of Chemistry n.p.).

Silica in crystalline form is as fine as dust, and when breathed in, it causes extensive health problems to miners and refiners. Common health implications of silica dust include silicosis (lung inflammation and scarring), lung cancer, chronic bronchitis, and some autoimmune diseases ("Crystalline Silica" n.p.). A 2015 study of 57 silica mining sites of the Shankargarh region of India shows that there are environmental implications to mining silica as well (Mishra 151). Land deterioration occurs through soil pollution and ravaged abandoned mines, resulting in the reduced productivity of top soil to produce healthy vegetation and, in turn, affecting the local food chain (155–156). Pollution to plant surfaces also blocks them from sunshine and photosynthesis. Pollution to water through rain run-off and the "deterioration of ground water and natural drainage systems" is aggravated by the egregious amounts of water needed for mining, as much as 4,500–6,000 gallons of water per minute (154). Overall, biodiversity is greatly diminished.

Aluminum

Like silicon, aluminum is usually found in combination with other materials in composites called bauxite and cryolite; bauxite is more commonly mined today, as cryolite has almost been mined into disappearance (Royal Society of Chemistry "Aluminum" n.p.). The American Aluminum Association notes that there are reserves and mines of each material in multiple continents, but that most aluminum in the bauxite form is excavated in Australia, China, Brazil, India, and Guinea (n.p.).

To smelt aluminum, bauxite is dissolved in a molten version of cryolite, and is then refined by further decomposition with electrolysis, a purifying process in which a current passes through an electrolyte. The result is pure aluminum.

Mining, as noted in the American-based Human Rights Watch organization, possesses its own complex infrastructure. The organization describes the impact of mining on their case study, the Boké region of Guinea, a country that excavates 7% of the world's bauxite:

> A network of mining roads and railways, used to transport box out to ports, crisscross once isolated rural communities. Industrial ports, where bauxite is loaded onto barges or ships for export, are juxtaposed with the mangroves, paddy fields and local fishing ports that form to the backbone of riverside communities' livelihoods.
>
> (n.p.)

The report highlights the impact of bauxite mining on existing communities, detailing the sociocultural consequences as well. While Human Rights Watch notes that mining provides new jobs, they also outline the government-sanctioned expropriation of ancestral farmlands to mining companies, the reduction in local resources—including fresh water—for existing communities due to an influx of mining laborers, and the reduced air quality due to dust particles (Wormington n.p).

Copper

Like silicon and aluminum, copper does not occur naturally as a resource, but rather is found as a compound element in minerals such as chalcopyrite and bornite (Royal Society of Chemistry "Copper" n.p.). Copper is a critical metal for technological production, highly conductive, and found in many forms of wiring. However, our need for copper outweighs its availability: despite copper being more abundant than many other natural resources, and despite mining expansion and production rates that are recorded between 15 and 20 million tonnes a year ("Copper Production and Environmental Impact" n.p.), industry estimates note that copper supplies will not be enough to meet growing demands in electronics (Mills n.p.), particularly as we increasingly seek to use electric and so-called "green" forms of energy.

The process of mining copper involves open-pit mining through near-surface level quarries, but also the much more expensive and dangerous processes of underground mining, which involves burrowing into the earth to reach copper ores. Mining can expose laborers to silica dust particles, resulting in asthma, tuberculosis, and silicosis (Holland, EMRC, and Imperial College London 2019; García-Gómez and Pérez-Cebada 2020). Mining has been shown to cause land degradation from deforestation, habitat destruction, ground- and surface-water pollution, and the exposure of minerals to the air and water, which oxidizes them into acidic forms that are harmful to surrounding flora and fauna ("Copper Production and Environmental Impact" n.p.; Hudson, Fox, and Plumlee 2019).

Once copper ores are retrieved, they are refined and smelted with sulfuric acid, a process that also creates pollution in the form of sulfur dioxide. In the air, sulfur dioxide combines with rain to create acid rain, which has harmful effects on forests, agriculture, and natural ecosystems ("Copper Production and Environmental Impact" n.p), in addition to damaging buildings and statues.

Repurposing and Disposal

Round will continue running until one of two things happens: I end the program by closing the window, because I decide to stop waiting for new lines as my laptop struggles to calculate the next digit, or my laptop can no longer support the requests that it is being asked to make. Of the second possibility, Montfort notes that "since whatever computational resources one has will eventually be exhausted," *Round* is not a never-ending poem, despite the fact that it is conceptually infinite. There is no final line, Montfort notes, no code condition to stop the program (n.p.), so either I will make a decision or my laptop will make it for me.

The stages of infrastructure called Repurposing and Disposal describe what happens to devices once users are done with them, including the people who manage them and the processes through which precious materials are salvaged from them. Where possible, Repurposing is preferred over Disposal for the purpose of saving money on mining as much as for the purpose of resource sustainability. Through the stage of Repurposing, the materials are returned to the stage of Refinement, where they will be used again to make new hardware components. These devices may be broken or just in need of an upgrade, and sometimes users may keep them for archives, sentiment, nostalgia, research, and so forth. Yet, continued use is rarely an option because of the planned obsolescence of the device: given if a user keeps a device, eventually it will be negated. The company that distributes the device will make the software an active or eventually the device cannot update past a certain model number, as older models cannot support ever-increasing demands for higher functioning power (CPU), more space (hard drive), and more memory (RAM) to handle increasing standards of computation.[5] Like the Excavation and Refinement stages, the Repurposing and Disposal stages are also characterized by exploitation, invisible and erased labor, materiality, technocapitalism, and globalization. In addition, they foregrounds the unsustainability as well as resource dependency and depletion of global computational infrastructures.

I received my laptop in September 2019. Generally, my computational devices have a use time of about five years, as I have a history of spilling something on the keyboard and shorting it. I always try to replace their parts and get more use out of the device, and when it's well and truly over, I always save my devices for archival and future research purposes. I don't want to give up my device after the end of its perceived use-value and cultural death.

But, if I gave my device to an e-waste recycling program or an e-waste donation center, what would happen to the computer parts involved in *Round*—the CPU, fans, heat sink, transistor, wires, circuit board? Where do they go? Who handles them?

Recovery is a priority with computational and electronic devices because of the need for natural resources and especially precious metals to produce technological hardware. Precious metals such as gold, silver, platinum, and palladium are so named because, although they can be made from other elements through nuclear reactions, in general they are rare and there is a finite amount available on Earth.

For computational and electronic technologies, natural resources and precious metals are needed to produce many components, including printed circuit boards (gold, silver, aluminum, tin, and zinc), computer processors (gold, silver, copper, aluminum, and tin), hard drives (platinum, palladium, cobalt, and neodymium), and wires and cables (copper).

How much of each of these resources are found in digital devices? To offer a general impression, the Electronic Recyclers International (ERI) Direct reports that "for every 1 million cell phones recycled we can get these amounts of precious metals: 35,274 pounds of copper; 772 pounds of silver; 75 pounds of gold; 33 pounds of palladium" (n.p.).

However, recovery of the reusable materials is a costly process, and even more costly to perform safely. For this reason, most e-waste that is meant for "recycling" is shipped to other parts of the world for outsourced cheap labor, especially to East, South, and Southeast Asian countries.[6] Depending on the country and its safety regulations, laborers do not always have access to protective equipment such as gloves, facemasks, and goggles. This means that e-waste laborers in the Global South face exposure to harmful materials while recovering resources and disposing unwanted parts. For example, the process of retrieving precious metals may require that they physically interact with elements such as arsenic, cadmium, and lead, all of which are poisonous.

In addition, we may consider the poisonous *methods* through which resources are recovered. For example, the fastest ways to access the copper in many electronic components is to dip them in acids or to burn them to remove their polyvinyl chloride (PVC) coatings. A short video entitled "E Waste in India Short Documentary" explains the acid process:

> In [the pictured] recycling shop, workers dip circuit boards and electric cables into plastic drums full of acid. The bubbles from the acid are stripping the cables of their last remnants of copper and traces of silver. When the acid is depleted, the men dump it into the open sewer in the area.
>
> *(keekeesocean 3:20)*

The video also explains that the processes of resource recovery can occur in public and open spaces, where the method of burning in particular results in toxic fumes being released into the air, which are then inhaled by workers and other residents nearby. The narrator explains that:

> the residents [a neighborhood in East Delhi] say large piles of PVC-coated wires are burned here, a few times a month, in this open field in which children play cricket. They say a huge cloud of toxic smoke, containing organic chemicals such as brominated flame retardants and PCVs [sic], covers the school next to the playground, jeopardizing the health of children.
>
> *(4:15)*

Violet N. Pinto's "E-waste Hazard: The Impending Challenge" (2008) offers an excellent analysis and overview of the implications of toxic e-waste resources on the human body as well as on the environment. She reports that computer devices contain toxic materials and that they are processed through toxic chemicals that e-waste workers are regularly exposed to due to a lack of safe procedures and protective equipment. For instance, lead and mercury affect the central and peripheral nervous systems, the urinary and reproductive organs, and lead can cause anemia; cadmium, "a potentially long-term cumulative poison," accumulates in the kidneys and has also been shown to cause cancer; polycyclic aromatic hydrocarbons (PAHs) cause skin and lung cancers, also affecting the bladder (67).

Pinto reveals that there are recovery-based counterparts and thus deeply unethical implications in recycling processes, potential occupational hazards, and potential environmental hazards; she outlines these in a comprehensive chart on "Environment and Health Hazards" (67). Here, I specifically focus on the computer components covered in this chapter: CPU microprocessor chips, metal-based heatsinks and fan bearings, and wires.

To recover resources from CPUs, Pinto explains that chemical stripping occurs along riverbanks using nitric and hydrochloric acids, resulting in acid contact with the eyes in skin as well as inhalation of the acids' fumes, which "can cause respiratory irritation to severe effects, including pulmonary edema, circulatory failure and death" (67). The acids also pollute the water source, its inhabitants, and its ecosystem (67). The recovery process of metallic resources via smelting exposes workers to dioxins and heavy metals, and also emits these toxins into the air (67). The recovery process of copper in wires, through burning, releases "brominated and chlorinated dioxin and PAH ... to workers living in the burning works area" as well as "hydrocarbon and ashes, including PAHs [to be] discharged into air, water and soil" (67).

After silicon dioxide, bauxite, cryolite, chalcopyrite, and bornite are respectively refined into silicon, aluminum, and copper to become computer components such as wires, circuit boards, hard drives, keyboard matrixes, and so forth; these computer components can be taken apart to retrieve and salvage materials. They are re-refined to make them suitable for manufacturing once again and are re-inserted into the Production stage of the capital circuit.

[Refrain]

The final stages of the technocapital circuit, Repurposing and Disposal, and their refrain to the earlier stages of Refinement and Production, create a loop in computational infrastructure that is repeated. This loop disrupts the story of linearity and unidirectional consumption projected by technocapitalism, inundating and complicating the process by showing the repeated points of entry for natural resources to be expended over and over. Specifically, Repurposing troubles the linearity of Production by providing materials that have already gone through the capital circuit and that are re-refined, re-packaged, and re-imbued with new cultural value in the form of a technological commodity.

The inhumane conditions of labor that support and mobilize Excavation, Refinement, Repurposing, and Disposal are kept far from users' knowledge, photo negatives of the Immediate Experience. Repurposing in particular is greatly misunderstood because it is disguised under the ruse of consumer-friendly language, with the term "e-waste recycling" misleading users into thinking that this form of recycling can be performed under conditions that are local, clean, safe, humane, and sustainable.

That is not to say that e-waste recycling is worse than mining new natural resources for technological production; certainly, e-waste recycling is more sustainable than mining. However, e-waste is just as unethical in its labor practices, it does not entirely replace excavation, and it contributes to forms of technological pollution. As we have not yet found alternatives for many natural resources that we continue to mine or repurpose, and as there is a limit to their repurposing, it is entirely accurate to say that resource dependency as well as e-waste recycling are unsustainable.

Conclusion

Toward further use and application of BTS storytelling, artists, researchers, and everyday users may explore genres that encompass critical inquiries and/or creative representations of technological infrastructures, including academic writing, the fine arts, film, and media, creative non-fiction, and literary writing in various media formats. To further delineate these genres for application, in this conclusion, I will describe how to identify and organize BTS storytelling through form-based and/or content-based representation.

In content-based BTS storytelling, the content of a work—from journal articles to video games—uses textual, audio, visual, and interactive representation to explicitly address some or all stages of computational infrastructure, including by describing device design, history, function, and local or global politics; for example, see Molleindustria's video game *Phone Story* (2011). If a work also engages in form-based BTS storytelling, content-based storytelling may serve to complement, support, and explain those formal choices—such as Nick Montfort's *Round*, as has been explored in this chapter. Content-based BTS storytelling may also describe the connections between media materiality and various factors in media ecologies, from human impact to climate change, as seen in J.R. Carpenter's digital project *The Gathering Cloud* and Eugenio Tisselli's accompanying note on the video game *The Gate* (2020). That content-based BTS storytelling may take the form of games or the genre of electronic literature is no coincidence, increased interaction and choice can make a user feel more involved in the cause-and-effect of the content and can consequently make them feel complicit in making decisions relating to computational infrastructure.

In form-based BTS storytelling, two approaches dominate: the structure of computational infrastructure itself is represented or the physical features and embodiment of computational devices are brought to a user's attention.

The first approach has been explored in this chapter through the works of Bratton and Crawford and Joler. These methods of representing the structure of computational infrastructure occur through visual maps, flowcharts, and "architectural" models of infrastructural networks and assemblages. It is important to note that form-based BTS storytelling does not have to be digital; however, it often takes a digital form, which allows the work to critique its own physical apparatus in an embodied and immediate way.

In the second approach—being aware of the device—the content may not explicitly be about computational infrastructure; however, the user is still made aware of their own embodied relationship with devices, the material contexts and conditions of devices, and/or the global histories and implications of owning that device. *Active* versions of device awareness include Annie Abraham's *Séparation* (2002–2003), which draws attention to a user's embodied relationship with their device, including by thinking about how computational media affect the human body. This work is active in its form-based BTS storytelling because it occurs through physical input with the device. *Passive* versions of device awareness may not be interactive, but rather consist of user experiences that occur as the story unfolds over time, such as Nick Montfort's *Round*.

In outlining how BTS storytelling can be further identified and developed, I seek to encourage new ways of thinking, articulating, and practicing transparency in technocapitalism for everyday digital device users. This chapter has proposed BTS storytelling and the narrational and reflexive model that it offers as a way to help everyday users understand that for every on-screen action and experience, there is an underbelly. Through storytelling, users are in a more empowered position to negotiate the specific causes of computer activities and phenomena, the specific effects of their device input as well as their decisions as consumers, and the origins and afterlives of digital devices in a way that is intentionally non-linear.

Acknowledgements

Thank you to systems design engineer Lulu Liu for her expert insights and advice.

Notes

1 BTS storytelling is not based on Sarah T. Roberts' research in *Behind the Screen: Content Moderation in the Shadows of Social Media* (2019), though similar to Roberts, I am examining forms of exploitative and inhumane labor that are needed to support Big Tech infrastructure and capitalism. Where Roberts is scrutinizing content-based human labor, here I am focusing on the processes of producing computational hardware.
2 By examining the user's interaction with abstracted on-screen content, I do not imagine that the Immediate Experience is a solely *content*-driven part of computational infrastructure. On the contrary, it is important to connect the seemingly immaterial operations of "addresses" back to their material counterparts, including by connecting them to the equally abstracted notion of "the cloud." While such a task is beyond the scope of this chapter, it could begin by examining data centers and server farms, people who manage them, what servers are actually made of, the

physical lands that house server farms, and the exorbitant energy costs that keep them running. Creative examples of BTS storytelling that trace addresses and the cloud include J.R. Carpenter's *The Gathering Cloud* and Timo Arnall's film *Internet Machine*. Critical examples of BTS storytelling that trace address and the cloud are John Durham Peters' *The Marvelous Clouds: Toward a Philosophy of Elemental Media* (2015), Sean Cubitt's *Finite Media: Environmental Implications of Digital Technologies* (2016), and Christian Ulrik Andersen and Søren Bro Pold's *The Metainterface: The Art of Platforms, Cities, and Clouds* (2018).

3 Many people choose to void their warranty and to sidestep authorized vendors and dealers, repairing their devices on their own. These efforts can be done by hobbyists, as part of what is called the Right to Repair movement, or to save money.

4 However, cold environments are still used to maintain large collections of data servers, partially explaining why so many server farms are built in countries in the utmost Northern hemisphere.

5 For more information on these increasing standards over computational history, see the theory of Moore's Law.

6 Each country has its own rules of governance and regulation when it comes to e-waste, and countries such as India are trying to create more clean and safe forms of e-waste recycling (Pandve 2010; Turaga et al. 2019).

Works Cited

Abrahams, Annie. *Séparation. Electronic Literature Collection 2*. 2003. https://collection.eliterature.org/2/works/abrahams_separation/separation/.

"Aluminum." British Royal Society of Chemistry. Accessed December 16, 2020. https://www.rsc.org/periodic-table/element/13/aluminum.

Balsamo, Anne. *Designing Culture: The Technological Imagination at Work*. Durham, NC: Duke University Press, 2011.

"Bauxite." American Aluminum Association. Accessed December 10, 2020. https://www.aluminum.org/industries/production/bauxite.

Bolter, Jay David and Richard Grusin. *Remediation: Understanding New Media*. Cambridge, MA: MIT Press, 1999.

Bratton, Benjamin H. *The Stack: On Software and Sovereignty*. Cambridge, MA: MIT Press, 2015.

Burke, Steve. "Understanding CPU Heatsinks: Picking the Best CPU Cooler." Gamers Nexus. Accessed December 4, 2012. https://www.gamersnexus.net/guides/981-how-cpu-coolers-work.

Carpenter, J.R. *The Gathering Cloud*. LuckySoap. Last modified 2016, http://luckysoap.com/thegatheringcloud/.

"Copper." British Royal Society of Chemistry. Accessed December 16, 2020. https://www.rsc.org/periodic-table/element/29/copper.

"Copper Production and Environmental Impact." Greenspec. Accessed January 20, 2021. https://www.greenspec.co.uk/building-design/copper-production-environmental-impact/#:~:text=Common%20ailments%20include%20respiratory%20illnesses,process%20can%20also%20create%20pollution.pdf.

CPU Shack. "How a CPU Microprocessor Is Made." *The CPU Shack*. Accessed December 20, 2020. http://www.cpushack.com/EtchingWafers.html

Crawford, Kate and Vladan Joler. *Anatomy of an AI System*. 2018. https://anatomyof.ai/.

"Crystalline Silica in Air & Water, and Health Effects." Minnesota Department of Health. Accessed December 18, 2020. https://www.health.state.mn.us/communities/environment/hazardous/topics/silica.html.

Emerson, Lori. *Reading Writing Interfaces: From the Digital to the Bookbound*. Minneapolis: University of Minnesota Press, 2014.

Fan, Lai-Tze. "Digital Nature." In *Nature and Literary Studies*. Edited by Peter Remien and Scott Slovic. Cambridge: Cambridge University Press, forthcoming 2022.

García-Gómez, José Joaqúin and Juan Diego Pérez-Cebada. "A Socio-Environmental History of a Copper Mining Company: Rio-Tinto Company Limited (1874–1930)." *Sustainability* 12, no. 4521 (2020): 1–17.

Gordon, Whitson. "Hot Computers are Slow and Dangerous—Here's How to Fix Yours." *Popular Science*. Accessed September 15, 2018. https://www.popsci.com/prevent-computer-overheating.

Hayles, N. Katherine. *How We Became Posthuman*. Chicago, IL: University of Chicago Press, 1999.

"Helping Maintain Industry Leadership and Driving Innovation." Intel. Accessed December 22, 2020. https://www.intel.ca/content/www/ca/en/architecture-and-technology/global-manufacturing.html.

Holland, Mike, EMRC, and Imperial College London. "Reducing the Health Risks of the Copper, Rare Earth and Cobalt Industries: The Transition to a Low-Carbon Economy." OECD Better Policies for Better Lives. 2019. https://www.oecd.org/greengrowth/Reducing%20the%20health%20risks%20of%20the%20copper,%20rare%20earth%20and%20cobalt%20industries.pdf.

"How Many Precious Metals Are Found in Electronic Devices?" ERI Direct. Accessed June 23, 2015. https://eridirect.com/blog/2015/06/how-many-precious-metals-are-found-in-electronic-devices/.

Hudson, Travis L., Frederick D. Fox, and Geoffrey S. Plumlee. *Metal Mining and the Environment*. Alexandria: American Geosciences Institute, 1999.

"Intel Global Manufacturing Facts." Intel. Accessed December 22, 2020. https://www.intel.com/content/dam/www/public/us/en/documents/fact-sheets/standards-global-manufacturing-facts.pdf.

Kaplan, Daniel M. and Christopher G. White. *Hands-On Electronics: A Practical Introduction to Analog and Digital Circuits*. Cambridge: Cambridge University Press, 2003.

keekeesocean. 2012. "E Waste in India Short documentary." Accessed April 19, 2012. YouTube video, 7:50, https://www.youtube.com/watch?v=sFfaYc_pIx8.

Liu, Alan. "Transcendental Data: Toward a Cultural History and Aesthetics of the New Encoded Discourse." *Critical Inquiry* 31 (2004): 49–84.

Manovich, Lev. *The Language of New Media*. Cambridge, MA: MIT Press, 2000.

Mattern, Shannon. *Code and Clay, Data and Dirt: Five Thousand Years of Urban Media*. Minneapolis: University of Minnesota Press, 2017.

Mills, Rick. "Copper, the Most Critical Metal." *Mining.com*. Accessed December 6, 2020. https://www.mining.com/web/copper-the-most-critical-metal/.

Mishra, Ashutosh. "Impact of Silica Mining on Environment." *Journal of Geography and Regional Planning* 8, no. 6 (2015): 150–156.

Molleindustria. *Phone Story*. 2011. http://www.phonestory.org.

Montfort, Nick. 2013. *Round*. New Binary Press. http://round.newbinarypress.com.

Montfort, Nick. 2013. "A Note on *Round*." New Binary Press. http://round.newbinarypress.com/note.html.

Pandve, Harshal T. "Some Initiative in E-Waste Disposal, Management and Recycling." *Indian Journal of Occupational & Environmental Medicine* 12, no. 1 (2010): 20–21. https://www.conceptmanagement.co.uk/services/disposal/precious-metal.

Parikka, Jussi. *A Geology of Media*. Minneapolis: University of Minnesota Press, 2015.

Pinto, Violet N. "E-waste Hazard: The Impending Challenge." *Indian Journal of Occupational & Environmental Medicine* 12, no. 2 (2008): 65–70.

Rosner, Daniela K. *Critical Fabulations: Reworking the Methods and Margins of Design*. Cambridge: MIT Press, 2000.

"Silicon." British Royal Society of Chemistry. Accessed December 16, 2020. https://www.rsc.org/periodic-table/element/14/silicon.

Tisselli, Eugenio. "The Gate: A Game-Essay on Coexistence and Spectrality in the Anthropocene." *The Digital Review*. 2020. https://thedigitalreview.com/issue00/the-gate/index.html.

Turaga, Rama Mohana R., Kalyan Bhaskar, Satish Sinha, Daniel Hinchliffe, Morton Hemkhaus, Rachna Arora, Sandip Chatterjee, Deepali Sinha Khetriwal, Verena Radulovic, Pranshu Singhal, and Hitesh Sharma. "E-Waste Management in India: Issues and Strategies." *Vikalpa; The Journal for Decision Makers* 44, no. 3 (2019): 127–162.

"What is a Heatsink?" *Radian Heatsinks*. Accessed December 18, 2020. https://www.radianheatsinks.com/heatsink.

Wormington, Jim. "'What do We Get Out of It?': The Human Rights Impact of Bauxite Mining in Guinea." *Human Rights Watch*. Accessed October 4, 2018. https://www.hrw.org/report/2018/10/04/what-do-we-get-out-it/human-rights-impact-bauxite-mining-guinea.

6
THE DIGITAL TERRAIN OF THE LITERARY ANECDOTE

David Ciccoricco

If the most concrete way to attach a narrative to a particular place would be in the form of a commemorative historical plaque, something literally set in stone, then perhaps the most fleeting way would be an anecdote tied to that place that circulates through conversations and generations. At least that would have been the case before the proliferation of mobile micro-computing and global positioning systems (GPSs). These technologies anchor the evanescence of the anecdote, materializing its orality in the form of site-specific audio media, and allowing users new ways to "attach" stories to physical locations (Ryan, Foote, and Azaryahu 2016, 127). One increasingly popular application of this geo-narrative affordance is the domain of literary tourism (47). The imbrication of the literary arts and tourism is not new in itself. Although arguably as old as literature itself, the practice of literary cartography coalesced in the mid-1800s with the commercial publication of literary guidebooks and maps. It then saw a pronounced surge in activity in the early 1900s, when such cartographers were attempting to modernize works of nineteenth-century novelists, such as Charles Dickens, for new generations of readers (Bulson 2007).

The proliferation of digital applications (apps) that are conspicuously geo-narrative in nature, however, prompts a new set of (potentially media-specific) questions. What is the cultural status of the literary anecdote? More specifically, if the anecdote is both a literary form and a literary-critical method (Fineman 1991), then how have digital networks and GPS technology reshaped and arguably redefined it? In the age of obsessive online archiving and incessant self-publishing, has the anecdote become something much different to its more familiar (oral and ephemeral) origins? Finally, how have the virtual, non-spaces of digital terrain re-grounded or re-contextualized the relationship between anecdotes and accuracy or truth claims? Has the anecdote become something

DOI: 10.4324/9781003053880-7

ever more verifiable – and, by extension, less enchanting – in the age of perpetual Google searching and micro-blogging? Or rather have the same socially mediated, open-access, and often Artificially Intelligent platforms transformed the anecdote into fodder for "fake news" or "alternative facts," marking an intensification of (or return to) the radical relativism of postmodern historicism (Liu 2008)? These questions provide the impetus for the current chapter.

An actual literary tourism project will provide some empirical basis: an app developed for the city of Dunedin, New Zealand, following its designation as a UNESCO City of Literature in 2014. The development of the app, called "dtour," involved a research component in which the writers coded the anecdotes they collected about individual authors featuring in the app, in particular with regard to their source and verifiability. This data yielded observations about the anecdote – as form and method – across physical and digital spaces. More generally, the project served as a palpable illustration of what digital media – and its mediated geographies – do to established narrative forms.

Much of the scholarly focus on literary cartography is directed at the relationship between a fictional place and an actual map, for example, the practice of mapping a single novel per se, whether that practice is undertaken by a scholar as a function of critical analysis or by a reader as an expression and extension of their fandom. Such a focus often takes a deconstructive approach to the power dynamics re-inscribed in ostensibly neutral acts of mapping. These moves usefully remind us that such spatial representations are always ideological, "influenced by the culture, history, economy, and politics of a particular time and place, [and] they reflect ways of seeing the world and the scores of individuals who live, and have lived, and will live in it" (Bulson 2007, 11). Another development in the broader domain of literary cartography is its productive pairing with the digital humanities, which have brought computing power and computational methodologies to bear on the production and analysis of spatial representation. These practices remake the literary map from a static to an interactive, site-specific, and mobile resource, often one that is tied to an informational and archival database; in turn, they are markedly influencing "the ways literary scholars are 'thinking spatially'" (Cooper, Donaldson, and Murrieta-Flores 2016, 7). Finally, in recent years, narrative theory and geography has made a concerted effort to mutually enfold their methodologies, marking a formalization of ideas that have grown out of the so-called spatial and narrative turns of twentieth-century critical theory (Ryan, Foote, and Azaryahu 2016, 2).

My own focus is limited to the way in which anecdotes are recast – indeed, spatialized – in digital environments. I first outline a brief critical genealogy of the anecdote, more specifically its movement through literary history's periphery to the center stage of New Historicism, and then through media studies and on to its mobilization – in the dual sense of movement and (political) use – in digital culture. Next, I trace the development of literary tourism and the place of the anecdote within it, in order to establish a comparative media backdrop for the implication of digital anecdotes in the spatial and narrative imagination. Finally,

I make recourse to the dtour literary tourism app and the digital anecdotes it animates, connecting some of the specific observations that emerge from some modest empirical research on the app to the general trends visible in the broader comparative media backdrop. Our ever-shifting digital terrain has significant implications for how we create, consume, and circulate anecdotes. In terms of form, attending to anecdotes in a transmedial light allows us to see how media can shape genres, indeed either reanimating them or accelerating their obsolescence. Attention to anecdotes in terms of method, moreover, is attending to the way we communicate and theorize communication – the way stories move through space. To what extent a medium or technology can dictate or, in Fredric Jameson's terms, serve as the cultural dominant that defines a historical period remains up for debate (Jameson 1993; see also McHale 2015; Ciccoricco 2016). What is clear, however, is that in light of the current media landscape and the intellectual confluence of digital culture and new historicist thought more specifically, we will find the anecdote at the center rather than the periphery of critical concern. What is needed, in turn, is a critical discourse dexterous enough to map its terrain across media and across academic and public domains, and through which we learn recursively from the public humanities projects we create.

Remediating Anecdotes

The anecdote has arguably served as a discrete textual form and "literary resource" since classical antiquity (Bauman 2005, 22). But the literary-critical significance of anecdotes was certainly foregrounded in the 1980s with the rise of New Historicism, an approach to literary history that – as a kind of counterpoint to its more dominant, text-centric, and formalist predecessor of New Criticism – sought to inject social and cultural context back into the field of textual analysis and historiography (Greenblatt 1992). New Historicists understand the anecdote in a dual sense. In the first familiar sense, it is "a specific literary genre, with peculiar literary properties" (Fineman 1991, 60) that involves the narration of a singular event; it is a form that we might describe as a *historeme*, that is, "the smallest minimal unit of the historiographic fact" (67). In his essay on "The History of the Anecdote," however, Joel Fineman establishes another valuable sense: it is a methodological mode that "in significant ways, determines the practice of historiography" (60). This literary anecdote sustains an intricate relation to referentiality because, in Fineman's terms, it "uniquely refers to the real" (67). It disrupts narrative's teleological hold and instead introduces contingency; it "establishes an event as an event within and yet without the framing context of historical successivity, [and] it does so only in so far as its narration both comprises and refracts the narration it reports" (72). In a passage in dialogue with Fineman's essay from the introduction to *Learning to Curse*, Stephen Greenblatt describes anecdotes as:

> the encounter with something that I could not stand not understanding, that I could not quite finish with or finish off, that I had to get out of my

inner life where it had taken hold, that I could retell and contemplate and struggle with.

(1992, 5)

Thus, if anecdotes are playful it is also because they are also recalcitrant in the face of their two masters: history and narrative.

If Greenblatt's exposition points to a sense of hermeneutical challenge evoked by the nature of the form, one that translates readily into personal struggle, it also reminds us that personal struggle often motivates anecdotes. In fact, we can point more specifically to a suggestive relation in the context of mapping space. In his now paradigmatic account of his visit to the architecturally mystifying Bonaventure Hotel in Los Angeles, Fredric Jameson recounts his disorientation in a space that "transcends the capacities of the individual human body to locate itself, to organize its immediate surroundings perceptually" (1993, 83). He goes on to articulate his notion of cognitive mapping, which he casts as a socio-political strategy that would allow us to come to terms with the complexity and interconnectivity of global networks and position ourselves meaningfully within it. His account is framed as a subversion of the narrative stroll – a failure of the way in which our physical trajectories should more readily translate into narrative experience. Nonetheless, Jameson clearly renders his inability to map his surroundings as a personal anecdote. In a stronger reading, it is possible to suggest that Jameson's very concept of the cognitive map *derives* from his anecdotal experience.

As "a short, humorous narrative, purporting to recount a true incident involving real people" (Bauman 2005, 22), we still tend to associate the anecdote, in the popular conception, with oral and often dialogic transmission, and its etymology – derived from the Greek *anekdotos* and Latin *anecdota* (22) – would similarly connote the "unpublished." The proliferation of short, self-published micro-narratives coursing through global digital networks, however, would encourage us to revisit the nature of the anecdote yet again in twenty-first-century terms. If New Historicism added sophistication to our idea of anecdotes as simply *short*, *real*, and *spoken* (which is also to say ephemeral), then digital textuality further troubles these traits by virtue of its medium.[1] Picking up on Greenblatt and Fineman's focus on contingency, Alan Liu, for one, updates the anecdote in an expressly media-theoretical context. In his *Local Transcendence*, Liu identifies a "structural convergence between historicism and informationalism," whereby "critical approaches arose in both domains in parallel" (2008, 6). For example, Liu notes that New Historicism invented "its microhistorical anecdote" at the same time as computer revolutionaries were using personal computing to challenge the mainframe, and at the same time as hypertext enthusiasts were crafting micro-narratives with links and nodes that defied the linear (master) narrative (6).

Liu, moreover, identifies the same paradox that Fineman does in the way anecdotes are "at once contained *in* historical reality and admitting of freedom *from* that reality" (24). But he builds further on the New Historical conception, pushing the structural analogy pre- and post-digital forms, and framing the anecdote as a "media form," one that is derived from "oral culture, the post-Montaigne essay, the vignette, journalistic print culture, the electronic sound bite, and, more recently, the Internet blog post" (24). He states his "hypothesis" that:

> there is a link between such an understanding of history as semi-autonomous, 'subversive,' or never fully governable representational forms hosted in artifacts, arts, language, and other cultural substrates – *media* in my usage here – and the media form of the anecdote itself as it has become one of postmodernism historicism's own signature acts of representation.
>
> *(24)*

In short, anecdotes are a form of "random access"; if New Historicism is "a kind of relational database," Liu writes, "then the anecdote is its query" (259). Liu's musings on postmodern historicism factor in the complex "mediations" between our past and our future, either directly through actual (digital) media innovations or indirectly through varied allusions and analogies to prior media forms. He thus offers vital historicizing of the anecdote as form across media and establishes its role in a critical method designed to incorporate rather than avoid contingency.

If a media analysis of the anecdote as form and method instils historical continuity, then we must still account for fissures or breaks we encounter (but do not necessarily notice) in our experience of media over time – what N. Katherine Hayles calls the "cognitive-technical transformations" (2012, 121) that arise from confronting and crossing perceptual thresholds as we co-evolve with our technologies. As Hayles writes:

> when time is measured, it is frequently through spatialized practices that allow temporal progress to be visualized – hands moving around an analogue clock face, sand running through an hourglass, a sundial shadow that moves as the sun crosses the sky.
>
> *(2012, 111–112)*

Given that spatializing narrative is a subcategory of spatializing time, it is necessary to reflect further, in the fissure of the present moment, on the implications of digital and computational media in that process. Most machines keep time in some manner – they are inherently time machines.[2] Humans are time machines in this sense too, as our experience of time is inscribed biologically; moreover, as Hayles reminds us, our experience of time is multiple, right down to our neurological core(s). In the layered temporalities of neurology, a neuron fires in about 0.3–0.5 milliseconds; we register sensations in anywhere from 80 to 500 milliseconds; and we understand high-level faculties (like word recognition) in 200–250 milliseconds; and not all of these processes necessarily happen in a linear or sequential fashion (104).

In her later work *Unthought*, Hayles seizes on the example of trading algorithms in the global financial system, which operate autonomously at speeds that "far transcend the temporal regimes of human decision making" (2017, 4). Clearly, high frequency financial transactions that remain outside of conscious comprehension and intervention – occurring as fast as roughly once every tenth of a millisecond (165) – have profound consequences in a runaway capitalist context. But the same technological phenomenon also has consequences for how we map and spatialize narratives. Temporality inheres in narratives in multiple and nested ways: they can represent multiple temporalities through their storyworlds, fictional or non-fictional; the re-readability of narrative texts propagates them multiply over time and among readers; and the fact that texts can travel, either as physical or digital entities, also distributes them over time. The nature of anecdotes more specifically, which can spread casually, even virally, in unexpected surges, might be particularly prone to the kinds of spatialization – through database and networked formats – that visualize its paths through time. Locative narratives, arguably, are also always already anecdotal, for the anecdote appears in the very location that contextualizes it, recalling Greenblatt's formulation that it "exceeds the literary" and has "pointed, referential" access to "what lies beneath or beyond" it (1992, 5). Nonetheless, it is the *acceleration* of this process that takes us to, if not yet already beyond, another experiential threshold, and there is need for caution on the other side.

The practice of micro-narrative production has clearly intensified in recent years (as a historical marker, the micro-blogging platform Twitter was launched around the same time as Liu's book saw publication). Also intensifying is the (often corporate) practice of digital data-mining, whereby the material we post and view online is tracked in order that the same social media platforms that allow us to self-publish will feed us back information based on our online profiles and preferences. In this light, the technological phenomena of data-mining and the political phenomena of "fake news" conceivably mark a further critical shift in a contemporary post-digital conception of the anecdote. Of course, it would be logical to suggest that if narratives travel much faster these days, then truth would travel at pace with falsehood. But that position does not necessarily find empirical support. A 2018 study by three Massachusetts Institute of Technology (MIT) scholars working out of the "Laboratory for Social Machines" found that false news travels much faster and much farther than true news. Vosoughi, Roy, and Aral investigated "the verified true and false news stories distributed on Twitter from 2006 to 2017" with a data set of approximately 126,000 stories tweeted by three million people more than 4.5 million times (2018, 1). They classified news stories as objectively and verifiably "true" or "false" through six independent fact-checking organizations, and defined *news* as "any story or claim with an assertion in it" and *rumor* as "the social phenomena of a news story or claim spreading or diffusing through the Twitter network" (1). Specifically, their findings show that when tracing the way in which both true and false rumors spread over time and geographically through space, falsehood spread online "significantly farther, faster, deeper, and more broadly than the truth in all categories of information" (2). In order to attempt to account for these results, they conducted a further content analysis that categorized tweets based on associated emotional language in user responses; in turn, even though one cannot draw a direct causal link between the nature of tweets and why they are retweeted, they found that "false news is more novel and that novel information is more likely to be retweeted" (5).

Beyond their reportage of the data, the way in which the authors acknowledge the politicization of Twitter and the phrase "fake news" in particular is telling: "at one time, it may have been appropriate to think of fake news as referring to the veracity of a news story, we now believe that this phrase has been irredeemably polarized in our current political and media climate" (1). Moreover, the researchers address the scenario of those looking to explain away the results based on the inner workings of social media and the vagaries of artificial intelligence (AI), with "bots" ultimately to blame for irresponsible applications of the medium. Using a "sophisticated bot-detecting algorithm," they removed all bots from their analysis, and found that false news spreads "farther, faster, deeper, and more broadly than the truth *because humans, not robots, are more likely to spread it*" (5, my emphasis). The observation reminds us that rumors are "inherently social" (1), just like the humans who generate and propagate them.

Granted, anecdotes are arguably a special, liminal case, not strictly true or false to begin with. They are often embellished, and that quality is what endows them with rhetorical richness. (Literary anecdotes, especially those about long-deceased authors, might suggest a sense of fair game.) But it would be misguided to treat them as too special or insulate them from the perturbations of the political, corporate, or mass media sphere (now more likely to be called "crowd consciousness" or simply "what the Internet thinks"). After all, the same rhetorical strategies and effects that make false news "novel" and attractive can be found in both tweets and in literary fiction, regardless of where one sits on the question of "literary language" as distinct from everyday narrative communication. Ideally, further research and teaching on the topic, which oscillates self-consciously between these domains, can sharpen our collective analytical acumen.

Tourism in the Comfort of Your Own Phone

Though there were no bots to circulate anecdotes in the 1800s, there was a fascination with this literary form from the very origins of literary tourism. Literary tourism can be considered as an outgrowth of the preoccupations and practices of literary cartography, which is guided by the broad "critical conviction" that mapping is "a practice that enriches the reader's appreciation of the literary work of art" (Cooper, Donaldson, and Murrieta-Flores 2016, 8). With a comparably much older genealogy, the practice of literary cartography is interwoven inextricably into the history of literature in print. There are, nonetheless, notable examples from the early modern period, such as Alessandro Vellutello's landscape plan for Petrarch's *Provence*, published in 1525 and inspired by earlier maps of Dante's *Inferno* from the start of that century (see Cachey 2007, 455, for a reproduction of Vellutello's map). Literary tourism is typically tied to the literary travel guidebooks that date back to the mid-1800s, which came of age with "guidebook gurus" John Murray and Karl Baedeker; their popular publications served patrons in England, Italy, Germany, France, Belgium, Switzerland, and Holland from that time (Bulson 2007, 26–27). (Although the English Murray preceded and influenced the work of the German Baedeker, the Baedeker publishing house came to be a household name for global tourism books and the brand continues to this day.)

In English, the earliest works to be characterized as resources for the literary tourist were "literary itineraries, which, whether intended for the armchair or the field, were often embellished with maps and plans documenting sights of either literary-biographical or purely imaginative significance" (Cooper, Donaldson, and Murrieta-Flores 2016, 8). They were also embellished with anecdotes. Eric Bulson describes the literary guidebooks dedicated to major European cities of the 1840s as "topographical histories and poetic biographies," and notes that they "provided a collection of entertaining anecdotes for the well-educated 'literary man' about town" (2007, 27). The titles of these guidebooks reflect much of the same anecdotal spirit, such as John Smith's 1846 *An Antiquarian Ramble in the Streets of London with Anecdotes of the More Celebrated Residents* (27).

Later literary guidebooks included maps by default, marking a kind of innovation in terms of the representation of space. That is, these resources combine the two major conceptual structures in the textual presentation of space: the *tour* and the *map*, with the tour affording "a description of space from the point of view of a moving, embodied observer who visits locations in a temporal sequence" and the map affording the observer "a totalizing, simultaneous perception of the relations between objects" (Ryan, Foote, and Azaryahu 2016, 8–9). The same distinction still commonly structures approaches to literary tourism. In fact, many design aspects laid out during the literary tourism craze of the early 1900s have carried over conspicuously across decades and media. Consider this definition of "literary maps" put forth by the Library of Congress for a 1993 exhibit:

> A literary map records the location of places, associated with authors and their literary works or serves as a guide to their imaginative worlds. It may present places associated with a literary tradition, an individual author, or a specific work. Some maps highlight an entire country's literary heritage; others feature authors identified with a particular city, state, region, or country. Maps can feature real places connected with an individual author, literary character, or book, such as those featuring Jane Austen's England, the London of Sherlock Holmes or the settings in Herman Melville's *Moby Dick*, or they may show wholly imaginary landscapes such as Oz, Middle Earth, or Neverland.
>
> (cited in Bulson 2007, 22)

From literary guidebook maps to literary tourism apps for mobile devices, the organizing concept remains the same.[3] We can zoom in to literary authors or zoom out to literary cities. With regard to civic heritage and civic pride, moreover, we see the motivation for literary tourism projects run in parallel with increasing urbanization. As Bulson notes with regard to literary tourists of the early twentieth century, "by superimposing fictional plots on a map of England, readers were also participating in a more coded form of literary nationalism" (2007, 6). In the twenty-first century, literary tourism apps and resources are often mobilized by heritage organizations, such as the UNESCO City of Literature designation that supported the dtour project in Dunedin. In addition, we see the same governing design choice arise between factual, biographical locations, or fictional, imaginary ones. We see the same tensions arise, in turn. If a resource establishes a binary distinction between biographical and fictional sites, then some places will invariably fall in between the two. Furthermore, even prototypically realist authors were not bound to geographical accuracy in their own writing, and there are detailed accounts registering the shock of early literary tourists upon discovering that many of Dickens's sites were in fact "creative composites" (Bulson 2007, 138). Similar challenges arise, of course, for science fiction novels or those set in a familiar city, albeit at some point in the future.[4]

Nevertheless, the shift from print to digital media makes a palpable difference. If we return to the notion of the tour as a representation of one's experience of space from "the point of view of a moving, embodied observer who visits locations in a temporal sequence," then the literary tourism app effectively collapses the distinction of *map* and the *tour*, as we are represented – typically via a pulsing blue dot – at once spatially on the map and temporally, with the help from GPS satellite location tracking, as we move from site to site. A curious relation between maps and stories is thus foregrounded: conventional, topographical maps tend to efface temporality, whereas stories preserve it. In literary tourism apps, past and present literary figures can be mapped synchronically on a contemporary (Google) map as their own stories are spatialized, framed by the space of the screen but contained only by a function of the relative proximity of pins or markers clustering the sites. Experientially, time is flattened at the surface level of the map, whereas space "zooms" in and out and "scrolls" in all directions.[5]

Anecdotes themselves mediate, regardless of their medium. They mediate not only between past and present, but also between literary and popular culture. In their portability and accessibility, they are a literary form that can be said to serve an inherently socializing or communitizing role. They are not sealed off in academic (con)texts or academic classrooms, but instead extend out into and cut across communities. Again, for these reasons they are especially amenable to mapping through spatial and network forms in digital environments.[6] But in broader terms, when literary tourism takes to the digital medium, the result is a work of public humanities as well as digital humanities: such projects more specifically offer "new tools and methods for reestablishing communication between the humanities and the public" (Liu 2012).

An Empirical Detour

The accessibility and portability of anecdotes underscored the concept of Dunedin's dtour app from the start. Along with seeking out stories that showcased local color and local knowledge, the project writers were tasked with adopting a conversational, anecdotal style in creating the individual author entries. The impetus for the project came with Dunedin, New Zealand, becoming a UNESCO City of Literature in 2014, a world heritage designation that recognizes a city's past and present contributions to sustaining a rich literary culture. There are currently 39 Cities of Literature worldwide with two, Dunedin and Melbourne, located in Australasia. The Department of English and Linguistics at the University of Otago first partnered with the Dunedin City of Literature (formed as a branch of the city council's arts and culture program), next gained internal and external funding, and then contracted programmers, graphic designers, and writers to create the app. Production ran from 2018 to 2020, with over 40 names appearing on the credits list in total.[7] The writers took original photographs and worked closely with the Hocken Collections in Dunedin for archival images. Entries for individual authors included short (~400-word) scripts that were also voiced over by voice-actors. (One value that underpinned the design was the attempt to use a technological device to reunite us with natural and built environments rather that disconnect us from them, which explains why the audio option – allowing physical movement while listening – was crucial for the user experience.) There are currently over 100 authors featured in the app, with several of those having multiple entries at different site locations. To date, 20 of those entries have been translated into Māori and appear as bilingual options in the app.

In terms of the interface, the map view is the default starting screen. Users see a familiar Google map of the city, but with an unfamiliar overlay of literary markers. Conceptually, the idea was to link writers and their stories to sites in Dunedin and the Otago region, and exhibit Otago's signature landscapes in the process. Writers chosen for inclusion had some significant connection to Dunedin, either a physical imprint found in their biography or an imagined imprint found in their fiction or poetry.

As the dtour "About" page notes, playing up the connection between natural landscapes and literary expression, "All of the literary sites are underpinned by anecdotes – the understory, so to speak, that generates and regenerates the literary ecosystem of Dunedin, New Zealand." The entries contain anecdotes and sometimes multiple anecdotes in a single entry, which is also to say we cannot equate a single entry to a single anecdote. Some anecdotes reproduce already published and rather canonical exchanges between New Zealand's best-known literary figures. For example, the entry for the major New Zealand poet and editor Charles Brasch, who ran his progressive bookshop from downtown Dunedin in the mid-twentieth century, details his kind offer of a coat to a young Janet Frame (who would become one of the nation's most iconic literary figures) before she went out into the (arguably also iconic) Dunedin rain. Others allude to stories that would have been part of more local legend, such as the story of the mysterious anchor well known to locals in the nearby port town of Port Chalmers just outside of the city,[8] which is referenced in the entry for illustrator and children's author David Elliot:

> Elliot has worked for more than 30 years illustrating children and Young Adult favourites, including books in Brian Jacques' *Redwall* series,

FIGURE 6.1 Screenshot from the dtour map view. Brown pins are "biographical" and green ones are "literary" (encircled numbers indicate further concentrations of sites). The menu expands from the icon in the lower right, allowing users the option to toggle between map view, list of authors, and the credits and references information.

Margaret Mahy's *The Word Witch,* Janet Frame's *Mona Minim and the Smell of the Sun,* and his own award-winning books, including *Pigtails the Pirate, Henry's Map, Sydney and the Sea Monster,* and *Sydney and the Whalebird.* Flying whales and whimsy feature strongly, as do local mysteries.

(What are all those old ship's anchors holding down now? And what really happened to the Port Chalmers band rotunda? If you look closely at Elliot's drawings, you'll see at least one possibility.)

Before you leave Port Chalmers, walk up the short track from Church Street to Centenary Lookout and the Robert Scott Memorial for one last glimpse of the township and the port. Dodge or feed the wild chickens, as you prefer, and consider the mysterious anchor known only as "Nineteen Fathom Foul." It was for years a maritime hazard lost from an unknown vessel. If you imagine, for a moment, that this mystery anchor is attached to a soaring cetacean, then David Elliot has done his job.[9]

The script reflects the anecdotal style embraced by the dtour writers. We can also recall Greenblatt's comments on the denigration of anecdotes in conventional literary criticism, which he equates to the "enemy of wonder" in the exploration of literary works (1992, 5). Here, instead, we find the epitome of wonder: imaginary whales in the sky, not only unmoored from their ocean homes, but even carrying a mystical anchor.

The literary form of the anecdote was both a driving concept for the design of the app and an accompanying research component that grew out of it. We wanted to conduct an analysis on the digital state of the literary anecdote at the same time as researchers and writers created their entries for the dtour app, and we wanted to consider the ways in which digital environments have changed the very nature of that traditionally oral and ephemeral form. Specifically, in the first year of production, two researcher/writers, responsible for creating 30 entries each, were asked to code any anecdotes they included in their entries as either verifiable (V) or partially verifiable (PV). For the purposes of the analysis, *verifiable* anecdotes derive from and check out across two or more credible sources, whereas *partially verifiable* anecdotes derive from at least one source and may contain embellishments or exaggerations. The researchers, furthermore, recorded the source of the anecdote by simply answering yes or no on a form for whether the anecdote source was from (1) a verbal interview, (2) a formally published textual source, or (3) an informal account found online. Finally, they were asked to track instances in which online accounts were used to challenge or falsify verbal ones and the converse.

By any measure, our empirical study was unscientific. By contrast to the computational study of Twitter undertaken by Vosoughi, Roy, and Aral, which examines over 100,000 stories, we wound up with a corpus of 40 anecdotes in a pool of research on nearly 60 authors. The design of our analysis (which preceded the MIT study of Twitter by a year or so) was also constrained in several respects in practice. The production deadlines, for one, meant that the writers were perhaps less likely to seek out interviews. Online, there are of course no absolute cutting

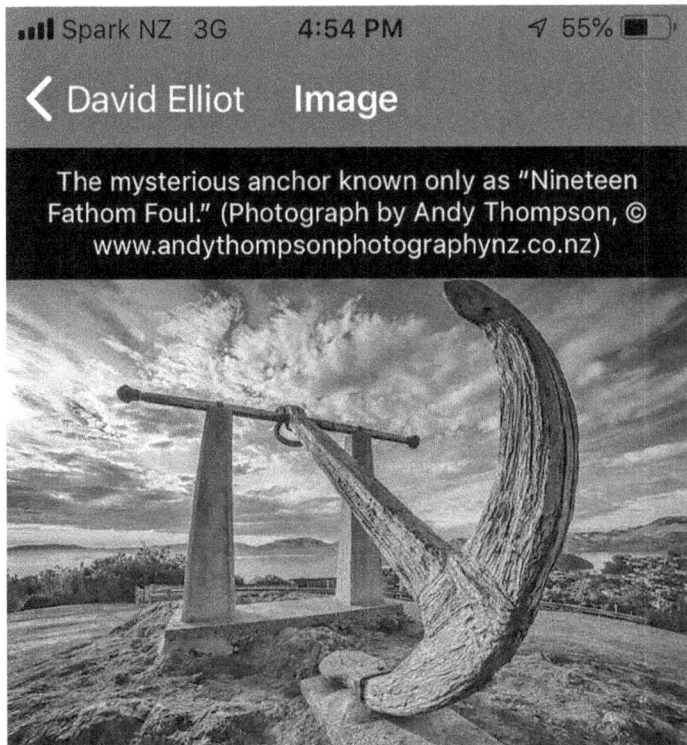

FIGURE 6.2 Screenshot from the dtour David Elliot entry, featuring a photograph by Andy Thompson of the "Nineteen Fathom Foul" anchor, now on display as a monument overlooking the Otago Harbour.

lines between formally and informally published sources. We were also intent to feature a high quality of creative writing, and previously published writers with English PhD degrees were typically doing the work. For the same reason, they were often hard-wired to locate reliable details from academic sources by default. Many of the interviews that were conducted involved representatives of literary estates, who had a vested interest in straightening our stories, so to speak.

There were, nonetheless, several illuminating outcomes. In fact, we were curious about the extent to which the mystique of anecdotes might be disappearing in the digital age, given the era of instant verifiability courtesy of the Google search box. (We can all relate to the scenario of say a grandfather telling tall tales of his war heroism to a grandson, who, smart tablet in hand, replies along the lines of "well grandpa that's not what it says here…") One hypothesis we had was that we would struggle to find any compelling embellishments in the first place, at least any that would not be instantly explained away online. That proved not to be the case. More than half of the total number of anecdotes the writers submitted for the analysis (25 from a total of 40) were coded as partially verifiable. A follow-on effect was the relatively low number of sources that were used to challenge or verify a partially verified anecdote (seven cases from the total, with three of those cases coming from the same interviewed source who was a literary executor). These exceptions to the overall pattern, however, yielded some valuable insights that return us to the broader questions around the nature of the anecdote as transmedial form.

In some cases, challenges to the accuracy of anecdotes arose from not enough information, in a manner analogous to the familiar type of narratorial unreliability of "under-reporting" (see Phelan 2005, 49–53). For example, we can consider John Caselberg, a Dunedin-based writer whose works ranged from poetry to playwriting and from short fiction to essays. He also collaborated with painters in his home or artistic enclave of Broad Bay, on the Otago Peninsula. His major works were, of course, published before the World Wide Web. But it was more the fact that Caselberg led an intensely private life, and his family were protective of his privacy, which makes it difficult to locate much beyond the same standard biographical details. In other cases, however, it might have been too much information that complicated the ability to excavate anecdotes. Known as the "Queen of Romance" in New Zealand, Essie Summers's romance novels sold over 19 million copies in over 100 countries from the middle of the twentieth century. There were over 50 novels in total, most of which she published under the Mills & Boon imprint. Summers's family remain active in managing her literary estate and work to maintain the integrity of her biographical record and celebrate her writing. Their gracious assistance in our dtour research thus presented a different kind of challenge: a wealth of details to condense, then attempt to independently verify. Where conflicts persisted, we proceeded with the verbal anecdotal account by family or by literary executors, which not only preserved the motivating spirit of the project in seeking out local and insider knowledge, but also ensured we had the appropriate clearances from stakeholders. A final example of twentieth-century author and entrepreneur A.H. Reed underscores the role of anecdotes in myth-making. In addition to his literary exploits, Reed was well known for his ambitious adventures walking New Zealand. He hiked Mount Taranaki in the North Island at age 80 and gained national notoriety for hiking the length of the country at age 85 (about 1,000 miles or 1,600 km north-south). He also continued hiking into his 90s, but the details of those exploits become less clear (and subject to some of his own calculations reported in his autobiography). Quite clearly, numbers and distances are amenable to embellishment and exaggeration, and they lay bare the mechanisms for myth-making over time and across media. In terms of the empirical analysis for dtour, the digital domain was just as responsible for blurring the record as it was in setting it straight.

By combining insights from narrative theory and geospatial practice, this chapter has offered a map and a tour of the literary anecdote. More specifically, it anchored the anecdote in the genealogy of literary cartography and then negotiated its transmedial journey to its place in digital culture, where it persists, albeit politicized. As Greenblatt writes, "our belief in language's capacity for reference is part of our contract with the world; the contract may be playfully suspended or broken altogether, but no abrogation is without consequences, and there are circumstances where the abrogation is unacceptable" (1992, 15). I would only add that for those working as educators and public intellectuals, we are also the keepers and guardians of that contract. While we can only ever provide temporary moorings for anecdotes, we might better learn how to take hold of them and indeed let them go, even when they take hold of us. If the phenomenon of fake news and the very notion of weaponizing genres serve as a reminder of our responsibility to remain vigilantly critical, they should also remind us of our own power to deploy the digital medium to propagate artistry, creativity, and imagination. Either way, however mystical it may appear, the way stories move through space is by no means beyond us.

Notes

1 As Amy Earhart adds,

>   The tensions between history and literature are nothing new […] yet certain periods heighten the anxiety. New historicism was one such moment where clashes between literature and history peaked, and the new age of digital archive work seems to have reignited the battle (2015, 59).

2 I credit Steve Tomasula's "new media novel" *TOC* (2009) for an extended, aesthetic elaboration of this idea.
3 For historical context, the Library of Congress exhibit happened around the same time as IBM launched the first smartphone.
4 In the dtour app, the site for Julius Vogel, for instance, refers to his novel *Anno Domini 2000*, which was published in 1889 and set in a Dunedin of the (then) future and by now recent past.
5 It is worth considering in a wider socioeconomic vein whether or not the digital media literary tourism guide is somehow more democratizing than its print predecessor. Literary guidebooks were typically the provenance of the bourgeoise leisure class who had the time and money to undertake such cultural pilgrimages. Many apps are indeed free to download, provided you own a device to download it and WIFI access in order to use it.
6 Digital projects that combine literary studies with geospatial methodologies are perhaps doing more than extending the humanities beyond these traditional boundaries, potentially displacing other formerly paradigmatic preoccupations. Writing in 2015 on the "era of the archive," Earhart observes that "the central position maintained by digital archives in the late 1990s and early 2000s is diminishing. Fewer digital projects are adopting the term archive, and scholars are turning their attention to data-mining and geospatial representations" (2015, 61).
7 The dtour app can be downloaded free on the AppStore or Google Play, and the full credits list is available there. I acted as creative director of the project, working with a steering group of two other executive members plus the director of the Dunedin City of Literature. I also edited all of the entries, researched and wrote eight author entries, and took a lot of photographs.

8 When we spoke to locals over the course of our research, we were treated to accounts by those who claimed to have had family members responsible for pulling the famous anchor out of the harbor waters.
9 Excerpted from the dtour entry for David Elliot, written by David Large.

Works Cited

Bauman, Richard. 2005. "Anecdote." *Routledge Encyclopedia of Narrative Theory*, eds. David Herman, Manfred Jahn, and Marie-Laure Ryan, 22. London: Routledge.

Bulson, Eric. 2007. *Novels, Maps, Modernity: The Spatial Imagination, 1850–2000*. New York: Routledge.

Cachey, Theodore J., Jr. 2007. "Maps and Literature in Renaissance Italy." *The History of Cartography, Volume Three: Cartography in the European Renaissance*, ed. David Woodward, 450–460. Chicago, IL: University of Chicago Press.

Ciccoricco, David. 2016. "What [in the World] was Postmodernism? An Introduction." *Electronic Book Review*, December 4, 2016. <https://electronicbookreview.com/essay/what-in-the-world-was-postmodernism-an-introduction/>

Cooper, David, Christopher Donaldson, and Patricia Murrieta-Flores (eds.). 2016. *Literary Mapping in the Digital Age (Digital Research in the Arts and Humanities)*. London: Routledge.

Earhart, Amy E. 2015. *Traces of the Old, Uses of the New: The Emergence of Digital Literary Studies*. Ann Arbor: University of Michigan Press.

Fineman, Joel. 1991. "The History of the Anecdote: Fiction and Fiction." *The Subjectivity Effect in Western Literary Tradition: Essays toward the Release of Shakespeare's Will*, 59–90. Cambridge, MA: MIT Press.

Greenblatt, Stephen. 1992. *Learning to Curse: Essays in Early Modern Culture*. London: Routledge.

Hayles, N. Katherine. 2012. *How We Think: Digital Media and Contemporary Technogenesis*. Chicago, IL: University of Chicago Press.

———. 2017. *Unthought: The Power of the Cognitive Nonconscious*. Chicago, IL: University of Chicago Press.

Jameson, Fredric. 1993. "Postmodernism, or the Cultural Logic of Late Capitalism." *Postmodernism: A Reader*, ed. Thomas Docherty, 62–92. New York: Columbia University Press.

Liu, Alan. 2008. *Local Transcendence: Essays on Postmodern Historicism and the Database*. Chicago, IL: University of Chicago Press.

———. 2012. "Where Is Cultural Criticism in the Digital Humanities?" *Debates in the Digital Humanities*, ed. Matthew Gold, 490–509. Minneapolis: University of Minnesota Press.

McHale, Brian. 2015. *The Cambridge Introduction to Postmodernism*. Cambridge: Cambridge University Press.

Phelan, James. 2005. *Living to Tell About It: A Rhetoric and Ethics of Character Narration*. Ithaca, NY: Cornell University Press.

Ryan, Marie-Laure, Kenneth Foote, and Maoz Azaryahu. 2016. *Narrating Space / Spatializing Narrative: Where Narrative Theory and Geography Meet*. Columbus: The Ohio State University Press.

Vosoughi, Soroush, Deb Roy, and Sinan Aral. 2018. "The Spread of True and False News Online." *Science* 359 (6380): 1–6.

7
FOOTPRINTS IN SPATIAL NARRATIVES

Wearable Technology, Active Reading, and a New Digital Literary Mapping of Dorothy Wordsworth's Scafell Pike Excursion

Joanna E. Taylor and Christopher Donaldson

> – and not simply by the fact that this shading of
> forest cannot show the fragrance of balsam,
> the gloom of cypresses
> is what I wish to prove.
>   (Boland 2012)

Eavan Boland's poem 'That the Science of Cartography is Limited' (1994) proves a truth about map reading: however detailed its visualisation, a map can never communicate the way it feels to stand in a place. A map might demonstrate what a place looks like and express a location's key features, but it 'cannot show' what it's like to be there: to smell the foliage; to feel the ground underfoot; or to understand the associations that make certain features expressive of gloom, like Boland's cypresses or, like Wordsworthian daffodils, joy. Places become more meaningful when we acknowledge the numberless interactions at macro and micro scales, and in geographical and phenomenological ways, that make it so. Cartography, as Boland's poem indicates, is good at representing where things are, but limited when it comes to showing why things matter. Poetry is the opposite: it often ekes out, foot by foot, the feeling of being somewhere – but where precisely can be difficult to pin down. There are three elements at play in the relationship Boland describes: location, body, and perception. The map's province is location, the poem's is perception. But what of the body, the entity that mediates between place and perception? How might we communicate the embodied experience of being somewhere in a spatial narrative?

    The limitations of analogue maps in capturing a sense of place are exaggerated by their digital counterparts. Notwithstanding attempts to represent

DOI: 10.4324/9781003053880-8

digitally the experience of standing in a location (Google's Street View being an obvious example), digital maps cannot comprehend an embodied sense of place. Indeed, on its own, no visual media can capture the complex and multisensory feeling of being at a particular place and in a particular body. And that matters, because our unique bodies influence the way we experience the world. Re-inserting the body into geographical discussion has long been a focus for feminist geographers; as Doreen Massey demonstrates, assuming a 'standard' body of either sex risks eliding the impact of difference – including in gender, health, or mobility – on every spatial experience (Massey 1994). Donna Haraway goes as far as to indicate that a feminist mapping practice would register the 'view from a body' as opposed to a 'view from above' (Haraway 2013). If conventional maps (at least, in Western cartographic traditions) flatten and elide the differences that define how people perceive and experience a place, then one important job for spatial narratives is to highlight such differences and to illuminate how multifarious human perceptions of places are. Previous work in digital literary studies has amply shown that combining maps with texts can enrich the science of cartography by aligning place with perception. But, in this chapter, we want to go a step further by demonstrating how new technologies afford a means of re-introducing the body as a crucial link between map and text.

Twenty-first-century mobile cartographic technologies have re-centred quotidian mapping practices on person rather than place. Wearable technologies and fitness apps have become almost ubiquitous in the last few years; in the US in 2013, 21% of adults reported using digital technology to track some aspect of their body (e.g. weight, heart rate, blood pressure). By 2018, this figure had risen to 70%. The data captured by these technologies threaten to disrupt understandings of subjectivity as being 'unified, rational, and static' (Mitchell 2013). Instead, they break down both body and place into a multifaceted series of cartographic marks, including Global Positioning System (GPS) tracks, step counts, heart rate, calories burned, or distance covered. We might consider these technologies as examples of mapmaking, which emphasise movement over stasis, line over point, and connection over individuation. The result, as Peta Mitchell has concluded, is 'a reassertion of local agency' (Mitchell 2013). Mitchell means the map *reader*. But wearables also make it possible for the map *writer* to reflect multivalent and individuated spatial subjectivities. In quantifying the individual's relationship to their location, recent research involving wearables has emphasised the extension of cartographic interest from geographic sciences towards the arts and humanities (Berglund, Duvall, and Dunne 2016; Broadhurst and Price 2017; Guler, Gannon, and Sicchio 2016; Horvath, Hoge, and Cameron 2016; Pedersen, Everrett, and Caldwell 2020; Pedersen and Iliadis 2020). Justin Tonra's project *Eververse* has introduced wearables into discussions of poetry; his interdisciplinary team investigated how data from the quantified self can be used alongside poetic theory and Natural

Language Generation to produce automatically a form of literally embodied poetry (Tonra et al. n.d.). Yet, outside of the performing arts, rhetoric, and fashion studies, wearable technologies are not yet widely used in humanities research. This chapter seeks to encourage more creative-critical experimentation with wearables by showing how they can contribute to the study of literary spatial narratives. Specifically, this chapter demonstrates how incorporating embodied data – including heart rate monitoring and GPS tracks – alongside a literary text in a mapping environment can transform not only how we read, but also how we understand the role of embodiment in historical and contemporary place-making.

To do so, this chapter takes as a case study one particular text: Dorothy Wordsworth's epistolary account of her pioneering ascent of England's highest mountain, Scafell Pike, on October 7, 1818. The letter in which Wordsworth described this feat is one of the earliest known records of a recreational ascent of England's highest mountain (the earliest occurred three years before) (Taylor and Gregory 2022), and it is the first known account written by a woman. The original manuscript of Wordsworth's letter does not survive, but her account was first published in her brother William's *Description of the Scenery of the Lakes* in 1822. This book later became William's bestselling *Guide through the District of the Lakes*, and the inclusion of Dorothy's letter in it inspired several generations of walkers to follow in her footsteps – even if, since the letter was published without attribution, these walkers thought they were following William. We read this letter alongside data gathered from a recreation of this walk by a party of researchers, artists, and mountaineers who retraced Wordsworth's footsteps on October 7, 2018. In part, this was a reimagining of an important moment in the history of British Romanticism and the history of mountaineering. But, as this chapter contends, the recreation was also an opportunity to reflect on the relationship between reading and digital technologies, wherein the maps created by walking this route might transform the ways we read and respond to the texts the initial ascent inspired. This chapter's ultimate claim is therefore that bringing these two types of data – those generated by author and by reader – together can foreground a phenomenology of place that induces new ways of reading both text and map, and that positions embodiment as a central element in scholarship on digital mapping.

This approach is well suited to Wordsworth. She was born in Cockermouth, Cumberland (now Cumbria), at the edge of the modern Lake District National Park and World Heritage Site (Figure 7.1) in 1771. She was nine years old when the earliest wearable fitness technology – a pedometer made by a Swiss watchmaker – was manufactured ('Perrelet' n.d.). By the 1790s, as her career as a prodigious walker was beginning (Andrews 2020), these devices were available in London. Wordsworth did not use a pedometer herself, but her letters prove that she kept track of the distances she walked and the pace at which she did so. Her decision to include such data in epistolary descriptions of her

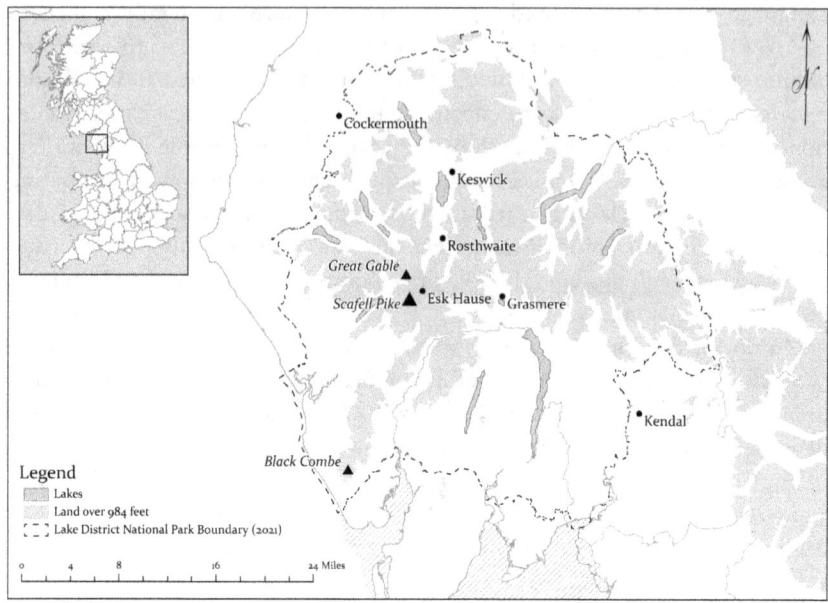

FIGURE 7.1 England's Lake District.

journeys reflects the role that counting and measuring played in her poetics of walking. Throughout her life, Wordsworth remained sensitive to the interplays between place and person, text and map. Her journals and letters in particular reveal her efforts in recreating something of the lived experience of place in text. Most of these works were not published during her lifetime, and in them we often find personal impressions and detailed accounts that connect place and perception through the body.

The new approaches to reading we present herein share much in common with historical reading practices, including the sort of participatory reading in which Wordsworth herself engaged. When William Wordsworth went on a walking tour of the Alps in 1790, he sent Dorothy letters that described his journey. While William 'march[ed]' at 'military speed' (*Prelude* VI.428) (Wordsworth 1926) through the Swiss mountains, Dorothy used his letters to trace his route on a map, an action which allowed her to partake vicariously in the excursion. Following William's journey on the map evidently helped her feel a connection with her absent brother and to share in the bodily experiences of the walking tour; she wrote to her friend Jane Pollard that when she 'trace[d] his paths upon the maps', she wondered 'that his strength and courage have not sunk under the fatigues he must have undergone' (De Selincourt 1935). William, for his part, was imagining that the landscape was a 'book' in which he 'could not chuse but read | A frequent lesson of sound tenderness' (*Prelude* VI.473–475) (Wordsworth 1926). Collectively, then, as brother and sister they developed a cyclical, reciprocal relationship between text and place. What both Wordsworths enacted in different ways in this example is what we call active reading. In her reading of William's letters, Dorothy not only dynamically participated in the creation of meaning, but also translated his descriptions into activity. By following the map's contour lines, she sensed the bodily 'fatigue' her brother must surely have felt. Her fingers replaced his feet and the map stood in for the landscape, and this enabled the siblings to share the journey through the medium of the letters. The data from wearable technologies, we suggest, can offer similar insights into the active reader's bodily engagement with both text and landscape and contribute to a spatial narrative which blends cartography and phenomenology.

Yet, the emergent analytical practices wearables might facilitate in studies of written works are underexplored. The connection between body, location, and text that our practice develops begins to move us towards the pinnacle of the spatial narrative as the highly curated peak of the deep map pyramid (Ridge, Lafreniere, and Sarma 2013): a mode of analysis based both on a particular text and/or location and its interactions with a specific body. Birringer and Danjoux discovered in 2009 that 'the mobilisation of smart technology concerns sensorial experience and expression' that can encourage 'a more experimental and playful adaptation of the digital medium as a wearable medium' (Birringer and Danjoux 2009). Here, we adapt this performance-focused approach to suggest that the mobilisation of this technology, which uniquely captures elements of the physical processes that inform perception, can lead to experimental and playful textual analyses that translate digital data into interpretative tools. Just like secondary reading can enhance our understandings of a literary work, so too can using digital data in this way augment our personal and critical relationships with the text.

Mapping the Body: Wearable Technologies and Spatial Narratives

Before we proceed to explain how wearables can contribute to the study of spatial narratives, a brief overview of wearable technology is in order. Such technology, as Catherine Gouge and John Jones have suggested, comprises an array of devices 'whose primary functionality requires that they be connected to bodies' (Gouge and Jones 2016). The design, manufacture, and use of these devices have grown rapidly over the past 20 years. Even taking into account a decline in the market thanks to the COVID pandemic (Hamblen 2020), the wearables market is on track to increase from $27 billion in 2019 to $64 billion by 2024 ('Wearable Tech Market Set to Grow' 2020). What the ongoing expansion of this industry indicates is that embodied experience matters and that, as Steve Benford puts it, 'our interaction with computers is not only a matter of abstract cognition, but also reaches out into the physical and material' (Benford

2017). The result is a concurrent machinisation of humans with the humanisation of machines (Zheng 2017) making 'digital humanity' less of an oxymoron than some might wish to believe.

Wearable devices tap into our fascination with observing ourselves (Chalfen 2014): they facilitate ways of recording our actions and of monitoring our habits towards the improvement of personal, even global, health by tracking information such as our calorie intake, exercise habits, or carbon footprint (Forrester 2014). As well as personal tracking, wearables have been experimented with to address global challenges; they have proved highly valuable throughout the COVID-19 pandemic, for instance ('Wearable Wonderland: How Tech Is Tackling Covid-19' 2020). Since around 2014, the most popular items on the market have been wristbands or watches (Berglund, Duvall, and Dunne 2016) that track elements like heart rate, oxygen saturation, stress levels, activity levels, footsteps, and – via GPS chips – location. At the same time as promising something like 'mastery of the organized complexity of bodily systems' (Gouge and Jones 2016), the physical data tracked by these devices can offer something more: a means of communicating and interpreting the user's emotional state (Zheng 2017) The result is something approaching a comprehensive account of what the physician Eric Topol calls the 'high definition human' (Topol 2015), although it is worth noting that, in most cases, being 'human' in the development of sports and wearable technologies usually means being a man (Criado Perez 2019).

The vocabulary applied to wearables indicates their centrality to the contemporary lives of affluent societies; in Johannes Birringer's words, 'you wore clothes, but now you wear a smart device', rhetoric that indicates how ubiquitous such devices are in day-to-day apparel. The dark side to this ubiquity is that it expands significantly the ability of those in power to understand and utilise our most intimate data; as Birringer continues, if you wear these devices, 'you wear sensors and wireless transmitters, and you can be tracked' (Baker 2017). Users' data is harvested – and, in fact, owned – by the device manufacturer, who may sell it to insurance or healthcare companies (Baker 2017). Data security has been consistently secondary – both for producers and consumers – to novelty, functionality, and fashion (Dwivedi et al. 2019). This laxity has consequences that reach beyond data protection: revelations that Huawei included in patents that its systems could help to track Uyghur Muslims indicate how such technologies can aid and abet the violation of human rights (*BBC News* 2021).

Nevertheless, wearables significantly impact the way we experience and respond to space. Users reporting changing their habits in response to their device, for example, consciously walking more to hit the '10,000-step' mark (Lemos and Bitencourt 2017), is perhaps the most obvious example, but the effects of marrying wearables with the body to navigate our place in the world are far-reaching. By moving away from perceiving wearables from what

N. Katherine Hayles describes as a posthuman view (Hayles 1999) that privileges the so-called quantified self and towards acknowledging wearables as what Jordynn Jack – promoting a feminist framework for assessing wearables in rhetoric studies – calls 'embodied rhetorics' (Jack 2016), we can incorporate wearables and the data they generate into a cohesive framework for producing literary spatial narratives. In fact, doing so can help us participate in the spatial narratives we investigate: wearable technologies, as Jason Kalin and Jordan Frith note, 'foreground the specificity of location and embodiment, the user's body in space and time' (Kalin and Frith 2016).

Incorporating data taken from a wearable device into literary analysis presents an intriguing opportunity to investigate a physiology of active reading in ways that are both deeply intimate – focused on one body and one text – and which have the potential to engage with big data. That might be physiological (data taken from other users of wearable technology tracked at the same location), textual (other written accounts of the place), or cartographic. In the latter case, wearables present a unique opportunity: by appearing to foreground individual interactions with and bodily responses to the environment, wearables can destabilise standardised cartographic hegemonies. They might be the best instance we have developed so far of what Guattari might recognise as chaosmotic maps (Guattari 1995): cartographies that reflect the multifaceted nature of subjective experience, challenge Cartesian dichotomies between mind and body or body and world, and facilitate new forms of exploration into the inherent plurality of spatial narratives.

If the human body is a 'key frontier for creating powerful and deeply engaging ways of interacting with computers' (Benford 2017), then wearable technologies offer a way of mediating between environment (including, as we demonstrate here, reading material), body, and machine. Positioning the data tracked, including location, pulse, elevation climbed, or pace, alongside an account of being in the same place at a different time (in our example, two centuries apart) might, we suggest, allow us to develop an approach to spatial narratives that acknowledges active reading as a physiological activity, at the same time as recognising the experience of space as a textual – or, at least, interpretative – one. Like Merleau-Ponty, we are suspicious of any suggestion that there is a straightforward 'point-by-point correspondence' between being and feeling; but like him, too, we want to explore physiology's role in the connection between the body and the 'idea of an external world' (Merleau-Ponty 2012).

The sort of active reading we outline below can provide an approach to a range of different spatial narratives, but it is especially suited to narratives, such as Wordsworth's, which dwell on the author's embodied experience. This is a point Simon Bainbridge has stressed in his recent study of Romanticism and mountaineering. Wordsworth's Scafell letter, as Bainbridge affirms, repeatedly draws attention to her 'awareness of her embodied state' (Bainbridge

2020). Our investigation of active reading aims to extend this line of enquiry into spatial narratives in general and Wordsworth's letter in particular. Accordingly, in what follows we demonstrate how interpreting the data wearables track can inform a new mode of spatially conscientious narrative analysis that acknowledges both the bodily and the intellectual experience of reading.

'Active' Reading: Following Dorothy Wordsworth Up Scafell Pike

Walking was central to Wordsworth's life and writing. She completed her first long-distance walk in 1794 with her brother, trekking from Kendal at the southern edge of the Lake District to Keswick at the northern end. In 1803, she, William, and (for a while at least) Samuel Taylor Coleridge undertook a tour of Scotland. Wordsworth recorded their impressions in her *Recollections of a Tour made in Scotland*, a text that, after its publication in 1874, became the most widely read account of pedestrian tours to Scotland (Leask 2020). Later, in 1820, she – with William, his wife Mary, and some family friends – completed a pedestrian tour of the Alps. This trip also inspired a travel journal, which Wordsworth circulated among friends. But Wordsworth's ascent of Scafell Pike is particularly notable for the daring it displayed. Wordsworth's description of this excursion captures her approach to mountaineering: it goes beyond tales of sporting prowess, preferring instead to examine the details of the mountainside and to reflect on the experience of the journey.

In 1818, Scafell Pike was an uncommon choice for a recreational climb. Wordsworth's letter, as we have mentioned, is the first known record of a recreational ascent by a woman. It is actually pre-dated only by a party led by the geologist, surveyor, and mechanic Jonathan Otley in 1815. The massif was even, in some cases, left off popular maps of the region; the profile map published by William Hutchinson in 1794 is not alone in dismissing the west of the Lake District as being uninterestingly 'desolate and mountainous' (Hutchinson 1794). It was not until Otley's publication of *A New Map of the District of the Lakes* in 1818 – mere weeks before Wordsworth's excursion – that the massif was properly mapped. After Wordsworth's account of the climb was published in her brother's *Guide*, it became a canonical text for the region's mountaineers; writer-walkers, including Thomas Wilkinson, Harriet Martineau, and Eliza Lynn Linton, all followed in her footsteps. Indeed, modern routes up the mountain still reflect the re-inscription of Wordsworth's route by readers on the mountainside. Figure 7.2 shows her route, modelled on the letter and with data taken from the Lake District National Park's Digital Public Rights of Way dataset (Lake District National Park Authority 2019).

Wordsworth's ascent of Scafell Pike, then, is even more remarkable in this context. She undertook the ascent with her friend Mary Barker, 'an unmarried Lady' who lived in Borrowdale. Also accompanying them were Barker's maid, Agnes, a porter, and a shepherd who served as their guide. Wordsworth reported that Barker had been 'bewitched with the charms of the rocks, &

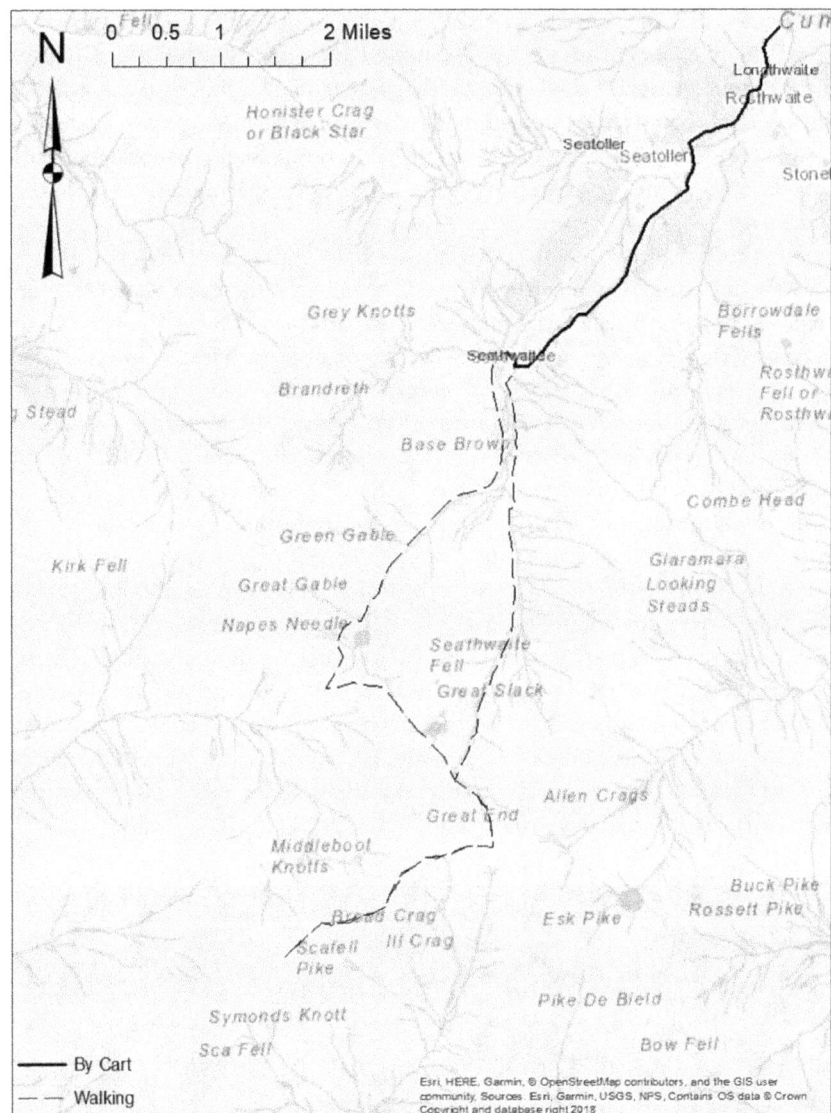

FIGURE 7.2 Dorothy Wordsworth's route up Scafell Pike, October 7, 1818, combining data from her letter with the Lake District National Park's Digital Public Rights of Way dataset.

streams, & Mountains, belonging to that secluded spot' and had 'there built herself a house'. Barker occupied herself with painting, music, reading, and, Wordsworth records, in becoming an 'active Climber of the hills' (Wordsworth 1967). This appellation recognised Barker's commitment to exploring the uplands; not only had she moved – like Wordsworth herself – to the region better to access the uplands, she deliberately sought out mountainous adventures. No passive consumers of the scenery, Barker and Wordsworth shared an 'active' appreciation of the landscape that situated embodiment at the heart of their spatial narratives. Moreover, both aimed to share the experiences that, in Bainbridge's words, they had 'found to be so rewarding' (Bainbridge 2020), whether by organising excursions with friends or by sharing written accounts of them.

It is this foregrounding of 'active' pursuit that inspired a recreation of Wordsworth and Barker's pioneering ascent, 200 years to the hour after the original. Part of the collaborative project *This Girl Did: Dorothy Wordsworth and Women's Mountaineering* (led by the Wordsworth Trust with an international group of academics and artists), the recreation had three aims: first, to promote Wordsworth's role in the development of women's mountaineering; second, to conduct an embodied exploration of what the ascent might have felt like for Wordsworth and her party; and third, to investigate how a recreation of this walk might guide new modes of reading Wordsworth's account. There were five principal actors at this event: Alex Jakob-Whitworth, a Cumbria-based artist, took on the role of Wordsworth; Harriet Fraser, poet and one half of the SomewhereNowhere collective, was Barker; Joanna Taylor (University of Manchester) was Agnes; Paul Westover (Brigham Young University) was the porter; and Paul Davies, a general practitioner (GP) and member of the Ambleside amateur dramatics group, was the shepherd guide. We were accompanied by a support team (including Jeff Cowton, Curator at Wordsworth Grasmere), and two filmmakers (who were also Mountain Rescuers), Jago Miller and Richard Berry, documented the event (Miller 2018).

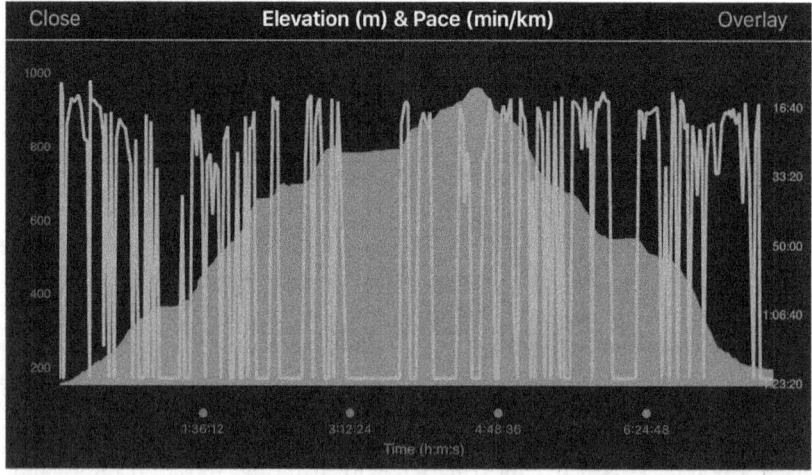

FIGURE 7.3 Pace and elevation data from Taylor's Garmin Vivoactive2, 7 October 2018.

October 7, 1818 was a glorious day, and Barker and Wordsworth set off by cart from Barker's home in Rosthwaite at around 9.30 in the morning, anticipating an invigorating climb up Esk Hawes, from which Barker had promised 'a magnificent prospect'. They acquired their guide from Seathwaite, at the foot of the mountain, and set off up the fell feeling refreshed by the autumn air and 'the sweet warmth of the unclouded sun'. Once they had lunched at Esk Hawes, though, they decided there was enough time – and that they had enough energy – left to keep going. Notwithstanding the miles they had already walked that day, they agreed to head over to Wasdale and up Scafell. They had climbed so high in any case that they seemed already to be 'three parts up that Mountain'. Although the distance turned out to be 'greater than it had appeared', still their 'courage did not fail'. As they reached the top of Scafell Pike, Wordsworth and Barker realised that they had climbed out of the reach of the Lake District's familiar sounds: they 'paused & kept silence to listen, & not a sound of any kind was to be heard'. Not even an insect 'hum[med] in the air'. They completed the descent, past Sprinkling Tarn, by the light of a full moon. Other than a brief rainstorm near Illgill Head, they had enjoyed the best of Britain's October weather.

October 7, 2018 was cold, wet, and exceptionally windy; the first edges of what would become Storm Callum were beginning to blow into the western Lakes. Having gathered at Barker's former home, now the Scafell Hotel, our party set off by car at around 9.30 to Seathwaite, following a near-identical route to Barker and Wordsworth's cart. We were wearing clothes similar to what Wordsworth's party would have worn (with the exception that we wore modern walking boots and carried waterproofs with us, and Taylor was wearing a smart watch), and the Scafell Hotel had generously provided a lunch of period-relevant eatables for the maid to carry up in her wicker basket, and the porter to take in his satchel. Up to Esk Hause, we enjoyed weather not dissimilar to the sort Wordsworth and Barker experienced in 1818, and we paused at points to enjoy the views, to talk, and to read excerpts of Wordsworth's letter. Like Wordsworth and Barker, we enjoyed the 'magnificent prospect' as we ate. But, as we ascended the ridge up to Illgill Head, from whence to proceed across boulders to Scafell Pike, the storm blew in. Given the kite-like nature of long skirts, and the worryingly decreasing visibility, we were forced to descend early. Sprinkling Tarn lived up to its name, spraying vertical jets of water up into the gales as we passed. A new moon made the last part of the journey rather more treacherous than it had been 200 years before.

Wordsworth's letter provided the information we needed to plan the route and, more than that, it offered a guide towards how we should experience the ascent. The letter emphasises how it feels to be moving on the mountain, and becoming part of it – for a time at least. Wordsworth's peculiarly forthright interest in the relationships between place, text – whether cartographic or written – and body emphasises the limitations of conventional cartographic visualisation. The recreation had also highlighted the limits of standard literary analysis; following in Wordsworth's footsteps had required an extraordinarily close reading of the text and in the chilly afterglow of the experience, a more usual analysis did not seem enough to capture adequately the experience, and the meaning, of being on the mountain. We had discovered what Dorothy had elsewhere described: that no written or visual representation can, alone, capture what it feels like to be at a place (Taylor 2019). Comparing the physiological data mapped through a wearable device with Wordsworth's account offered an opportunity to address the limitations of both cartography and literary analysis to generate a spatial narrative that combined digital and literary material with criticism mediated through an embodied experience of place.

Beyond Description: Incorporating Wearables into Literary Analysis

During the recreation, Taylor had been wearing a Garmin Vivosmart 2, a smart watch brand that has been praised, among other things, for offering accurate measurements and being waterproof (a feature that proved essential on our rain-sodden excursion; Guler, Gannon, and Sicchio 2016). Tracking the route on the watch served two purposes: first, it allowed us to compare our actual route with the original; second, and more significantly, it offered a way of experimenting with how to create a form of mapping that combined reading, embodiment, and digital data. The aim was to embed an ecosystem – to adapt a phrase from Adam Hammond, Julian Brooke, and Graeme Hirst – of embodied close reading (Hammond, Brooke, and Hirst 2016) into the construction of a spatial narrative that linked 1818 with 2018 via footprints over the same mountain. In documenting the performance of this excursion, the watch recorded the creation of what Schwartz and Halegoua call the 'spatial self', a character created by 'intentional socio-cultural practices of self-presentation that result in dynamic, curated, sometimes idealized performances of who a user is, based on where they go' (Schwartz and Halegoua 2015). In this case, the 'spatial self' was a hybrid identity: a mixture of the modern walker and the historical figure in whose footsteps we, quite literally, followed. The watch data documented the process of inserting an individual into a transhistorical group: this was not simply a case of sharing social data among our contemporaries as such devices are designed to do (Kalin and Frith 2016). More, it recorded a physical experience shared, however vicariously, across centuries.

The watch data – route, elevation, pace, and heart rate – articulated an intimate connection between body, text, and landscape. For instance, overlaying the pace data onto the elevation indicated the places where we – mimicking the 1818 party – paused to talk, admire the views, or eat (Figure 7.3). In doing so, the pace data begins to reflect the letter's structure: the places where the pace data indicates we slowed down or paused recalls the longer sentences and paragraphs that, in the letter, reveal a moment where Wordsworth had also slowed down to more carefully document her impressions. The top of Esk Hawes – Wordsworth and Barker's original destination – offered such a moment. Two long sentences record a physical pause as Wordsworth, exhilarated, looked out across the region:

> The green Vale of Esk deep & green, with its glittering serpent stream was below us; and on we looked to the Mountains near the sea – Black Coombe and others and still beyond to the sea itself in dazzling brightness. Turning round we saw the Mountains of Wasdale in tumult; and Great Gavel [sic], though the middle of the Mountain, was to us as its base, looked very grand.
>
> *(Wordsworth 1967)*

The embodied connection between herself and the mountains that Wordsworth recounts seems to have physically invigorated her. Maria Jane Jewsbury described Dorothy as being 'an embodied spell', and passages like this give some indication of where that magic came from: she seemed almost to draw up energy from the ground. Each main clause here – distinguished by the semicolons, dashes, and full stops – follow Wordsworth's 'turning round' so that the experience of standing at a particular location is encoded into the text. The commas, meanwhile, mimic the effect of place on perception; they distinguish the groups of objects or impressions that came together in one view, from the 'serpent stream' winding its way through the lush valley, to the mountains along the Furness peninsula seeming to join with the sea, to Great Gable's deceptive base, appearing from her viewpoint as though it rose up from the centre of Scafell. The letter here records the realisation of a monumental connection between body, perception, and place – and the watch records a similar effect. The peaks and troughs of the pace data are a counterpart to Wordsworth's broken-up sentences, and reflect both the challenges of negotiating a difficult landscape and the moments of pause and reflection that these negotiations facilitate. As we reach Esk Hause, our pace data slackens and lengthens out to match the plateau at the summit. Like Wordsworth's long sentences, this pause records a moment of tranquillity to take in the multifaceted view.

The heart rate data makes this reciprocity between body, place, perception, and text even clearer. Wordsworth had recorded that the climb up to Esk Hause was 'invigorating', and the quickening of the heart rate data from the watch corroborates a shared experience. The climb is so 'invigorating' in part because it documents – in text for Wordsworth and data for the recreation – a mutual connection between geology and physiology (Figure 7.4): that degree of physical exertion rises and falls with that of the terrain. At the top of Esk Hause, though, the heart rate data goes further: it allows us to develop Wordsworth's account beyond words. She wrote of this moment that:

We found ourselves at the top of Ash Course without a weary limb, having had the fresh air of autumn to help us up, & the sweet warmth of the unclouded sun to tempt us to sit and rest by the way. From the top of Ash Course we beheld a prospect which would indeed have amply repaid me for a toilsome journey, if such it had been; and a sense of thankfulness for the continuance of that vigour of body, which enabled me to climb the high mountain, as in the days of my youth, inspiring me with fresh chearfulness, added a delight, a charm to the contemplation of the magnificent scenes before me which I cannot describe[.].

(Wordsworth 1967)

She cannot describe the 'delight, [the] charm' of the moment because it is deeply embodied; but that is precisely where the data from the wearable steps in: it visualises the indescribable. The heart rate captures something similar to what Wordsworth recalls: a sense of repose, but not rest. What Wordsworth articulates here is an active appreciation of the view that self-consciously unites perception and place with a deeply embodied experience where the text and the landscape are united in the same breath. The data represents a profound experience of a deep and embodied close reading that transforms Wordsworth's writing from a generic description of a location into something micro-mappable that registers, evidently, in each heartbeat. This embodied data closes the gap between the body and the digital, the person and the place, and between the reader and the writer. It becomes the text through which we can read a personal ecology as part of three wider ecosystems: the natural, the historical, and the computational.

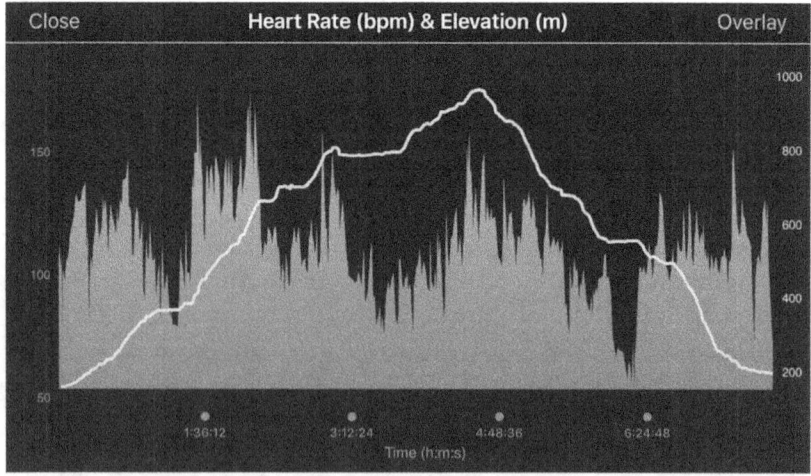

FIGURE 7.4 Heartrate and elevation data from Taylor's Garmin Vivoactive2, 7 October 2018.

The approach we have outlined here offers new possibilities for the study of each of these ecosystems. Recognising the uniqueness of the body being tracked, including both the vital statistics captured by the wearable and the body's historical, social, and political situation, is crucial for challenging the homogenisation of the body-as-big-data that wearables risk promoting (Gouge and Jones 2018; Happe 2013). More than this, though, it encourages the recognition of this data as narratives in themselves, and therefore as texts to be analysed carefully. At a larger scale, using data from a wearable offers the possibility of comparing individual results with those of other users, potentially on a massive scale (the limitation being the availability of that data from private companies). Exploring the relationships we've outlined here – between pace, heart rate, and landscape – would allow us to ask how or to what extent other users engage, knowingly or not, with the cultural landscape generated through Wordsworth and others' writing. Moreover, understanding the intersection between person, perception, and place may be one of the 'previously unidentified relations' that Gouge and Jones suggest would allow wearers better to engage with 'an expanded range of potential relations with bodily processes' (Gouge and Jones 2018). What, for instance, would a device that tracked the kind of physiological poetics that we have addressed here – moments of pause, of attention, registered in the slowing down of the body's actions – look like? How might that data allow us to develop our understandings of people's interactions with and feelings towards particular locations or environments? And how might that data feed in to both the development of affective computing (Picard 2000) and to the ways we understand perceptions of the non-human world at a large scale? How, in other words, might such questions help to close the gap between person, perception, and place?

These are important questions. If treating wearables as no more than representations of the body elides the embodiment that characterises individual experience (Gouge and Jones 2018), then it also risks perpetuating a divorce between the body and its environment (Kalin and Frith 2016). Might understanding wearable data as a new form of spatial narrative move us towards situating wearables as an everyday, everywhere reminder to connect differently with the places through which we move? Might they initiate new opportunities not only for aligning historical texts with present spatial experiences, but for cohering anew the active body with the long histories and projected futures of a particular place? In short, might interpreting the data from wearables as and alongside text allow for more widespread acknowledgement that, in Bruno Latour's words, 'there are not organisms on one side and an environment on the other, but a coproduction by both' (Latour 2018)? A spatial narrative that blurs the boundaries between where the landscape ends and the body begins might offer a unique opportunity for a new kind of ecocritical storytelling.

Acknowledgements

We would like to thank attendees of the 2018 RSAA conference in Canberra for their considered reflections about the ideas embedded in this chapter. Thanks are due to the This Girl Did team – Alex Jakob-Whitworth, Harriet Fraser, Paul Westover, and Melissa Mitchell and Jeff Cowton – for their collective enthusiasm and generosity in collaborating on the reimagining of the Scafell excursion. Kerri Andrews and Jonny Huck both offered thoughtful feedback on a draft of this piece. We are also grateful to support received from the Faculty of Arts and Social Sciences at Lancaster University.

Works Cited

Andrews, Kerri. 2020. *Wanderers: A History of Women Walking*. London: Reaktion Books.
Bainbridge, Simon. 2020. *Mountaineering and British Romanticism: The Literary Cultures of Climbing, 1770–1836*. Oxford: Oxford University Press.
Baker, Camille. 2017. 'Critical Interventions in Wearable Tech, Smart Fashion and Textiles in Art and Performance'. In *Digital Bodies: Creativity and Technology in the Arts and Humanities*, edited by Susan Broadhurst and Sara Price, 175–190. Basingstoke: Palgrave Macmillan.
BBC News. 2021. 'Huawei Patent Mentions Use of Uighur-Spotting Tech', 13 January 2021, sec. Technology. https://www.bbc.com/news/technology-55634388.
Benford, Steve. 2017. 'Foreward'. In *Digital Bodies: Creativity and Technology in the Arts and Humanities*, edited by Susan Broadhurst and Sara Price, v–ix. Basingstoke: Palgrave Macmillan.
Berglund, Mary Ellen, Julia Duvall, and Lucy E Dunne. 2016. 'A Survey of the Historical Scope and Current Trends of Wearable Technology Applications'. In *Proceedings of the 2016 ACM International Symposium on Wearable Computers*, 40–43. ISWC '16. New York, NY, USA: Association for Computing Machinery. https://doi.org/10.1145/2971763.2971796.
Birringer, Johannes, and Michèle Danjoux. 2009. 'Wearable Performance'. *Digital Creativity* 20 (1–2): 95–113. https://doi.org/10.1080/14626260902868095.
Boland, Eavan. 2012. *New Collected Poems*. Carcanet.
Broadhurst, Susan, and Sara Price, eds. 2017. *Digital Bodies: Creativity and Technology in the Arts and Humanities*. Basingstoke: Palgrave Macmillan UK. https://doi.org/10.1057/978-1-349-95241-0.
Chalfen, Richard. 2014. '"Your Panopticon or Mine?" Incorporating Wearable Technology's Glass and GoPro into Visual Social Science'. *Visual Studies* 29 (3): 299–310. https://doi.org/10.1080/1472586X.2014.941547.
Criado Perez, Caroline. 2019. *Invisible Women: Exposing Data Bias in a World Designed for Men*. London: Chatto & Windus.
De Selincourt, Ernest, ed. 1935. *The Letters of William and Dorothy Wordsworth: The Early Years 1787–1805*. Oxford: Clarendon Press.
Dwivedi, Yogesh, Emmanuel Ayaburi, Richard Boateng, and John Effah, eds. 2019. *ICT Unbounded, Social Impact of Bright ICT Adoption: IFIP WG 8.6 International Conference on Transfer and Diffusion of IT, TDIT 2019, Accra, Ghana, June 21–22, 2019,*

Proceedings. Vol. 558. IFIP Advances in Information and Communication Technology. Cham: Springer International Publishing. https://doi.org/10.1007/978-3-030-20671-0.

Forrester, Ian. 2014. 'Quantified Self and the Ethics of Personal Data'. BBC R&D. https://www.bbc.co.uk/rd/blog/2014-06-qs-ethics-of-data.

Gouge, Catherine, and John Jones. 2016. 'Wearables, Wearing, and the Rhetorics that Attend to Them'. *Rhetoric Society Quarterly* 46 (3): 199–206. https://doi.org/10.1080/02773945.2016.1171689.

———. 2018. 'Wearable Technologies and Invention'. *Rhetoric Review* 37 (4): 421–433. https://doi.org/10.1080/07350198.2018.1497887.

Guattari, Félix. 1995. *Chaosmosis: An Ethico-Aesthetic Paradigm*. Bloomington, IN: Indiana University Press.

Guler, Sibel Deren, Madeline Gannon, and Kate Sicchio. 2016. *Crafting Wearables*. Berkeley, CA: Apress. https://doi.org/10.1007/978-1-4842-1808-2.

Hamblen, Matt. 2020. 'Wearables, Wearable Sensors Gain Popularity with Pandemic, Despite 2020 Revenue Lull'. FierceElectronics. 23 November 2020. https://www.fierceelectronics.com/electronics/wearables-wearable-sensors-gain-popularity-pandemic-despite-2020-revenue-lull.

Hammond, Adam, Julian Brooke, and Graeme Hirst. 2016. 'Modeling Modernist Dialogism: Close Reading with Big Data'. In *Reading Modernism with Machines: Digital Humanities and Modernist Literature*, edited by Shawna Ross and James O'Sullivan, 49–78. Basingstoke: Palgrave Macmillan.

Happe, Kelly E. 2013. *The Material Gene: Gender, Race, and Heredity after the Human Genome Project*. New York: New York University Press.

Haraway, Donna. 2013. *Simians, Cyborgs, and Women: The Reinvention of Nature*. New York: Routledge.

Hayles, N. Katherine. 1999. *How We Became Posthuman: Virtual Bodies in Cybernetics, Literature, and Informatics*. Chicago, IL: University of Chicago Press.

Horvath, Joan, Lyn Hoge, and Rich Cameron. 2016. *Practical Fashion Tech*. Berkeley, CA: Apress. https://doi.org/10.1007/978-1-4842-1662-0.

Hutchinson, William. 1794. *The History of the County of Cumberland: And Some Places Adjacent, from the Earliest Accounts to the Present Time*. Carlisle: F. Jollie.

Jack, Jordynn. 2016. 'Leviathan and the Breast Pump: Toward an Embodied Rhetoric of Wearable Technology'. *Rhetoric Society Quarterly* 46 (3): 207–221. https://doi.org/10.1080/02773945.2016.1171691.

Kalin, Jason, and Jordan Frith. 2016. 'Wearing the City: Memory P(a)Laces, Smartphones, and the Rhetorical Invention of Embodied Space'. *Rhetoric Society Quarterly* 46 (3): 222–235. https://doi.org/10.1080/02773945.2016.1171692.

Lake District National Park Authority. 2019. 'LDNPA Public Rights Of Way'. 5 July 2019. https://data.gov.uk/dataset/767931ee-c98a-4030-bb87-eb6b6512fb1f/ldnpa-public-rights-of-way.

Latour, Bruno. 2018. *Down to Earth : Politics in the New Climatic Regime*. Cambridge: Polity Press. http://web.a.ebscohost.com.manchester.idm.oclc.org/ehost/ebookviewer/ebook/bmxlYmtfXzE5ODUzMDZfX0FO0?sid=388adc0f-76dc-43f7-9480-ec178f1f9597@sessionmgr4006&vid=0&format=EK&lpid=navPoint-19&rid=0.

Leask, Nigel. 2020. *Stepping Westward: Writing the Highland Tour c.1720–1830*. Oxford: Oxford University Press.

Lemos, André Luiz Martins, and Elias Bitencourt. 2017. 'Smartbody and Performative Sensibility in Fitbit Devices'. *Galaxia* 36: 5–17.

Massey, Doreen B. 1994. *Space, Place, and Gender*. Minneapolis: University of Minnesota Press.

Merleau-Ponty, Maurice. 2012. *Phenomenology of Perception*. London: Taylor & Francis Group.

Miller, Jago. 2018. *Journeywoman - Walking in the Footsteps of Dorothy Wordsworth*. https://vimeo.com/301608226.

Mitchell, Peta. 2013. *Cartographic Strategies of Postmodernity: The Figure of the Map in Contemporary Theory and Fiction*. London: Routledge.

Pedersen, Isabel, Tom Everrett, and Sharon Caldwell. 2020. 'The Wearable Past: Integrating a Physical Museum Collection of Wearables into a Database of Born-Digital Artifacts'. *Digital Studies/Le Champ Numérique* 10 (1). https://doi.org/10.16995/dscn.366.

Pedersen, Isabel, and Andrew Iliadis. 2020. *Embodied Computing: Wearables, Implantables, Embeddables, Ingestibles*. Cambridge, MA and London: MIT Press.

'Perrelet'. n.d. 19 January 2021. https://perrelet.com/en/content/14-history.

Picard, Rosalind W. 2000. *Affective Computing*. MIT Press.

Ridge, Mia, Donald Lafreniere, and Sisira Sarma. 2013. 'Creating Deep Maps and Spatial Narratives through Design'. *International Journal of Arts and Humanities Computing* 7 (1–2): 176–189.

Schwartz, Raz, and Germaine R. Halegoua. 2015. 'The Spatial Self: Location-Based Identity Performance on Social Media'. *New Media & Society* 17 (10): 1643–1660. https://doi.org/10.1177/1461444814531364.

Taylor, Joanna E. 2019. 'Mountain Matter(s): Anticipatory Cartography in Nineteenth-Century Mountain Literature'. In *Anticipatory Materialisms in Literature and Philosophy, 1790–1930*, edited by Jo Carruthers, Nour Dakkak, and Rebecca Spence, 23–44. Basingstoke: Palgrave Macmillan.

Taylor, Joanna E., and Ian N. Gregory. 2022. *Deep Mapping the Literary Lake District*. Lewisburg, PA: Bucknell University Press.

Tonra, Justin, Brian Davis, David Kelly, and Waqas Khawaja. n.d. 'Eververse'. Text. NUI Galway. Moore Institute @ NUI Galway. Global. 13 January 2021. https://eververse.nuigalway.ie.

Topol, Eric. 2015. *The Patient Will See You Now: The Future of Medicine Is in Your Hands*. New York: Basic Books.

'Wearable Tech Market Set to Grow'. 2020. *GlobalData* (blog). 13 August 2020. https://www.globaldata.com/wearable-tech-market-set-to-grow-137-by-2024-but-smartwatches-to-see-a-10-decline-in-revenue-this-year-due-to-shipment-delays-and-tighter-consumer-wallets-says-globaldata/.

'Wearable Wonderland: How Tech Is Tackling Covid-19'. 2020. Medical Technology. October 2020. https://medical-technology.nridigital.com/medical_technology_oct20/wearable_tech_covid-19.

Wordsworth, William. 1926. *The Prelude, or Growth of a Poet's Mind (1850)*. Edited by Ernest De Selincourt. Oxford: Oxford University Press.

———. 1967. *The Letters of William and Dorothy Wordsworth: The Middle Years: Pt. 2, 1812–1820*. Oxford: Clarendon P.

Zheng, Caroline Yan. 2017. 'Machinising Humans and Humanising Machines: Emotional Relationships Mediated by Technology and Material Experience'. In *Digital Bodies: Creativity and Technology in the Arts and Humanities*, edited by Susan Broadhurst and Sara Price, 111–127. Basingstoke: Palgrave Macmillan.

8
ARCHIVAL INTERFACE AND NATIONALIST MEMORIALIZATIONS OF 9/11

Dhanashree Thorat

In his work on archives and silences, Michel-Rolph Truillot writes that power not only informs "the moment of fact assembly" when the archive is constructed, but in fact "precedes the narrative proper, contributes to its creation and to its interpretation" (Truillot 29). Archives, as meaning-making systems, are instrumental in reproducing ideological orientations and narrativizing history while covering over that mediation. What emerges from the archive then appears to be a priori knowledge rather than a constructed narrative built from selected documents (Foucault 129). These cautionary reminders about the embedding of archival processes in asymmetrical power relations are important in this contemporary moment when digital archives have proliferated. Digital archiving has proven to be a scalable digital project, undertaken by private individuals or large educational institutions with varying socio-technical infrastructures. Historicizing and studying these exclusionary tendencies of the colonial archives is crucial so that they are not replicated in digital archives.

In this chapter, I trace these concerns with power, ideology, and memorialization in the September 11 Digital Archive, the largest 9/11-related archive today. The September 11 Digital Archive was founded in 2002 to "collect, preserve, and present the history of the September 11, 2001 attacks ... and the public responses to them" (About). Developed as a collaboration between the American Social History Project at City University of New York (CUNY) and the Roy Rosenzweig Center for History and New Media at George Mason University, the project has since been supported by a number of grants and institutional partners. In 2003, the Library of Congress incorporated the archive into its own permanent collection, marking the cultural significance of the archive and the implied necessity for its long-term preservation. Focusing not only on the content of the September 11 Digital Archive but also on the

DOI: 10.4324/9781003053880-9

socio-technical structure of the archive, I argue that the digitally mediated archival interface constructs a nationalist history presenting 9/11 as a national trauma and operationalizing a melancholic nostalgia about the role of white, male citizen heroes in aiding the recovery of the American nation-state.

First, I examine the emergence of two intertwined nationalist narratives, of 9/11 as a national trauma and of the 'citizen hero', by undertaking a chronological tracing of changes to the archive interface. Second, I read photographs in the First Responders sub-collection to show how the archive marks 9/11 as a schismatic event indelibly marking the national psyche. The narrative of the 'citizen hero' arises to ameliorate the effects of national trauma as it presents the nation with a unifying figure around whom the traumatized nation and its people can coalesce. The September 11 Digital Archive struggles to meet the conflicting pressures of a memorial space, which largely eulogizes victims, and a critical (digital) public sphere, where marginalized Muslims and other minoritized groups can speak of their encounters with racism after 9/11 due to jingoistic fervor. Instead, the archival interface acts as an extension and reflection of nationalist anxieties unfolding in American culture after 9/11. In performing a critical reading of archival structure, I take up Alan Liu's challenge to digital humanities scholars to read digital technologies and tools within the "register of society, economics, politics, or culture," and to bring the technical under the ambit of cultural criticism (Liu).

The structure of the digital archive (and not just the content of the archive) aids in the construction of this nationalist memorialization of 9/11. The material structure of the digital archive is the organizing framework which houses the content of the digital archive. This schema includes the underlying code and database which form the backbone of the archive. Structure also includes technical features, including capacities such as search and retrieval, hyperlinking, and metadata, which are those aspects that support and enhance the viewer's interaction with the archive. Finally, structure includes interface and design, which refer to the aesthetic and ideological choices made in the presentation of archival content. The material framework of the digital archive organizes the assembly of information in the archive and informs how that information is retrieved by users. This means that the socio-technical structure of a digital archive also plays a critical role in what Truillot identifies as the stage of narrative-making, as it mediates how marginalized subjects are re/presented as well as how the user/viewer accesses that re/presentation. I draw particularly on the work of Johanna Drucker (2011), Cynthia Selfe and Richard Selfe (1994), and Brenda Laurel (1990) on the aesthetic-ideological orientations of digital interfaces.

As digital archiving constitutes a major area of interest in digital humanities, libraries, and cultural heritage institutions, it is important to consider how the egalitarian potential of digital archives is constantly undermined by inequalities in infrastructure, lack of access to digital technologies, and uneven capacities to shape digital infrastructures, technologies, and spaces. Although digital archives that are open access and can be constructed with relatively few resources and technical skills promise to be more democratic than colonial archives, they are not inherently progressive or neutral. The September 11 Digital Archive, which has been termed as "virtual presence of collective memory shared by American people," operates as a socio-political space linked to the biopolitical regime of the American state and rooted in its racial anxieties (Zhang). While Benedict Anderson attributed print capitalism as the cause for the emergence of the nation-state, we must now examine those forms of digital media which support and recreate the contemporary nation-state today.

Reading the Interface of the September 11 Digital Archive

Reading the interface of the September 11 Digital Archive historically, since the archive went live in 2002, shows the gradual emergence of insular nationalist narratives, particularly of the citizen hero, after 9/11. Archival structure, and not just archival content, plays a key role in the hypervisibility of this one narrative until alternative narratives are buried. I read the interface as a techno-ideological space and a map of the underlying system. The interface makes interpretive choices about how to represent the system for the user. Studying the interface then presents a way to understand how underlying elements such as code, metadata, page design, hyperlinks, search features, and database structures are ideologically and politically constructed. For Drucker, the interface is "a zone of affordances organized to support and provoke activities and behaviors" where elements are grouped, separated, juxtaposed, highlighted, and organized in ways to compel the user's interaction with the system in specific ways (Drucker 7). Hidden underneath the interface, but informing it, are the logics of system structure and design which are, in turn, shaped by ideas of how knowledge should be represented in computational systems and cultural ideologies of design.

In the September 11 Digital Archive, the visual layout of the landing page and the Collections page indicates shifts in the operationalized meanings and memorializations of 9/11 in the (almost) 20 years since the attacks. Tracing the various iterations of the September 11 Digital Archive website through the Internet Wayback Machine since it was launched in 2002 shows how the narrative of the citizen hero gradually came to prominence. I use the term "citizen heroes" in the context of 9/11 attacks to refers to three groups: (1) civilians who died in the World Trade Center and Pentagon attacks, (2) the passengers who seized control of United Airlines 93 from the hijackers, and (3) first responders (firefighters, police, rescue workers, and others), including those who died during the early rescue efforts. As the term suggests, citizen heroes are average citizens who did something extraordinary during and after the 9/11 attacks. I call on this term to speak to the American search for heroes of 9/11, for a narrative of hope amidst the bleakness and horror of the tragedy. One op-ed published in October 2001 in *The New York Times* noted that "in the benumbed first days after Sept 11, America went on a hero hunt" to "balance out the grief" (Dubner). This cultural and political drive to produce heroes after 9/11 has been studied by scholars like Thomas Riegler, who wrote about the filmic tropes of 'citizen soldier' and 'heroic rescue worker' in films like *United 93* and *World Trade Center*. These tropes evince American myths of "average citizens rising to the challenge, while political and military command centers fail[ed] to grasp the situation" (Riegler 157, 158). As narratives of hope and uplift, they construct a shared identity around which the traumatized nation can rally.

The archival website has gone through a number of updates and changes that can be tracked through the Wayback Machine.[1] When the September 11 Digital Archive was published online in 2002, the narrative of the citizen heroes was one of several featured narrative under Special Collections (see Figures 8.1 and 8.2 of the landing page and Special Collections page). The website at that point had a landing page, which allowed users to browse the collection by *document type* (Email Repository and Image Repository), or through the featured Special Collections. The Special Collections page highlighted items, which had presumably been selected by the curators of the archive Highlighted video content, included a tribute to 9/11 heroes, a video on the impact of 9/11 on airline workers, Arab American responses to 9/11, and South Asian leaders addressing hate crimes. In other highlighted categories, the curators highlighted satire, comedy, calls for military retaliation, the Anthrax crisis, and digital artwork memorializing 9/11.

As this list indicates, the Special Collections page initially enshrined a diversity of responses ranging from hypernationalist responses to outrage about the civil rights violations of Muslims. Although tributes to victims and references to heroes was the first item at the top of the page, one of the advantages of this Special Collections page was that users were encouraged (by the layout of the page) to see that calls for retribution (against a broadly constructed and nebulous 'enemy') and the culture of fear visible in the Anthrax scares were linked to hate crimes against Muslims. These cultural narratives co-existed and informed each other. Moreover, the grouping of these items together on the interface allowed the reader to question how one narrative might shape another or affect public action. This Special Collections page from 2002 illustrates the importance of the visual layout of the interface combined with curatorial agency to the interpretation of archived materials. The archival interface reflected the curatorial decision to do determined outreach to ethnic and national groups. As Brier and Brown write, the archivists and historians creating this archive realized very early that digital submissions largely came from "white and middle class" individuals and groups and sought to "encompass a wide range of individual and collective responses" (105).

Towards the end of 2002, the website was updated, and one prominent shift was the apparent de-narrativization of the landing page. The link to the

Archival Interface of 9/11 **147**

THE SEPTEMBER 11 DIGITAL ARCHIVE

SAVING THE HISTORIES OF SEPTEMBER 11, 2001

The September 11 Digital Archive uses electronic media to collect, preserve, and present the history of the September 11, 2001 attacks in New York, Virginia, and Pennsylvania and the public responses to them. The Archive is working with the Smithsonian Institution's National Museum of American History, Behring Center; Museum of the City of New York; New-York Historical Society; City Lore; and other local and national institutions.

 current highlights

SEPTEMBER 11: BEARING WITNESS TO HISTORY

Help the Smithsonian commemorate the first anniversary of the terrorist attacks by sharing your September 11 experience. Submissions will be permanently archived in the September 11 Digital Archive and will be made available online on September 11, 2002, when the exhibition "September 11: Bearing Witness to History" opens at the National Museum of American History, Behring Center. [more]

VIDEO TRIBUTE

Three weeks after the attack, Paul Michael Gordon—a 20-year-old from Seattle—returned with his mother to her childhood neighborhood near the World Trade Center site. Moved by what he witnessed, Paul produced and directed this short video tribute to those he says are the "true heroes of our society." It has been nominated for a local Emmy Award.

The September 11 Digital Archive is funded by a major grant from the Alfred P. Sloan Foundation and organized by the American Social History Project at the City University of New York Graduate Center and the Center for History and New Media at George Mason University. Affiliated institutions include:

FIGURE 8.1 Landing Page in 2002.

Special Collections page disappeared from the main menu on the landing page, and this menu was now solely organized by *document type*: Stories, E-mails, Still Images, Moving Images, Audio, Documents. This absence of Special Collections was noteworthy as this was used previously by curators to feature particular stories and narratives about 9/11. Curatorial agency played an important role here in determining what was important and worthy of being highlighted, and this shift in the website layout curtailed curatorial power. In other words, the assembly and presentation of pre-formed narratives was removed from the archival interface and this new layout aspired to neutrality and objectivity. It appeared that, at least on the surface, the user now had more agency in navigating disparate items of the document type collections and deciding how to interpret and organize the material they could browse into distinct narratives and stories about 9/11.

It is likely however that the reader's interpretation of the event was still overdetermined by whatever material were already predominant in the archive. For

SPECIAL COLLECTIONS

Contact us about submitting document collections, digital creations, video, audio, or other unique materials that will help tell the history of 9/11 and its aftermath. You can also browse or search contributions in the public collection.

VIDEO

September 11 Hero Tribute
[video, Paul Michael Gordon, 2001, 2:41 minutes]
Three weeks after the attack, Paul Michael Gordon - a twenty year old from Seattle - returned with his mother to her childhood neighborhood near the World Trade Center site. Moved by what he witnessed, Paul produced and directed this short video tribute to those he says are the "true heroes of our society." It has been nominated for a local Emmy Award.

Salt Peanuts
[video, Labor at the Crossroads Productions, 2001, 4:56 minutes]
A five minute video about the impact of 9/11 on airline workers. An interview with former US Air flight Attendant Joshua Freeze (AFA) is juxtaposed with a dramatization concerning the recent government airline bailouts. "Salt Peanuts" was screened in December 2001 at the Museum of Modern Art and at the Art in General Gallery, both in New York City. Produced by Simin Farkhondeh and directed by Alonzo Speight.

Arab-American Responses
[video excerpt, sight sea productions, inc, 2001, 5:31 minutes]
In the days following the September 11th attacks, Mark Landsman and Tia Lessin interviewed a diverse group of residents of Bay Ridge, Brooklyn, a neighborhood that is home to a large middle-eastern immigrant community. The documentary captures both the immigrants' patriotism and their response to the hate attacks against them in the wake of 9/11. Email: lands@mindspring.com

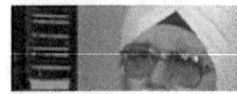

Raising Our Voices: South Asians Address Hate Crimes
[video excerpt, Omusha Communications, 2001, 1:45 minutes]
Sponsored by South Asian American Leaders of Tomorrow, this 25

FIGURE 8.2 Special Collections page in 2002.

example, the archive has always had a larger sample size of self-submitted testimonies than newspaper articles, of photographs of the Twin Towers than of the Pentagon, of American responses to 9/11 than of international ones. The user's arbitrary navigation through the archive would likely yield, in probabilistic terms, those narratives, ideas, and documents, which were over-present at the moment of "fact assembly" (Truillot 29). The invisible structural logic of the archive would continue to shape the reader's understanding of 9/11, even when the interface presented a seemingly unbiased visual choices and browsing structure.

In 2007, six years after the attacks, the website was updated again and the changes now reflected an increasing urgency in preserving memories of the attacks. The digital archive's orientation as a space for collective mourning became more emphasized with these changes. Special Collections returned to the main website layout, and again presented narrativized topics, mostly concerned with witnessing and testifying. These sub-collections under Special Collections, again selected by curators, included material acquired from the Smithsonian and the Library of Congress as well as user-submitted photographs and other digital items. Highlighted sub-collections included "Bearing Witness to History," "Here is New York," "Witness and Response," and "Voices of Chinatown." The re-emergence of this topic-oriented Special Collections included the narrative of the citizen hero. These sub-collections fall under the genre of the testimonial (as indicated in phrases like "bearing witness"), with citizens reflecting on their experiences of 9/11 and recording them for posterity. The testimonial also offers space for grieving the losses of 9/11. By reading the testimonies of other traumatized subjects, users can cope with the tragedy of the event collectively and within the bounds of the imagined community that constitutes the nation. In general, the very names of these collections reflect a broader concern that memories of the attacks were fragile and in need of preservation.

In 2014, the Special Collections page was updated again, and the changes again emphasized the importance of testimony and bearing witness to national trauma. The new page, now called "Collections," was organized by a mix of *document type* (e.g., Video), *source of content* (e.g., Library of Congress), and *topic* (e.g., First Responders). The curatorial choices in selecting this relatively arbitrary organization are unclear. The First Responders collection and the September 11: Bearing Witness to History Exhibition collection stand out here because they are the only remaining collections which are organized around thematic content.

The 2014 update shapes the user's perception of 9/11 by further making narratives of trauma and of the citizen hero hypervisible. First, 9/11 is upheld as a historic event for the nation-state, and Americans are drafted into the subject position of the "witness." By evoking "witnesses" to this traumatic event, the archive creates national subjects who are both affected by the event and yet somewhat distanced from it. The term enfolds the related subject position of the "victim" of trauma, but gives that subject the distance needed to reflect on the event. Kali Tal's observation that trauma survivors experience "the urge to bear witness, to carry the tale of horror back to the halls of 'normalcy' and to testify to the people the truth of their experience" stands true in this case (Tal 120). Although the traumatic event defies adequate representation in language, the survivor experiences a responsibility to narrate it nonetheless. In the context of the digital archive, viewers of 9/11 and its aftermath are pressed into service as witnesses tasked with the role of preserving their memories of the event, as a part of their contract to the nation-state.

By bearing witness and offering their testimony, citizens engage in the construction of a national memory and of an emergent historiography of 9/11. Such recitation and repetition is crucial not only in consolidating historiography, but also in the amalgamation of the archive itself. Derrida poses repetition as a necessary archival impulse to protect against the destructive force of the death drive (*Archive Fever* 14). If the archive exerts an archontic power, to name the law and consign or gather signs, in other words, engage in knowledge production, the death drive is anarchontic as it incites "forgetfulness, amnesia and the annihilation of memory" (10, 14). This anarchontic force is situated at the very heart of the archive and destabilizes its consignment. Repetition, as it occurs in the September 11 Digital Archive to shore up national memories, forms a corrective against this destructive force, affirming the archive's knowledge production processes and the knowledge authorized by the archive.

In late 2016, the Collections layout shifted again and the current website largely maintains those changes. This new layout whittled down collections organized around thematic content again. The collection on "September 11: Bearing Witness to History exhibition" has been removed, leaving only the First Responders as a topical idea on the browsing page. The other collections are either organized by *genre, type*, or *source of content*. While these other collections ask the user to browse and understand 9/11 on their own, the continuing presence of the First Responders collection presents a pre-formed narrative: that first responders, who are among the group counted as citizen heroes, as more crucial to understanding 9/11 than any other group of individuals affected by 9/11. The search for heroes noted by editorials in *The Washington Post* and *New York Times* in 2001 continues to be echoed in this archival space in 2020 in these aesthetic choices. This layout does not feature, for example, stories about New Yorkers, memorials to those who died in the attacks, Muslims who faced prejudice and racism, and other groups whose stories could be considered part of the memory of 9/11. Neither is the presence of these archival documents suggested by the interface and menu choices.

It is useful here to think of the interface of the digital archive as a "contact surface" that maintains a "balance of power and control" (Laurel xii). The interface is built atop the code for a non-technical user who cannot directly engage with the system at the level of code. The interface directs the user's experience of the archive by determining what the user can access and how the user accesses content. Due to the important role that the interface plays in use experience, Cynthia Selfe and Richard Selfe write that computer interfaces should be "mapped as complex political landscapes" that define border spaces (481). Borders are points of contact, but they also foreclose meetings and hinder circulation. This metaphor of the border is particularly amenable to the digital archive because the interface shapes what the user looks at, and both helps and hinders access to particular material. In the case of the 9/11 Digital Archive, the interface, particularly the layout and organization of the Collections page, reveals contested national narratives about 9/11. The archival interface tracks and responds to shifts in public memory while also playing a role in how 9/11 is remembered and shaping its meaning for the public.

While the regular updates to the website highlight that connection between interface and nationalist memorialization, the current form of the website presents another example of how layout informs interpretation and is, in turn, informed by public shifts in discourse. As it stands, the layout contains an apparent paradox: the hypervisibility of citizen heroes contrasts with the gradual disappearance of overt trauma narratives on the Collections page. Collection names that invoked "witnessing" are no longer prominent on the main collections page. Almost 20 years since the attacks, the psychic wound has become submerged in the collective national unconscious, even as its presence is indicated by the need for the narrative of the citizen hero.

While the national memory of 9/11 has moved into institutional spaces for codification (the memorial in New York, digital archives, state legislation like the PATRIOT Act, etc.), its public presence (in films, books, pop culture) has become somewhat muted until events like anniversary celebrations or the invocation of 9/11 era laws becomes public focus again. By enacting this shift in the location of memory, the memorialization of 9/11 is entrusted to hegemonic institutions for safe-keeping precisely so it can erased from the public consciousness. Thus, the security state apparatus constructed after 9/11 can become normalized in American society even as the events which called it into being become removed from public attention. Recently, the COVID-19 pandemic has accelerated this shift – the loss of life due to the 9/11 attacks is now compared to the number of Americans who have died due to COVID-19. This evokes not the national trauma of 9/11, but rather minimizes the impact of 9/11 on American life in comparison to the pandemic.

By shifting focus away from the wound, mythologization upholds celebratory ideas about the resilience of the American nation exemplified by its citizen heroes while covering over the initial traumatic loss. The hypervisibility of the citizen heroes in this updated Collections menu is part of the mythologization that Tal deems as a strategy of cultural coping (6). Mythologization, she writes, "works by reducing a traumatic event to a set of standardized narratives … turning it from a frightening and uncontrollable event into a contained and predictable narrative" (6). This process of codification reduces the traumatic event to recognizable narratives, tropes, and symbols. While the traumatic event cannot be contained entirely, as it extends past psychic capabilities of assimilation, the standardized narratives resulting from mythologization allow traumatized subjects to begin coping with the event.

National Trauma and the First Responders Collection

Thus far, my analysis of the interface of the September 11 Digital Archive indicates prevalent narratives about trauma and citizen heroes in the visual layout of the Collections menu. To pursue the specific ways in which these narratives are developed and their psychic function in the American cultural imaginary, the contents of the First Responders Collection offer a suitable site of study. The First Responders Collection, as noted above, is prominently featured on the Collections page, and it is the only collection that explicitly refers to a group of people affected by 9/11. Its prominent placement suggests that first responders are crucial to the cultural imaginary of 9/11, and users who want to learn more about 9/11 should engage with the experiences of this group of people. The collection mainly houses action plans and reports about the clean-up efforts at Ground Zero, emergency medical technician (EMT) photos at Ground Zero for a length of time after 9/11, and messages and photos thanking the first responders.

The photographs, namely the "EMT photos at Ground Zero," are an ideal site to examine the valorization of first responders for a number of reasons. Perhaps because 9/11 was one of the most visualized tragedies in the contemporary world, the digital archive overall contains thousands of images collected from other institutions and self-submitted by users. The EMT photos also promise unfiltered access, first-hand and close-up, to the tragedy at the site of the World Trade Center. Drawing on Susan Sontag's assertion that photographs enable viewers to have "an imaginary possession of a past that is unreal ... [and] to take possession of space in which they are insecure," I argue that these EMT photos offer users a means of juxtaposing the past glory of the World Trade Center towers in the New York skyline against the traumatic wound marked on the site after 9/11 (Sontag 9). In this section, I show that the valorization of first responders, while expected given their work after 9/11, constructs rescue work as gendered labor, mainly open to white men, and occludes the tensions within the respective organizations (especially the Fire Department of New York) over their racial and gender gatekeeping efforts.

In the "EMT photos at Ground Zero" sub-collection, most of the photos appear to depict not workers but wreckage, and evoke repetition, a trope of trauma narratives. These photos record Ground Zero as a wound in the psychic fabric of the nation and a scar in the material landscape of New York. As the photos were taken by an EMT who helped with rescue efforts after 9/11, they show not only workers at Ground Zero but also the workers' perspective of working at Ground Zero as a monumental endeavor. The photographs capture the harsh and discouraging work that workers faced at Ground Zero as it became clear that live victims would not be found in the rubble. In a large set of these photos, the rubble is always set in the background but it looms over the miniscule subjects in the foreground. The sheer heat and violence which brought the buildings down is visible in the metal, which is shorn, bent, and broken into unrecognizable parts. The smoke rising over the rubble is ominous, and signals how recently the towers came down and the dangers incipient in the rescue and clean-up efforts. The debris shown in the photographs is itself a site of horror as it contains the remains of those who were not able to escape the collapsing towers. The first responders' efforts at clean-up are not then as straightforward as they appear to be, and the photographs draw the spectator into gazing at the horrors of the site cordoned off from public viewing at the physical site in New York. Yaeger explains that this debris is "frightening and animated" as it begs a haunting question of the spectator and of the first responders: "Is it rubble or body part?" (Yaeger in Trauma at Home 191).

The indistinct boundaries between the two become apparent in the fact that powdered debris was collected and offered to victims' families in urns. The sacralized dust becomes the only remaining trace of human bodies, and at the same time, human remains face the possibility of being reduced to dust and carted from the site as debris. Yaeger thus imbues the debris with the "power of the uncanny" as it shifts and assumes different meanings: rubbish to be cleared away, hallowed matter handled respectfully, a contaminating and polluting agent for the living, and a weapon capable of killing (190, 191). In the context of the photographs, the debris constitutes what Barthes might label as the 'punctum, meaning a "wound, this prick, this mark made by a pointed instrument" (Barthes 26–27). The punctum is experienced on the affective register, and it disturbs and punctuates the studium which is recorded on the cultural, historical, and political register on which an image might be read. The uncanny nature of the debris, as the punctum of the photographs, stems from the fact that it draws the viewer's attention even when the cause of that lingering is unknown.

With the added implication of its constitutive elements, the looming debris in the photographs takes on darker overtones as it becomes apparent that the first responders were not dealing solely with debris, but with this fused horror of inanimate-animate matter. The first responders cleared away, trod upon, and even inhaled this in/animate matter, subsuming its horrors onto themselves. In relation to the horrifying symbols contained within the debris, the first responders are variously rescue workers, clean-up crew, interlopers and exhumers on a burial site, and mediators between the external world and the horrors of Ground Zero. Their role as mediators is particularly significant, because they screen the nation from further traumatization and sanitize the site of Ground

Zero until it can be re-opened for public consumption. They are charged with removing the material signs of a psychic wound, until the wound is rendered invisible, and present only in its absence. The September 11 Digital Archive itself performs this same function through its interface: allowing users to cope with the trauma of the event through witnessing and testimony until those collections slowly disappear from the browsing menu.

The wound is a reminder of the new-found vulnerability of the nation-state and the loss of life linked with 9/11. Several scholars have since defined the Ground Zero site as an absence; Greenberg calls the site "an enormous, smoldering … hole of the missing," while Stamelman terms it a void that must be filled with meaning and narrative (Greenberg 25, Stamelman 15). As a traumatic wound, the site resists closure or healing and compels the return of the spectator to witness loss. Dozens of photos capture the site of the wound from different perspectives, angles, and at different times of the day, in an attempt to contain the monumentality of the event which escaped psychic assimilation. Some photos pan the site widely to capture its size, while others zoom in on the chaos of the rubble. Such repetition is part of the aftermath of trauma: because the traumatic event fails to be assimilated into the subject's consciousness at the moment of occurrence, it repeats "itself, exactly, unremittingly, through the unknowing acts of the survivor and against his very well" (Caruth 2). The photographs represent that unconscious impetus to return to the site of the trauma and the struggle to cope with it.

Traumatized subjects can then revisit a personal and national wound together and attempt to make sense of it. The debris-littered site evokes not only the traumatic wound, but also the nostalgia for an idealized time before the traumatic event when the towers were still standing and an iconic representation of New York's status as a global capital of finance. And if the traumatic event disrupts signification and psychic assimilation, then the photograph presents an opportunity to grapple with the event. These photographs of the wreckage also suggest a temporal rupture, as the user is locked into the past, in a never-ending repetition of 9/11 and its immediate aftermath. A future without the traumatic event cannot be fully imagined within the scope of these photos as they maintain the effects of 9/11 in suspended animation: the photos only document, after all, early clean-up efforts rather than picturing the site after the clean-up was completed. Within the bounds of the collection, the clean-up effort is never-ending, and the site of the wound remains raw, open, and covered in debris. The relative bleakness of this vision of the past and its looming impact on the future is partially offset, however, by the workers who appear in the images.

When first responders are present in most of the images in this sub-collection, they are so dwarfed by the scale of the smoldering wreckage that surrounds them that they are recognizable only by their bright safety clothing and they appear not to be valorized at all. The perspective of the photographs indicates the vast scope of the work facing the first responders. Barely distinguishable from the rubble, the workers become part of the rubble, of the violence and tragedy of the event. The workers are rendered so small in comparison to the size of the rubble that their usefulness is also called into question. The photographs only record in absentia the shock, dismay, and helplessness that workers might have experienced in the immediate days after 9/11 when they confronted the task before them. It was not time yet for the workers to process or record their own emotions, or perhaps the workers temporarily deflect a confrontation with traumatic emotions by investing themselves in Ground Zero. In the photos with the looming rubble, the workers lack any individuality, and individual differences are coded as unimportant in comparison to the tragedy they are a part of.

Such lack of individuality is not at odds though with the celebratory rhetoric around the first responders, as this rhetoric does not rely on individualized portraiture or narratives. Rather, it is the work performed by the first responders collectively that forms the core of the celebratory rhetoric around citizen heroes. Even though they are confronted by this enormous labor, the workers are undaunted and continue to work away at the rubble. When workers are portrayed in close-up photographs, they are generally depicted at work or in motion. The workers embody a sense of purpose and intensity, even though their actions in the photograph appear to be small or mundane. One worker is shown in a ruined corridor scrubbing or marking a pillar. Another photograph shows workers amidst medical stretchers and boxes with trucks and an ambulance in the background. This photo foregrounds two workers who are walking past each other in opposite directions. One of them wears an American flag pinned to their safety hat and is captured midstride in the photograph. The workers never look at the camera (or the viewer), but they look evenly ahead or up, and never down at the ground. Their forward gaze into an unseen future directs attention away from the traumatic gash on the ground, which anchors the nation in the present moment and hinders progress towards imagining a future without trauma. There are no posed portraits, as though to suggest that the work to be done at Ground Zero is too important and serious to draw the workers' attention away from it.

The collection favors the depiction of blue-collar workers. Working willingly in a dangerous work environment, these workers offer their labor to the nation, for the eventual rebuilding of the site, and of America. Clearing the rubble is an act of faith and an investment in the future of the nation. When the workers are individually distinguishable, they appear to be coded as male and white. The workers are also marked in terms of work and nationality. The safety clothing and uniform reflects the kind of work they performed at the site of the wound. The presence of the American flag on their uniforms or in their immediate surroundings putatively marks them as American. The iconography of the flag on or around the workers is significant in their mythologization as

American heroes. The ubiquitous presence of the flag asks readers to put aside the other aspects of their identity in favor of asserting an American identity and national unity during a troubled time.

It is perhaps not unusual that a digital collection devoted to First Responders will, to some extent, mythologize their efforts during and after the 9/11 attacks. These workers did risk their lives and continued to work in dangerous conditions. Their work is commendable, and that there is a concerted attempt to document their efforts and preserve this record for posterity is to be expected. The issue, however, is that this narrative of the citizen hero is repeated in other collections in the digital archive to the occlusion of other narratives of 9/11. There is digital artwork commemorating rescue workers, audio and video content discussing the bravery of these heroes, and photos of ash-covered firemen across all the collections (especially in User Submitted Content Collection, in various Photography sub-collections, and the tenth Anniversary Collection). In the commemorative space of the digital archive, the narrative of first responders as citizen heroes and its recuperative function for national trauma dominates other possible avenues of understanding 9/11.

As pre-eminent American symbols, these workers are celebrated and mourned by the public at large. Graffiti, artwork, thank you letters, and pictures of street memorials, which are included in the digital collection, issue a call to "never forget" the loss of citizen heroes in the 9/11 attacks. In other words, viewers are instructed on who is constituted as worthy of being celebrated and mourned after 9/11. Judith Butler's questions about the bounds of empathy are particularly resonant here when she asks, "Who counts as human? Whose lives count as lives? And finally, [what] makes for a grievable life?" (Butler 20). Butler's questions suggest that mourning is premised on the attachment of personhood and value to a life. The category of the "victim" or the "hero" is not given a priori to the nation. Rather, it is constituted in various collective space (public and virtual), such as the September 11 Digital Archive which collects the necessary documents for the formation of these categories in relation to post-9/11 America.

The terrorist attacks on American soil disrupted the idea of the home(land) as a safe space and raised national anxieties about the American empire, specifically the possible decline of American global power and the diminishing of the cultural brand of America. The narrative of the citizen hero recuperates these anxieties by suggesting that common civilians, with their uncowed spirit and acts of courage, form the nucleus of the American nation-state. The nation borrows strength from their actions during a vulnerable time. Riegler's term, "citizen soldiers," evokes the interpellation of citizens into the military order of the state, to take offensive and defense actions to protect the nation, and to even sacrifice their lives to protect the American way of life. The term suggests that the state is capable of militarizing all its citizens in times of war and deploy them to protect itself.

The citizen heroes of 9/11 perform in multiple capacities as citizens, heroes, victims, soldiers, and sacrifices. David Simpson comments on the congruency of these subject positions when they are collapsed together in his work on commemorative narratives of 9/11. He argues that civilians have been interpellated as heroes to create patriotic icons for the wounded nation to mourn. In particular, he notes that the civilian dead of 9/11 "have been made to figure in grander narratives of national futures and civic virtues" (Simpson 29). As such, they were "at once victims and heroes, those who made a sacrifice and who were the objects of a sacrifice invented by others in the aftermath of their deaths" (49). These civilians had not volunteered their lives for a patriotic cause, but they became patriots in death – implicitly American, even though they represented many different nationalities. Their sacrifices bring the nation together in collective mourning and eventually, in collective retribution.

Further, the celebratory rhetoric of this narrative covers over issues of race and gender within the institutions represented in the photographs and in America. For instance, there are almost no photos or other forms of documentation that specifically document and draw attention to women firefighters who were also involved in rescue efforts after 9/11. The documents in the digital archive reiterate rescue work as a gendered labor, which is open mostly to men. As the Franklin photograph (of the three white firefighters raising the flag) further shows, rescue work is crafted as the domain of white men. The New York City Fire Department (FDNY) has historically been white, and over the years it has faced accusations of discriminating against non-white applicants. In the September 11 Digital Archive, these racial tensions are rendered invisible because the emphasis after 9/11 was to stand as a united nation and celebrate firefighters. Connor writes in a related context that these heroic visualizations of the FDNY reiterated the historical ascription of heroism to white men after 9/11 (95). Since most of the documents in this archive come from the early and mid-2000s, what is also missing from the celebratory discourse around the rescue workers is that many of them suffered from health issues related to their 9/11 rescue work. As public and state attention turned away, these workers now suffer in relative obscurity.

Conclusion

The hypervisibility of the citizen heroes in the September 11 Digital Archive, who are mostly white, male, and American, raises troubling concerns about whose trauma is articulated within the archive, and the possible limitations of the persistent national trauma narrative of 9/11. As a memorial space, the digital archive codes 9/11 as a loss that is felt individually and nationally. That this same ideological construction of national trauma is reflected across different genres and national spaces is to be expected as these sites support the imagined community that is the nation. Writing about this framing of the American nation-state and its citizens as victims of trauma, Bennett notes that it is crucial to interrogate "the imagined political boundaries of victim communities and of their exclusionary effects." If this trauma is defined around the American nation-state and its citizens, is there scope to understand the trauma of citizens in Iraq and Afghanistan due to the wars following 9/11? Can Muslims in America be framed as victims of racialized hate crimes, if victimhood is selectively constructed by nationalist rhetoric? The digital archive cannot support the conflicting tendencies of a memorial space and the needs of a critical and self-reflexive space as a memorial, by definition, forestalls critique.

In the case of 9/11, these elisions can encourage a dangerous historical amnesia, rejecting reflection and accountability of the nation-state's reactionary policies and actions after 9/11. The digital archive is invested in the nationalist memorialization of 9/11 at several levels: it collects and consolidates material into collections and it presents those collections in particular visual form. In other words, the archive does not simply re-produce existing narratives of 9/11. Rather, it codifies and naturalizes selected narratives and preserves them for future generations. Just as the colonial archive was self-propagating – it emerged from that system which it simultaneously codified and brought into being – this digital archive reflects and reproduces the political, racial, and gendered ideologies of the American nation-state. In 2021, on the cusp of the 20th anniversary of the 9/11 attacks, the implications of this nationalist codification remain important. Even as the initial shock of 9/11 has faded from public memory and an entire generation has grown up in America since the attacks, the security state apparatus constructed after 9/11 remains in place and the racialized stereotypes about Muslims continue to be peddled in popular culture. Digital archives about 9/11 are uniquely positioned to contextualize and historicize these shifts to ensure a digital public sphere that enables critical and thoughtful conversation about 9/11 as a cultural touchstone in American memory and its continuing reverberations in American domestic and foreign policy.

Note

1 Images of the interface and photographs which correspond with the analysis below can be found on the writer's website (dhanashreethorat.com/research).

Works Cited

Anderson, Benedict R. O. G. *Imagined Communities: Reflections on the Origin and Spread of Nationalism*. 1983. Print.
Barthes, Roland. *Camera Lucida: Reflections on Photography*. New York: Hill and Wang, 1981.
Bennett, Jill. "The Limits of Empathy and the Global Politics of Belonging." *Trauma at Home*. Ed. Judith Greenberg. Nebraska: Nebraska UP, 2003. 132–139.
Brier, Stephen, and Joshua Brown. "The September 11 Digital Archive: Saving the Histories of September 11, 2001." *Radical History Review*. 111 (2011): 101–109.
Butler, Judith. *Precarious Life: The Powers of Mourning and Violence*. New York: Verso, 2004.

Caruth, Cathy. *Unclaimed Experience: Trauma, Narrative and History*. New York: Johns Hopkins Press, 1996.
Connor, Michan Andrew. "Real American Heroes: Attacking Multiculturalism through the Discourse of Heroic Sacrifice." *American Multiculturalism after 9/11: Transatlantic Perspectives*. Eds. Derek Rubin and Jaap Verheul. Amsterdam: Amsterdam UP, 2011.
Derrida, Jacques. "Diacritics." Trans. Eric Prenowitz. *Archive Fever: A Freudian Impression*. 25.2 (1995): 9–63.
Drucker, Johanna. "Humanistic Approaches to Interface Theory." *Culture Machine* 12 (2011): 1–20.
Dubner, Stephen J. "Looking for Heroes – and Finding Them." *The New York Times*. 6 October 2001. Accessed on 20 April 2017. https://www.nytimes.com/2001/10/06/opinion/looking-for-heroes-and-finding-them.html
Foucoult, Michel. *The Archaeology of Knowledge*. New York: Vintage, 1982.
Gardiner, Aidan. "Fire Dept. Doubles Minority and Female Applicants." *The New York Times*. 8 May 2012. Web. https://www.nytimes.com/2012/05/09/nyregion/new-york-fire-department-gains-minority-and-female-applicants.html. Accessed on 20 July 2017.
Greenberg, Judith. "Wounded New York." In *Trauma at Home*. Ed. Judith Greenberg. Nebraska: Nebraska UP, 2003. 21–38.
Laurel, Brenda. *The Art of Human-Computer Interface Design*. Addison-Wesley, 1990.
Liu, Alan. "Where Is Cultural Criticism in the Digital Humanities." *Debates in the Digital Humanities*. Ed. Matthew Gold. Minneapolis: U Minnesota P, 2012. 490–509.
Riegler, Thomas. "9/11 on the Screen: Giving Memory and Meaning to All that' Howling Space' at Ground Zero." *Radical History Review*. 111 (2002): 155–165.
Selfe, Cynthia, and Richard Selfe. "The Politics of the Interface: Power and Its Exercise in Electronic Contact Zones." *College Composition and Communication*. 45.4 (December 1994): 480–504.
September 11 Digital Archive: Saving the Histories of September 11, 2001. Roy Rosenzweig Center for History and New Media, 2002. Web. Accessed 1 April 2017.
Simpson, David. *9/11: The Culture of Commemoration*. Chicago: U of Chicago P, 2006.
Sontag, Susan. *On Photography*. London: Penguin Books. 1978.
Stamelman, Richard. "Between Memory and History." In *Trauma at Home*. Ed. Judith Greenberg. Nebraska: Nebraska UP, 2003. 11–20.
Stoler, Ann Laura. "Colonial Archives and the Arts of Governance." *Archival Science*. 2 (2002): 87–109.
Tal, Kali. *Worlds of Hurt: Reading the Literatures of Trauma*. New York: Cambridge UP, 1995.
Trouillot, Michel-Rolph. *Silencing the Past: Power and the Production of History*. Boston: Beacon Press, 1995.
Yaegar, Patricia. "Rubble as Archive, or 9/11 as Dust, Debris, and Bodily Vanishing." In *Trauma at Home*. Ed. Judith Greenberg. Nebraska: Nebraska UP, 2003. 187–194.
Waldman, Amy. "A Nation Challenged: Mementos; With Solemn Detail, Dust of Ground Zero Is Put in Urns." *The New York Times*. 15 October 2001. Web. https://www.nytimes.com/2001/10/15/nyregion/nation-challenged-mementos-with-solemn-detail-dust-ground-zero-put-urns.html. Accessed 20 April 2017.
Zhang, Jane. "Remembered History, Archival Discourse, and the September 11 Digital Archive." In *Society of American Archivists – Research Forum*. San Francisco. 2008. https://www2.archivists.org/publications/research-forum/2008

CONCLUSION

Digital Space and the Keyword

Daniel Punday

The concept of the keyword has emerged across a wide variety of disciplines. We can trace its modern usage back to Raymond Williams's 1976 *Keywords: A Vocabulary of Culture and Society*, but it was generalized by the 1990 *Critical Terms for Literary Study*. The idea embodied in this approach is that there are key concepts that organize a discipline, and that can be studied as an intersection of a variety of independent theoretical claims. *Narrative,* or *discourse,* or *representation*—to take some examples from *Critical Terms*—have a history whose meaning and variations are a vector for understanding the larger field of literary study.

It would seem that *space* within the field of digital narrative would function as a similar keyword. And yet as we look back on the chapters that have made up this collection, it is worthwhile to unpack some of the tensions and implications of this keyword approach. Williams's initial framing in *Keywords* emphasizes the generality of vocabulary. Williams tells the story of returning to the university after serving in World War II and being struck by the way that certain terms were being used:

> But I found myself being preoccupied by a single word, culture, which it seemed I was hearing very much more often: not only, obviously, by comparison with the talk of an artillery regiment of my own family, but by direct comparison within the university over just those few years. I had heard it previously in two senses: one at the fringes, in teashops and places like that, where it seemed the preferred word for a kind of social superiority, not in ideas or learning, and not only in money or position, but in a more intangible area, relating to behavior; yet also, secondly,

among my own friends, where it was an active word for writing poems
and novels, making films and paintings, working in theaters.

(12)

Williams's focus in *Keywords* is firmly on the common meaning of everyday language—the way that he hears terms being used in "teashops." And yet the way that such keywords have been framed subsequently has emphasized a very particular disciplinary orientation. Thomas McLaughlin opens *Critical Terms* with this example:

> Literary theory, which as a deserved reputation for its stylistic and conceptual difficulty, has escaped from the academy and become part of popular culture. "Deconstruction" is a word that gets used in *Newsweek*. A current British pop group, Scritti Pollitti, publishes its lyrics under the copyright of "Jouissance Music," adapting for their own purposes the term that the French critic Roland Barthes used to describe the pleasure of reading.
>
> *(1)*

McLaughlin frames these critical terms precisely by their disciplinary orientation, and the fact that they have escaped literary theory to become the subject of a *Newsweek* article or a pop band demonstrates the need to clarify their meaning. In the years since, we have seen a proliferation of keywords approaches that have followed a similar pattern in exploring the way that terms have accrued meaning within a disciplinary field. New York University Press has launched a whole book series of keywords for various fields. As they explain in the inaugural volume, *Keywords for American Cultural Studies*, the essays contained there will "synthesize a great deal of information about the historical and contemporary meanings of terms that will structure the fields of American studies and cultural studies" and "map the fissures and fault lines of the past, present, and future, treating the terms within it as sites of unresolved conflict and contestation" (1).

Although the emphasis in these kinds of keyword studies has been on disciplinary structure, other critics have been sensitive to the way that terms can move between fields. In *Traveling Concepts in the Humanities*, Mieke Bal explores the way that concepts "travel" between disciplines in the humanities. She opens with the example of the performative drawn from Jonathan Culler:

> the concept of the *performative*, travels first back and forth between philosophy—where the concept was first used—and literature—where it solved major problems but at the same time challenged the limitations of the philosophical proposal—then back to philosophy, on to cultural studies, and back to philosophy again.
>
> *(4)*

Bal's account of these travels is more sophisticated than the keyword model, which looks inward to the configuration of a single discipline. But at the same time, this traveling metaphor takes for granted a certain kind of stability for these various fields: philosophy, literature, cultural studies each have their own dynamics and identity, which allows the word performative to then take on a different meaning and have particular effects in this new environment. As she writes:

> after returning from your travels, the object constructed turns out to be no longer be the 'thing' that so fascinated you when you chose it. It has become a living creature, embedded in all the questions and considerations that the mud of your travels spattered onto it, and that surround it like a 'field'.
>
> *(4)*

Instead of Bal's traveling metaphor, it might be more productive to invoke Bruno Latour's idea of the contingent nature of groups and the controversies that reveal their temporary nature. He explains how we are "enrolled" in groups:

> For ANT [actor network theory], if you stop making and remaking groups, you stop having groups. No reservoir flowing from "social forces" will help you. For sociologists of the social, the rule is order while decay, change, or creation are the exceptions. For the sociologists of associations, the rule is performance and what has to be explained, the troubling exceptions, are any type of stability over the long term and on a larger scale. It is as if, in the two schools, background and foreground are reversed.
>
> *(35)*

The idea here is the groups are formed through temporary "associations" and that the work of those associations is ongoing rather than assuming a ground of disciplinary stability in which individuals choose to join a group. This is the essential insight that Latour brings to the language around keywords. As a critical concept, keywords work to explain and organize a stable discipline; indeed, this is why the concept is so useful in a classroom context, since introducing students to keywords is in and of itself a method by which they can come to understand the field and its dynamics. Even Bal's more complex notion of concepts that travel between disciplines assumes that there are stable boundaries that we can use to understand when a concept "leaves" or "returns." Latour, in contrast, would see this sort of keyword approach as itself a component of establishing "associations" that can change and evolve over time. Indeed, it allows us to reframe Bal's notion of traveling as itself a matter of "making and remaking groups," of constantly negotiating the boundaries of disciplines.

This kind of negotiation of boundaries is on full display in this collection, and we can see the power and effects of this movement from chapter to chapter. Marie-Laure Ryan's introduction provides a framework for the essays that follow by extending theoretical work grounded narrative theory and digital media to generalize about space as a whole. I would suggest that this synthetic work depends on a certain kind of analogy between disciplines. She opens with Joseph Frank's famous concept of spatial form, which itself is an example of this kind of work by analogy. She describes Frank's essay as describing how some works are "constructing a network of relations— semantic, phonic, visual, thematic—between elements separated in the temporal flow of discourse" (1). In the debates that have followed around Frank's work, many critics have questioned the term "spatial" here, since it gathers together a variety of organizational principles that appear to work against the temporality of the text, but aren't themselves necessarily spaces.[1] After all, to what extent is a network a space? Ryan, then, naturally links this organizational "space" to the more literal "typographical realization of language and the arrangement of words on the page" (2). She makes a similar analogy in discussing the "architecture of the underlying code that controls the navigation of the user through a digital text" (3), where a somewhat metaphorical understanding of the design of a digital work is articulated in more explicitly spatial terms as an "architecture" that then allows her to link the underlying code of these works to the spatiality of the page and the literal real-world spaces that she discusses around locative narrative and even plaques that commemorate events during World War II.

In pointing out the way that these analogies work, I am not of course criticizing Ryan's introduction. In fact, I would argue that her essay is the ideal place for this collection to begin because it captures the intellectual movement of terms between contexts and disciplines. I would go further and say that the functioning of a "keyword" like *space* is only possible because it depends on these analogies that stretch it into different contexts. When we review any common keyword collection today, we are struck by exactly this tension: that the terms mentioned are keywords precisely because they are not jargon in the traditional sense. If we compare the contents of a keyword book like *Keywords for American Cultural Studies* to a more traditional technical dictionary like Gerald Prince's *Dictionary of Narratology*, what we are struck by is that the former depends on terms that are used in a variety of ways across fields: *normal, rural, finance, marriage*. Prince's *Dictionary*, by contrast, is full of technical terms that have no usage outside of the field: *analepsis, free indirect discourse, heterodiegetic narrative*. The functioning of a keyword, even within an inward-looking book like *Keywords for American Cultural Studies*, depends on tension with other non-disciplinary uses of these same terms.

As an exploration of a single term that moves between a variety of disciplines, we would expect that the discussion of space in this volume would look different from either of these two types of work. Unlike Ryan's introduction, the contributors in the essays that follow do not depend as much on the work of analogy that creates a synthesis between different kinds of fields and usages. Instead, what we can see is that as this term moves across fields—from literary tourism through locative narratives and 9/11 memorials—the spatiality of this space takes on different flavors without insisting on the synthetic links that Frank's essay so well embodies. The effect of these various flavors, I would argue, allows us to see the tensions within our ideas of digital space that are often suppressed within essays and collections that try to create coherence and unity. In the remainder of this conclusion, I want to focus on seven main tensions that I argue define the nature of the interdisciplinary use of digital space.

Bodies

One of the central topics that emerges in this volume that falls outside of Ryan's introduction is the issue of the body that navigates these spaces. It's not hard to see how the body was marginal to Ryan's introduction, since she begins with Frank's abstract idea of a spatial form in narrative and moves on to the physical form of the book. Later, in her introduction, she turns to some issues that invokes corporeality when she addresses locative narrative and the kinds of physical spaces of the landscape, but the topic of the body remains more implicit than explicit.

The way that the body structures our experience of digital spaces is, however, essential in several of the chapters in this volume. Taylor and Donaldson are most central in identifying the body as a crucial gap in the way that we think about mapping, of "Re-inserting the body into geographical discussion" (126). Looking at space through the physical experience of movement is, as they show, a crucial element of our modern forms of digital tracking of the "high definition human" (130) that we can assemble by knowing things like "heart rate, oxygen saturation, stress levels, activity levels, footsteps, and—via GPS chips—location" (130). This information is of course fully digital—Dorothy Wordsworth's analog pedometer aside (127)—and yet this kind of data about corporal experience has largely been absent from our analysis of other forms of locative narrative, which are almost always based on Global Positioning System (GPS) location. Taylor and Donaldson reveal that beginning from a different understanding of the digital information based in space, one based in the physical experience of the body rather than a purely cartographic one, reveals an entirely different way to construct the digital spaces.

Gregory Whistance-Smith similarly centers the body, albeit to very different effect. Body focusing on the "walking simulator," Whistance-Smith reveals the way that models of corporality as built into digital spaces that, on first glance, might seem cartographic in a more abstract sense. As he writes at the outset of his chapter:

How do structures of embodied spatial experience inform the ways that readers engage with walking simulators and interpret their narratives? This article proposes an approach for analyzing walking simulators' expressive worlds using theories of embodied cognition, an emerging multidisciplinary field which argues that cognition is grounded in the body's interactions with its environment.

(50)

That corporeality as an element is, in retrospect, surprisingly under-examined in our thinking about topics like "spatial form," which usually works by removing the physical location of the reader (or character) for the sake of an abstract structure of meaningful relations. Indeed, we might say that spatial form itself depends on a lack of corporeal location that makes possible the apprehension of these networked relations. To grasp the spatial form of the text, we need to be outside the time of reading and the particular physical perceptions of page.

Both of these disciplinary orientations—the mapping of physical experience via personal data trackers and the conceptual models through which we make sense of spaces—depart from the cartographical orientation of our thinking about digital spaces. Indeed, there is something about the body that itself resists the models of the "architecture" of code or spatial forms, and that provides an opening for a radically different set of "associations" that we can form with disciplines to understand digital spaces.

Mapping

Taylor and Donaldson's critique of the cartographical orientation of our thinking about space raises the issue of the activity of mapping itself. As that critique implies, it is easy to see cartography as a matter that merely reveals the nature of space. Indeed, one way to think about Ryan's fourth type of space, the mimetic space of the storyworld, is as a confirmation of the kind of mapping that she discusses around the *Cartographer's Confession*, which she describes as a story about a "boy's attempt to manage both the city and his loss by becoming a cartographer and ultimately by confronting the part of his history that has caused him pain" (13).

Paul Wake's chapter picks up this thread on the activity of mapping that Ryan invokes. His focus is on the creation of maps as an activity in and of itself rather than focusing simply on the spaces that those maps reveal. Indeed, he evokes Ryan's discussion of mapping as comprehension in *Narrative Space/Spatializing Narrative* before unpacking an unlikely undertone: this "shifts attention from approaches that validate maps in terms of their interpretative force towards their potential to support immersion" (71). He shows that the creation of maps themselves reflects certain ways of using these digital and analog texts, distinguishing between database texts and "folk maps," which are "are expressions of unique encounters with the geography of a text's storyworld" (78). As he explains,

"Connecting games and their player-cartographers, these maps are 'private' paratexts, the creation of which is central to, and a vital expression of, the gameplay experience" (80). Such private paratexts will remind us of the way that Taylor and Donaldson represent the experience of movement across the landscape through physical data of heart rate and steps. In both cases, it is the activity that arises from our encounter with space that is central rather than some abstraction about the space itself. More broadly, we can see that focus on usage as itself a confirmation of Latour's emphasis on temporary associations that emerge within disciplines. Mapping is an activity that takes particular forms based on different communities, through which relations are formed. This is, of course, the point on which Wake ends his chapter, evoking Latour explicitly: "mapmaking initiates a series of relationships, placing players within networks of objects that form and reform, decentering the imaginative world of the text and exploring the fluidity of the constellation of author, text, reader and world" (84).

We see a similar theme emerge in other chapters as well. David Ciccoricco's chapter on literary tourism draws attention to the role of "fandom" in our use of literary spaces:

> Much of the scholarly focus on literary cartography is directed at the relationship between a fictional place and an actual map, for example, the practice of mapping a single novel per se, whether that practice is undertaken by a scholar as a function of critical analysis or by a reader as an expression and extension of their fandom.
>
> *(110)*

This emphasis on the use of spaces, and the way that individuals can write their experiences and stories on to them, is one thread that promises to move the discussion of digital narrative spaces in new directions. And those, in turn, help to build and extend communities. As Ciccoricco writes:

> Anecdotes themselves mediate, regardless of their medium. They mediate not only between past and present, but also between literary and popular culture. In their portability and accessibility, they are a literary form that can be said to serve an inherently socializing or communitizing role. They are not sealed off in academic (con)texts or academic classrooms but instead extend out into and cut across communities.
>
> *(117)*

Coherence

Astrid Ensslin makes an important contribution to our thinking about digital space by drawing attention to the fact that so much of our thinking about space depends on the search for coherence, through the kinds of mapping that Wake describes, or the way that Whistance-Smith develops a model of bodily experience into digital spaces. But Ensslin makes clear that spatial impossibilities are an important part of these texts as well. In particular, she notes that even seemingly mimetic narratives that seek to be immersive depend on impossible spatial elements: "spatial and gravitational impossibilities and other types of immersive and mechanically challenging non-mimetic structures form an integral part of the imaginative and interactive appeal of blockbuster game design" (24).

In particular, she notes the way that we depend on "conventionalization and naturalization" to make contradictions in digital spaces less disruptive. Her discussion of *The Pickle Index* explores an intentionally anti-mimetic digital fiction, but the broader point has far-reaching implications: the "constructedness" of digital works means that there will always be an incoherence in the space of these works. To take an example from Whistance-Smith, for all that we import a model of corporeality into the fictional world of these "walking simulators" that coherence depends on ignoring the corporeality of touching the keyboard and mouse. Different kinds of works can make reference to their constructedness, and one way of thinking about Wake's chapter on the topic of player mapmaking is that it is emphasizing the activity of constructing maps for particular purposes and by particular people. Most of the time our emphasis is on techniques that allow these digital narratives to seem "natural" and draw our attention away from these incoherences, but the potential for quite the opposite approach is an important and somewhat under-explored component of work on digital spaces.

Data

Going back to Ciccoricco's chapter, it is hard not to be struck by the way his discussion of the literary anecdote extends our understanding of the data that organizes our experience of digital space. The locative narratives discussed by Brian Greenspan make the most obvious use of spatial data for narrative, but we have also seen that Taylor and Donaldson significantly expand our sense of spatial data by emphasizing the information recorded by our bodily experience of moving through spaces.

Ciccoricco links the anecdote as a "special, liminal case, not strictly true or false to begin with" (115) to debates about the "fake news" that may be reported on Twitter. In particular, this liminal narrative is of interest because it departs from the official historical commemorations that Ryan discusses in the context of the plaque or museum. For Ciccoricco, the anecdote is related to "myth making" and is central to the way that communities are built around this kind of insider knowledge. He notes one of the challenges of the dtour app:

> a wealth of details to condense then attempt to independently verify. Where conflicts persisted, we proceeded with the verbal anecdotal

account by family or by literary executors, which not only preserved the motivating spirit of the project in seeking out local and insider knowledge, but also ensured we had the appropriate clearances from stakeholders.

(122)

Like Wake's discussion of the activity of mapping, this negotiation of the data that makes up the meaning of the spaces mapped digitally marks a departure from much of our debates around digital cartography.

Finally, Dhanashree Thorat draws our attention to the way the data that organizes digital spaces of commemoration are always a political act that structures a narrative around spaces in a particular way: "how underlying elements such as code, metadata, page design, hyperlinks, search features, and database structures are ideologically and politically constructed" (145). In particular, her analysis of the way that commemoration is written onto the space of ground zero through the September 11 Digital Archive makes clear that the relationship between mapped physical space and its digital archive is always designed to produce a specific goal: "the archive creates national subjects who are both affected by the event and yet somewhat distanced from it" (149) built around particular characters. The "narrative of the citizen hero" in particular organizes the early structure of the archive and, in turn, draws attention to narratives above the level of the individual anecdotes that Ciccoricco discusses. Both chapters reveal the way that stories, with a particular, variable claim to authenticity, are woven into the spaces mapped by digital media.

Sites of Commitment

A particularly striking theme has emerged across many of the chapters in this collection: the force that particular historical locations exert on our ability to impose narratives on them. Brian Greenspan helpfully evokes John Searle's concept of the "nonfictional commitments" that provide a structure against which novelists must work. As Searle says:

> if Sherlock Holmes and Watson go from Baker Street to Paddington Station by a route which is geographically impossible, we will know that Conan Doyle blundered even though he has not blundered if there never was a veteran of the Afghan campaign answering to the description of John Watson, M.D.
>
> *(331; quoted 39)*

Greenspan takes away from this the tension between fiction's ability to give new meaning to places and the "referents in the material city as they are (or will be) experienced by a contemporary user at any given future instance" (39). Of course, any locative narrative will work with the data provided by GPS, and thus is bounded by the way this material system processes movement and space. Ryan's introduction of course invoked the nature of historical sites and how they can be memorialized by plaques and other kinds of markers. But Greenspan's more comprehensive and flexible notion of spatial "commitments" strikes me as having the potential to generate sophisticated analysis.

We can see this issue of spatial commitments in two other chapters. Drawing on Alan Liu, David Ciccoricco notes that the anecdote is "random access" (113) and thus "at once contained in historical reality and admitting of freedom *from that reality*" (24; quoted 112). Read against Greenspan's notion of historical commitments, this raises the issue of how different genres imply different relationships to the material spaces that digital narratives will organize. The anecdote has a different relationship to a specific site and the kinds of historical markers that Ryan discusses in her introduction, which, in turn, have a different relationship to the kinds of infrastructural navigation that Searle notes in Sherlock Holmes. These genres organize our way of interacting with the space and account for the differences in our experiences between visiting a battlefield and walking the route of Bloomsday in Dublin. But these genres also, in turn, depend on different models for the data that make up these maps, as I discussed in the previous section.

Dhanashree Thorat's chapter on ground zero and 9/11 draws out a different element of these historical commitments. She notes that Ground Zero functions as a reference for this archive, even though it has no physical relationship to the space. Indeed, Ground Zero is a particularly rich and complex space in the context of these historical commitments, since it is defined by absence: "As a traumatic wound, the site resists closure or healing and compels the return of the spectator to witness loss" (154). While Greenspan's example of Sherlock Holmes in London focuses on the presence of known spaces and the way that they are then implemented in the Rebus app, Thorat draws our attention to the way historical events can exercise a more complex relation to our sense of the spatial realities represented in digital narrative, including national memory, trauma, and loss. This is an understudied element of our sense of digital media's relationship to space, which so often is organized around GPS and mapping, rather than these more complex affective relations to symbolic sites and these absences.

Scale

The language of mapping and cartography can sometimes make us overlook the issue of scale in digital narrative spaces. Indeed, the common focus on geolocation can make the scale of these spaces seem inevitably grounded in the scale of the individual moving through urban space.

Thorat's discussion of ground zero is the most direct confrontation with the issue of scale, since the gap between the human and global scale is so central for her analysis. As she writes:

> When first responders are present in most of the images in this sub-collection, they are so dwarfed by the scale of the smoldering wreckage

that surrounds them that they are recognizable only by their bright safety clothing and they appear not to be valorized at all. The perspective of the photographs indicates the vast scope of the work facing the first responders. Barely distinguishable from the rubble, the workers become part of the rubble, of the violence and tragedy of the event.

(154)

For Thorat, scale itself becomes an issue in the representation of the consequences of 9/11; it is precisely the gap between the images of airplanes and skyscrapers falling and the individual humans who are working to respond to that event that grounds the affective structure of the archive. This is an ideal example of the way in which our focus on mapping and geolocation is incapable of articulating the meaning of these memorial spaces.

In my discussion of the body in this conclusion, I noted the way that this scale grounds so much of the thinking about digital space. In particular, Whistance-Smith's model of the "walking simulator" depends on individual corporeality to ground our cognitive models, even though that scale is entirely arbitrary within the design of these games. Indeed, he notices that games can subtly shift scale at times to address larger landscape structures:

> Buildings can also embody metaphorical associations through their use of materials and the general articulation of their forms; a large brutalist concrete building evokes vastly different things than a small wooden one. At the scale of a landscape, peculiar landforms can evoke metaphoric readings (many mountains are named after the images they evoke), as can highly patterned landscapes which suggest some kind of cosmic ordering through their forms.

(58)

Although both these examples are relatively specific to their particular genre, Ciccoricco reminds us that "zooming" is central to most of our modern app models:

> From literary guidebook maps to literary tourism apps for mobile devices, the organizing concept remains the same. We can zoom in to literary authors or zoom out to literary cities. With regard to civic heritage and civic pride, moreover, we see the motivation for literary tourism projects run in parallel with increasing urbanization.

(117)

At precisely the moment that we are focused on the experience of particular locations through such locative programs, part of their appeal as well is that reference to a larger city or country map. Indeed, there appears to be a fundamental tension in such geolocative works in evoking both the particular location of the anecdote, narrative site, or memorial and at the same time offering a global "zoomed out" map that connects individual sites and a national or global imaginary.

Materialities

Finally, Lai-Tze Fan's chapter on "behind the scenes storytelling" draws attention to an element of digital narrative space that is so easy to overlook: the material conditions that make computing possible. As she writes, "As a result of these practices of design and abstract language, many everyday users have an equally surface-level understanding of the political, industrial, and sociocultural implications of technocapitalism on a global scale, including the true complexities of computational infrastructures" (89). Telling the story of the material technologies not only reveals conditions that we sometimes would prefer to ignore, but also reminds us that "digital space" is not an abstraction, but rather a distribution of physical servers across the whole, which are connected in particular ways through IP addresses and which, in turn, depend on a whole system of resource harvesting that is spatial in nature, even though digital media often work to hide those physical sites behind the idea of "cloud" computing.

The material structures behind digital spaces is invoked by Ryan's idea of the "architecture" of computing environments. But others in this collection have drawn attention to the way in which these underlying systems can be in tension with the user-facing systems that seem like such a natural part of our interaction with them. Dhanashree Thorat, in particular, draws our attention to the material basis or the 9/11 archive, which includes:

> underlying code and database which form the backbone of the archive. Structure also includes technical features, including capacities such as search and retrieval, hyperlinking, and metadata, which are those aspects that support and enhance the viewer's interaction with the archive. Finally, structure includes interface and design, which refer to the aesthetic and ideological choices made in the presentation of archival content. The material framework of the digital archive organizes the assembly of information in the archive and informs how that information is retrieved by users.
>
> *(225)*

Fan's invocation of Benjamin Bratton's *The Stack* is especially relevant because it reminds us that what we mean by "space" in a digital environment often depends of spatial relationships that the particular works are designed to obfuscate.

Note

1 I discuss the contradictions and multiplicity of Frank's concept of space in *Narrative After Deconstruction* (78–82).

Works Cited

Bal, Mieke. *Traveling Concepts in the Humanities: A Rough Guide.* Toronto: The University of Toronto Press, 2002.

Burgett, Bruce and Glenn Helder. *Keywords for American Cultural Studies.* 2nd ed. New York: New York University Press, 2014.

Latour, Bruno. *Reassembling the Social: An Introduction to Actor-Network-Theory.* Oxford: Oxford University Press, 2005.

Lentricchia, Frank and Thomas McLaughlin. *Critical Terms for Literary Study.* 2nd ed. Chicago, IL: University of Chicago Press, 1995.

Punday, Daniel. *Narrative After Deconstruction.* Albany: State University of New York Press, 2003.

Williams, Raymond. *Keywords: A Vocabulary of Culture and Society.* Rev. ed. Oxford: Oxford University Press, 1983.

INDEX

Note: *Italic* page numbers refer to figures; Page numbers followed by "n" denote endnotes.

Aarseth, Espen 21, 71
Age of Empires III 72
Ahmed, Sara 72
Alber, Jan 20, 22, 23, 24, 25, 26, 30, 32
"The Aleph" (Borges) 20–21
Alhrthi, Sultan 72
ambient literature 12
Andersen, Ulrik 106
Anderson, Benedict 145
anecdote, literary 109–115, 120–123, 167–168
Annalena (Bouillot), 4–5, *5*
Aral, Sinan 114
architecture (textual) 3–5
architecture in game spaces 51
archive 143–158
Arora, Rachna 106n6
augmented reality (AR) 9, 17, 21
Avedon, Elliot 78
Ayaburi, Emmanuel 130
Azaryahu, Maoz 60–61, 76–77, 109–110, 116

Baedeker, Karl 116
Bainbridge, Simon 131–132
Baker, Camille 130
Bal, Mieke 161–162
Balsamo, Anne 91
Barad, Karen 82

Bargh, John 56
Barker, May 132–138
Barthes, Roland 153
Bats of the Republic (Dodson) 6
Bauman, Richard 111, 112
The Beginner's Guide 56
behind the scenes storytelling 90, 93, 104, 171
Bell, Alice 21, 22, 23, 24, 25, 26, 32
Bell, Eleanor 44
Benford, Steve 129–130
Bennett, Jane 81
Bergland, Mary Ellen 126, 130
Berry, Richard 134
Bhaskar, Kalyan 106n6
Birringer, Johannes 129, 130
Bitencourt, Elias 130
Boateng, Richard 130
body 164–165, 166–167; body navigation 52–53, 169; embodiment in Merleau-Ponty 49; and environment 139; in mapping 125–126, 136–139; remains at Ground Zero 153; user 16
Boland, Evan 125
Bolter, J. David 2, 88–89
Bonner, Marc 57
BotFighters 11
Bouchardon Serge 21
Bratton, Benjamin 89–90, 91–93, 104, 171

Breathe (Pullinger) 12, 25
Brier, Stephen 146
Broadhurst, Susan 126
Brooke, Julian 136
Brooks, Peter 78
Brown, Joshua 146
Buckley, Ghloé Germaine 84
Bulson, Eric 10, 109, 110, 116, 117
Burgett, Bruce 160, 163
Butler, Judith 156

Cahill, Holger 79–80
Caillois, Roger 78
Caldwell, Sharon 126
Calligrammes (Apollinaire) 2
Cameron, Rich 126
Campbell, Keith 80
Carbo-Mascarell, Rosa 51
Carcassonne (Wrede) 83
Carne y Arena (Iñarritu) 8–9
A Cartographer's Confession (Attlee) 13, 165
Cartographers: A Roll Player Tale (Adan) 83
cartography 73, 125–126, 131, 135–136; folk 70, 78–82; literary 110, 117
Caselberg, John 122
CAVE 7, 17
Chandler, Raymond 41
Chaouli, Michel 40
Chartrand, Tanya 67
Chatterjee, Sandip 106n6
cheat 14
Choose Your Own Adventure (book series) 23–24, 78
Ciccoricco, David 111
citizen heroes 145–146, 149, 150, 156, 168
Civilization IV 72
Clandfield, Peter 38
Clark, Andy 50, 52
cloud computing 89, 105–106n2, 171
cognitive primitives (or cogs) *see* image schema
Coleridge, Samuel Taylor 132
colonialism 143
conceptual metaphor 58
Connor, Michan Andrew 157
Consalvo, Mia 80
Cooper, David 71, 110, 115
"Un Coup de Dés" (Mallarmé) 2
Cowton, Jeff 134
Crawford, Kate 89–90, 92–93, 104
Criado Perez, Caroline 130
Cubitt, Sean 106

Culler, Jonathan 161
cultural imaginary 152, 171

Dade-Robertson, Martyn 54
Danjoux, Michèle 129
Dante 116
data mining 114, 131–132, 139
database 74
Davies, Paul 134
De Certeau, Michel 54, 81
Dear Esther 15–16, 50–51, 55, 56, 59–62
dérive 10, 41
Derrida, Jacques 150
detective fiction 36, 42–44
digital humanities 144–145
digital narrative 2, 21–22
Dobson, Teresa 40
Domsch, Sebastian 56
Donaldson, Christopher 71, 110–111, 116
Dreamaphage (Nelson) 25–26
Drucker, Johanna 82, 144, 145
dtour app 110, 118–123
Dubner, Stephen 146
Dunne, Lucy 125, 130
Duvall, Julia 125, 130
Dwivedi, Yogesh 130

"Easter Wings" (Herbert)
Easterlin, Nancy 71
Effah, John 130
Elliot, David 119
Ensslin, Astrid 21, 22, 23, 24, 25, 26, 32
Entrances & Exits 27
environments, navigation of 53
Etrian Odyssey 83
Everest VR 17
Everett, Tom 126
Eververse (Tonra) 126–127
Everybody's Gone to the Rapture 25

fake news 114–115, 167
Fan, Lai-Tze 43, 89
Fernández-Vara, Clara 56
fictional discourse 49, 46; nonfictional commitments 39
Fineman, Joel 109–113
first person shooter (FPS) 50
first responders 145, 150, 151–157
flânerie 10
folk art 79–81
Foote, Kenneth 9, 70–71, 76–77, 109–110, 116

Forceville, Charles 57
Forrester, Ian 130
Foucault, Michel 143
Foursquare 41
Fox, Frederick 100
frames 55–56
Frank, Joseph 1–2, 4
Fraser, Harriet 134
Frith, Jordan 131, 136, 139

game engines 51
Gannon, Madeline 126, 136
García-Gómez, José Joaquín 100
Gardner, Jared 26
The Gate (Tisselli) 104
The Gathering Cloud (Carpenter) 104, 106n2
Genette, Gérard 72–73
Genius Loci 64–66
Gibson, James 52, 53
Goffman, Erving 55
Goldhagen, Sarah Williams 56, 58
Gomel, Elana 42
Gone Home 49
Google Maps 36, 40, 117, 118, 125–126
Gouge, Catherine 129, 130, 139
GPS 10, 17, 39–40, 41, 45, 109, 117, 126–127, 130, 164, 168, 169
Gray, Jonathan 73
Greenberg, Judith 153–154
Greenblatt, Stephen 111, 112, 114, 120, 123
Greenspan, Brian 41, 47
Gregory, Ian 127
Ground Zero 152–157
Grusin, Richard 2, 88–89
Gualeni, Stefano 49
Guattari, Félix 131
GUI 2, 25
Guler, Sibel Deren 126, 136
Gulliver's Travels (Swift) 21
Günzel, Stephan 71

Halegoua, Germain 136
Half-Life 50
Hamblen, Matt 129
Hamilton, Bill 72
Hammond, Adam 136
Hampe, Beate 57
Happe, Kelly 139
Haraway, Donna 126
hardware, computer 94–97
Harley, J.B. 73

Harry Potter (Rowling) 20
Hayles, Katherine 6, 88–89, 113, 114, 131
Helder, Glenn 160, 163
Hemkhaus, Morton 106n6
Herman, David 17, 71
Hiatt, Alfred 81
Hinchliffe, Daniel 106n6
Hirst, Graeme 136
Hoge, Lyn 126
Horowitz, Eli 33
Horvath, Joan 126
House of Leaves (Danielewski) 2, 27
Hudson, Travis 100
Human Rights Watch 99
Hurni, Lorenz 71
Hutchinson, William 132
hypertext 3–5, 23–24, 40

image schema 56–58
In a House of Lies (Rankin) 41
infrastructure, digital 89–105, 143–144
Ingress 11
Internet Machine (Arnall) 106n2

Jack, Jordynn 131
Jakob-Whitworth, Alex 134
Jameson, Frederic 37, 41–42, 45, 46, 47n2, 111, 112
Jenkins, Henry 21, 26, 49, 73
Johnson, Mark 52–53, 53–54, 55, 57, 58
Joler, Vladan 92–93, 104
Jones, John 129, 130, 139

Kafka, Franz 16–17
Kalin, Jason 131, 136, 139
keyword 160–171
Kermode, Frank 78
Khetriwal, Sinha 106n6
King's Quest (William) 74–75
Kirsh, David 52–53
Kromhout, Roelf 57

Lafreniere, Donald 129
Lakoff, George 52–53, 55, 56–57, 58
LaLone, Nicholas 72
Lammes, Sybille 72
landmarks 9, 38
Latour, Bruno 73, 82, 139, 162
Laurel, Brenda 144, 150
Leder, Drew 51
Lemos, André Luiz Martins 130
Lentricchia, Frank 160
Linton, Eliza Lynn 132

Liu, Alan 94, 110, 112–113, 114, 117, 144, 169
locative narrative 9–13, 36–47; and allegory 38–39, 46
Lunenfeld, Peter 82
Luscombe, Richard 45
Lynch, Daniel 27

Manovich, Lev 49, 74, 88–89
mapping 70, 165–167; cognitive (Jameson) 45, 112; database maps 76–78; digital *vs.* analog 125–126; extraction and entanglement 84; folk maps 78–82; literary maps definition 116–117; literary spaces 71; as paratext 72–73; *see also* body in mapping
Martineau, Harriet 132
Marvel Universe (Disney) 26
Massey, Doreen 126
materials in computing 98–103
Mattern, Shannon 91
Maziarczik, Grzegorz 26–27
McHale, Brian 111
McLaughlin, Thomas 160, 161
media archaeology 74, 91
Merleau-Ponty 49, 76, 131
Miall, David 40
Miller, Daniel 55
Miller, Jago 134
Mills, Rick 100
mimetic impulse (and anti-mimetic worlds) 23, 29–30; anti-mimesis 26
Mitchell, Peta 126
Monmonier, Mark 77
Moretti, Franco 71
mourning, collective 148–149
multimodality 40, 52
[*Murmur*] 10–11
Murray, Janet 71, 73, 81–82
Murray, John 116
Murrieta-Flores, Patricia 71, 110, 116

NaissanceE 54, 55
narration: omniscient 21; player 52
narrativity 11, 12, 6; de-narrativization 147; *vs.* experiences 17; in walking simulator 59
narratology 21
national memory 149–151, 153–157, 169
network protocols 47, 93, 171
new historicism 110, 111, 112–113
Newman, James 82
Nitsche, Michael 14, 24, 71

Noë, Alva 52–53
non-player characters (NPCs) 52
Norberg-Schultz, Christian 54–55

Otley, Jonathan 132
Owens, Craig 38–39

Pandve, Harshal 106n6
Paradise Lost (Milton) 21
paratext 72–73, 82
Parikka, Jussi 74, 91
Parlett, David 78
The Path (Samyn and Harvey) 14–15
Pederson, Isabel 126
Pérez-Cebada, Duan Diego 100
perspective, first *vs.* third 54
Peters, John Durham 106
Petrarch 116
Phelan, James 122
phenomenology 49–50, 51
Phone Story 104
The Pickle Index (Horowitz, Quinn, and Huebert) 20–21, 26–33, *29, 31*, 167
The Plague (Camus) 46
Plumlee, Geoffrey 100
Picard, Rosalind 139
Pieber, Darryl 41
Pinto, Violet N. 102
Pirates! (Meier) 83
Pokemon 26
Pokémon Go 11, 12, 41
Pold, Søren Bro 106
Pope, James 40
Price, Sara 126
Prince, Gerald 163
Pry (Cannizzaro and Gorman) 26–27
public humanities 111
Punday, Daniel 3, 26, 71–72, 172n1

Radulovic, Pranshu Singal 106n6
Rayley, Rita 8, 25
Reed, A.H. 122
Reynolds, Daniel 82
Richardson, Brian 21, 23, 24
Ricoeur, Paul 75
Ridge, Mia 129
Riegler, Thomas 146
Right to Repair movement 106n3
Roberts, Sarah 105n1
Ronen, Ruth 13–14
Rosner, Daniela 91
Round (Montfort) 90, 93, 95–97, 100–101, 104–105

Roy, Deb 114
Ruston, Scott 10–12
Ryan, Marie-Laure 3, 20, 22, 24, 25, 32, 40, 49, 70, 71, 76–77, 109–110, 116

S (Abrams and Dorst) 2, 6
Salter, Anastasia 80
Sample, Mark 36–37
Sarma, Sisira 129
scale 169–171
Schwartz, Raz 136
Screen (Wardrip-Fruin) 7–8, 25
Searle, John 39
Selfe, Cynthia 144, 150
Selfe, Richard 144, 150
Séparation (Abraham) 105
September 11 Digital Archive 143–158, 147, *148*, 168
Set in Darkness (Rankin) 37–39, 43–45
setting 14
The 7th Continent (Roudy and Sautter) 83
Shapiro, Lawrence 52
Sharma, Hitesh Nidhi 72, 102n6
Sicchio, Kate 126, 136
Simpson, David 156–157
Sinha, Satish 106n6
site of commitment 39, 168–169
Smith, John 116
Son et Lumière 9–10
space: as atmosphere 54–55, 56 (*see also* conceptual metaphor); embodied or lived spatial experience 49–50, 76 (*see also* body in mapping); mimetic 1, 13–17, 25, 71; physical space of text 6–9, 25, 78; primary *vs.* orienting 3; spatial context of work 9–13, 25, 109; spatial form 1–6, 25–26, 164–165, 172n1; spatial self 136
Space Quest 75
spatial form 1, 4
Spiel, Katta 72
The Stack see Bratton, Benjamin
Stamelman, Richard 153–154
The Stanley Parable (Wreden) 15, 21, 49, 50–51, 62–64
Sternberg, Meir 1
Storyspace 24
StoryTrek 36, 43
storyworld 1, 28, 73, 74, 78
Stuckey, Helen 82
Suits, Bernard 78
Summers, Essie 122

Sutton-Smith, Brian 78
System Shock 2 50

Taylor, Joanna 127, 134, 136
Tetris 7
threshold 73, 81
time 75, 113–114
Topol, Eric 130
Toups, Z.O. 72
tourism, literary 10, 109–110, 116–123, 166
Trailing Rebus 36–47, 169
transmedia 20, 23, 26–27, 28–33, 37, 73–74, 82
trauma, national 143–144, 149, 151–157, 169
Tree of Codes (Foer) 6, 7
Truillot, Michael -Rolph 143, 148
Tuan, Yi-Fu 14
Turaga, Rama Mohana 106n6
Twelve Blue (Joyce) 3–4, *4*
Twitter 114–115, 120–121
typography 2

Ulysses (Joyce) 2
The Unfortunates (Johnson) 27
United 93 (film) 146
unnatural narrative 20–21, 22–23, 24, 28–33; disruption more generally 40
urban storytelling 36, 38
user interface 21, 44–45, 54, 82, 90, 93–94, 105, 144, 145–151; intrafaces 82

virtual reality (VR) 7, 16–18, 21
Vlach, John Michael 80
Vosoughi, Soroush 114
VRwandlung 16–17

walking simulator 15, 49–57, 164, 170
War on Terror 33
Wardrip-Fruin, Noah 7, *8*
The Warlock of Firetop Mountain (Jackson and Livingstone) 70, 73–84, *77*–*80*
wearables 126–132
Webb, Andrew 72
Weber, Anne-Kathrin 71
Wegner, Philip 43–44
Westover, Paul 134
What Remains of Edith Finch 15
Williams, Raymond 160–161

The Wire 41
The Witness 49, 54
Wolf, Mark 71
Wood, Denis 81
Wordsworth, Dorothy 127–129, 132–138
Wordsworth, William 127–129, 132
World of Warcraft 14
World Trade Center (film) 146

Yaegar, Patricia 153

Zelda: Breath of the Wild 83
Zhang, Jane 145
Zheng, Caroline Yan 130
Žižek, Slavoj 45–46, 47
Zoran, Gabriel 13–14, 70
ZORK I 74
Zunshine, Lisa 21

For Product Safety Concerns and Information please contact our EU representative GPSR@taylorandfrancis.com
Taylor & Francis Verlag GmbH, Kaufingerstraße 24, 80331 München, Germany

www.ingramcontent.com/pod-product-compliance
Lightning Source LLC
Chambersburg PA
CBHW061349300426
44116CB00011B/2052